EIGHTH EDITION

OFF THE BEATEN PATH®
NEW HAMPSHIRE →

A GUIDE TO UNIQUE PLACES

BARBARA RADCLIFFE ROGERS

AND

STILLMAN ROGERS

gPP®

travel

Guilford, Connecticut

In loving memory of George Radcliffe and Norman Rogers,
the fathers who chose New Hampshire as our childhood home,
and of James C. Cleveland, who as a U.S. congressman worked
so long and hard to preserve its character and protect its land.

All the information in this guidebook is subject to change. We recommend
that you call ahead to obtain current information before traveling.

To buy books in quantity for corporate use
or incentives, call **(800) 962-0973**
or e-mail **premiums@GlobePequot.com**.

Text design: Linda R. Loiewski
Maps: Equator Graphics © Morris Book Publishing, LLC
Layout: Joanna Beyer

ISSN 1540-1537
ISBN 978-0-7627-5048-1

Printed in the United States of America
10 9 8 7 6 5 4 3 2 1

Contents

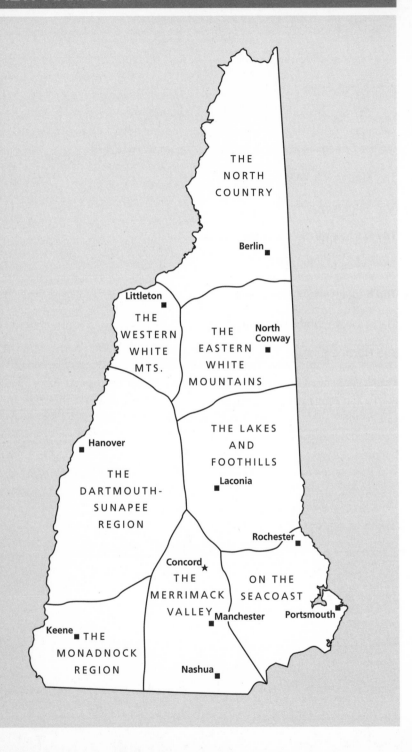

Acknowledgments

Any book is a joint effort, but this one has profited from the help of friends and family all over New Hampshire—and from a number of others who were strangers when we began but are now counted as friends.

They have shared with us their favorite off-the-beaten-path places, those restaurants, inns, hiking trails, and backroads that even a traveler used to poking into all the corners might miss. Our gratitude goes to Joan Farrel, Judy Hampe, Chris Hamm, Joanne Lemieux, Ted and Elsie Miner, Pauline and Frank Mooney, Lee Stark, Larry Pletcher, Nina Gardner, Dennis and Sandy Brennan, Kathleen Hatt, Philip Hollman, Mike and Merri Hern, Marti Mayne, Ray Gorman, Betty Falton, Art and Nancy Brennan, Alice Pearce, Karl Stone, Bonnie MacPherson, Stacy Lopes, Denise and Thom Perkins, Hilary Nangle, David Emerson, Nadine and Ed King, Mikey Duprey, and Lisa Rogak.

Very special thanks go to Dick Hamilton for his vast knowledge of the White Mountains that he so readily shared with us and to Jayne O'Connor for her invaluable help and support.

We have shared our travels over the years with many friends: hikes and backroads with Pat Hanson, mountain trails and fishing boats with Carole Belsky and John Norton, campfires with Fred and Sta Gursky, kayaking with Emma McKenny, campsites with Mark and Marge Davis, and miles of trails above the timberline with Howard and Sue Poore. Possibly the most hilarious of these adventures we have shared with Frank and Maria Sibley, as we searched for gorges, boulders, and ghost towns. Julie and Lura have always been fun to travel with, whether we were slipping over rocky trails in search of a waterfall in a downpour of rain or enjoying a leisurely second cup of tea at a Portsmouth bakery.

Our fondest appreciation goes to Dee Radcliffe, who has explored every corner of the state and whose notes and suggestions led us to places even the locals didn't know about. Her good humor and enthusiasm will always place her among life's best traveling companions.

Introduction

How do you introduce a friend, one with whom you've shared many of life's pleasures, one whose company never fails you? What can you possibly say of your friend that will capture those qualities that are most endearing and most enduring?

New Hampshire is that friend to us. The first memories of our childhoods are set here. The first ocean waves we played in broke on New Hampshire beaches; the first mountains we climbed and slopes and trails we skied—they were New Hampshire's. We've lived and traveled in many other parts of the world, but when asked a few days ago which of all the places we've traveled is our favorite, we said in unison, and without second thought, New Hampshire.

The tremendous diversity of New Hampshire's landscapes makes it visually exciting and also provides a wide variety of activities, particularly for those who enjoy the outdoors. The challenges of its terrain, soil, and climate have given its people a unique character—or perhaps such a place has always attracted those of independent and self-sufficient spirit.

New Hampshire people do tend to be an independent lot; most of them say exactly what they think. Another disconcerting trait to those who don't know us well is that you can't always tell about us by our looks. The size of a person's fortune often bears no relation to the size of one's home or the make of one's car. It is often said of Boston ladies that they don't buy their hats; they have them. New Hampshire people are like that, too. The beautiful farmhouse may be all that's left several generations later and may be kept up by a lot of hard work alone; the tiny cottage with the gate askew may be the home of a millionaire. We tend to live in what we have.

You Can't Get There from Here

As a rule of thumb, you can get north and south, but not east and west, on public buses. The main routes run from Boston to Montreal or Portland, Maine, passing through Portsmouth, Concord, Keene, Manchester, Nashua, and a few other cities farther north. But you can't get from Portsmouth to Keene without going back to Boston. The major bus lines are Concord Trailways (800-639-3317; www.concord trailways.com) and Greyhound (800-231-2222; www.greyhound.com). You can fly into the modern Manchester Airport, served by a variety of airlines.

If You Don't Like It, Wait a Minute

Mark Twain (and just about everyone else) had some choice words about the "infinite variety" of New England weather. Most of the exaggerated stories you've heard are probably true. Average temperatures don't tell you much. One day it may be sunny and 80 degrees, the next day may be 50 degrees and raining, but the average temperature for the period will be calculated at 65, although neither day was 65. And the twenty-four-hour averages don't tell you what the daytime temperature was. That in mind, you may find the following "official" average temperatures remotely helpful: Jan, 21 degrees Fahrenheit; Feb, 23 degrees Fahrenheit; Mar, 32 degrees Fahrenheit; Apr, 44 degrees Fahrenheit; May, 56 degrees Fahrenheit; June, 65 degrees Fahrenheit; July, 70 degrees Fahrenheit; Aug, 67 degrees Fahrenheit; Sept, 60 degrees Fahrenheit; Oct, 49 degrees Fahrenheit; Nov, 38 degrees Fahrenheit; and Dec, 25 degrees Fahrenheit. In reality, expect most summer days to be in the 70s, spring and fall in the 50s and 60s, winter in the 20s and 30s. Humidity tends to be high year-round, which makes the cold seem colder and the hot seem hotter. The nice thing, as Mark Twain suggests, is that it never stays any way for very long. In general, the best weather tends to be in August, September, and October, with less rain than in the spring and fewer hot, humid days than earlier in the summer. The worst cold spells usually come in December and January. November is gray and March muddy, but both have some glorious days.

The same trait is true of restaurants, which is very confusing to the traveler used to decorator interiors and flashy exteriors. You can't always judge a restaurant by its cover, and very often the plainest place or the most staid of inns may have a chef who retired to the country from a four-star bastion of haute cuisine. Surprises are what New Hampshire is full of, and they make each day a happy adventure.

"Off the beaten path" is a relative thing. By most standards, the whole state is off the beaten path. There are only three areas that are congested by traffic, even in the height of tourist season. If lodging is heavily booked during the most popular weeks, it is not because there are too many people here, but because resorts do not line our roads. Reservations are always a good idea during July and August and around the first week of October. Places such as **Garfield Falls,** which even many local people have not seen, require travel on unpaved roads. But none of these require four-wheel-drive vehicles, except in winter or early spring when some roads are muddy or not plowed.

Which brings us to the question of when to come. New Hampshire is a seasonal state, and each month has its attractions. The best time for you to explore the Granite State depends upon your tastes and interests. Winter is glorious, filled with crystal-cold days for skiing or snowshoeing across white meadows with clear views of mountains through leafless trees. Night brings the stars so close you can spot constellations you never saw before and is a good time for a sleigh ride and a blazing fire in the hearth. Snow covers all the hardscrabble farms and rock-filled fields, and the air is clear and smells of wood smoke. But if you like little museums or want to hike to waterfalls, winter is not the best season.

Spring is good for country walks and hikes. Sugar houses come briefly to life, shrouded in steam and smelling of sweet maple syrup. With the end of the sap run, spring wildflowers carpet the woodlands, and the view of the mountains is softened, but not obscured, by leaves the size of mouse ears. Spring peepers fill the evening air with chirping. A lot of the little places aren't open yet, but people in the ones that are have time to chat and tell you about local places. Bed-and-breakfast hosts have time to share a glass of sherry with you after dinner. Spring comes so fast that you can almost watch the apple blossoms unfold.

Summer is full of festivals celebrating almost everything from blueberries to zucchinis, and every little town has its historical society open. Days are long and not too hot to enjoy hikes and climbs. Lakeshores and mountain brooks offer swimming.

After Labor Day the weather is still summery, but there is a lull in the number of tourists until the end of the month. Farmers' markets are filled with produce and jars of glistening jellies. Hiking is at its very best, and the roadsides are brightened by patches of turning swamp maples.

Foliage paints the state, from north to south, in brilliant shades of red and gold. It begins in mid-September in the north country and lasts until mid- to late October in the Monadnock region. The peak can vary by a week or so,

What's Going on Here?

The major cities have daily newspapers, and every area has its free weekly paper listing local events, festivals, church suppers, and just about everything else. The daily papers have special sections, usually late in the week, with entertainment and events calendars for the coming week. Many papers also print special summer sections, which are available free at information centers early in the summer. The major newspapers are the *Union Leader* and *New Hampshire Sunday News* (Manchester), *Keene Sentinel, Foster's Daily Democrat* (Dover), *Portsmouth Herald, Concord Monitor, Valley News* (Lebanon), *Nashua Telegraph, Laconia Citizen, News and Sentinel* (Colebrook), and *Coos County Democrat* (the north country).

Save on Dining Out

A number of New Hampshire restaurants are included in an annual book of dining discounts called *Entertainment*. Participants change with each edition but always cover all price ranges and styles, from fine dining to fast foods. New Hampshire is included in two different books, one covering southern New Hampshire and south coastal Maine, the other covering Vermont and bordering areas, which includes the entire Connecticut River valley. The books cost about $30, and discounts are usually the price of one entree, which can be as much as a $24 savings on one dinner. In the back of the book are discount coupons for sports, such as kayak or ski rentals, and admission to museums and attractions in the area. For information call (508) 620-5600 or (800) 374-4464 or visit www.entertainment.com.

depending on the weather, but any area will have at least two weeks of good color, usually more.

So plan your travel dates according to your own interests, or better yet, come often and enjoy the best of each season. You will, of course, need a good road map in order to plan your travels and to keep from getting lost on our wonderful winding country roads—although getting lost has its rewards, too, and may actually be the best way to see the state. But it's nice to know where you are when you finally emerge onto a main road. We'd like to tell you to use the state's own free road map, but, sadly, it has changed and (maybe to save money on ink?) has left off many roads that you will want to take—or avoid. Being Yankees, we hate to suggest that you spend money, but we can't think of a better investment than the *New Hampshire Atlas and Gazetteer,* published by DeLorme map company.

Prices are a tricky thing to provide in a guidebook, but we have done it anyway. They change with economic conditions, even seasons and weather conditions, since restaurants depend on the markets for fresh produce and seafood. Lodging rates usually rise during the busiest times and drop during the slower ones. We have given dollar amounts when they seemed fairly likely to remain constant and elsewhere have used general ranges. For bed-and-breakfast places we consider $100 to $150 a night for two people to be moderate; for inns and hotels without breakfast, $90 to $125 is moderate. In restaurants, $15 to $25 is moderate for the main course, and we've further broken that into a high and low if the prices fall into a close range. How you add to that with other courses and wine will affect your bill, of course, but the entree price sets the base. Sometimes we've been even more specific, especially if the prices are exceptional.

To Find Out More

Write the New Hampshire Office of Travel and Tourism, P.O. Box 856, Concord 03302, or call (800) 386-4664 to order a copy of *The Official New Hampshire Guidebook,* a handy compilation of advertising and listings. To speak to a live voice, call (603) 271-2343 or (800) 258-3608. The state's Web site at www.visitnh.gov gives general information on events, weather, and attractions. For an update on fall foliage conditions, call (800) 258-3608; www.yankeefoliage.com. For alpine ski conditions call (800) 258-3608; www.skinh.com. For a listing of private campgrounds, call (800) 822-6764 or (603) 846-5511; www.ucampnh.com.

White Mountains Attractions, North Woodstock 03262 (800-346-3687 or 603-745-8720), can send you information on the northern part of the state, as will the Mount Washington Valley Chamber of Commerce, North Conway 03860 (800-367-3364; www.mtwashingtonvalley.org).

Now to all the usual disclaimers, add the caveat emptor endemic to travel guides: Things change, especially in the restaurant business. We've tried to choose places with consistent ownership, but when we discover a great new spot, we can't wait five years to share it with you. If you find our recommendations not up to our descriptions, there are several possible reasons. The restaurant in question may have changed owners or chefs, or it may have just plain gone downhill. Your taste in food may not be the same as ours. One person's pâté is another's "ptoooi," as Confucius wisely observed. There is no substitute for your own good judgment. If you get inside and don't think it's the right place for you, leave. In those memorable cases where a place we've recommended doesn't look like what it tastes like, we've mentioned that fact so that you will expect it. If in doubt, don't be embarrassed to ask to see a menu before you're seated. New Hampshire people don't buy pigs in a poke, and they don't expect you to either.

Enjoy New Hampshire as we do. We think that you'll agree after you've met the state in person that it's a place where familiarity breeds both respect and love.

ON THE SEACOAST

New Hampshire has the shortest seacoast of any coastal state—only 18 miles long—but it's also one of the most historic. The first European inhabitants established a settlement at **Odiorne Point** in 1623, and later the same year a fishing village was established at Dover Point on the northern banks of the Piscataqua River on Little Bay. The Odiorne Point settlement was abandoned, but the Dover settlers built a meetinghouse and homes, which became the first permanent settlement in the colony.

The histories of this area, the American colonies, and the young nation are inextricably intertwined. The first American flag to be saluted by a foreign power flew from the mast of the *Ranger,* which sailed from Portsmouth in 1777. The flag was sewn by Portsmouth ladies of fabric cut from their dresses. Portsmouth today, for all of its funky shops and bright eateries, still has the air of a prosperous eighteenth-century seaport.

Exeter, too, was a shipbuilding town and a lively port. Although it has now lost its navigable link with the sea, its fine buildings still speak of the profitable West Indian trade. Inland from the shores of the Great Bay stretched almost unbroken farmland, and, although more heavily settled than other parts of the state, the area is still rich in farms and orchards.

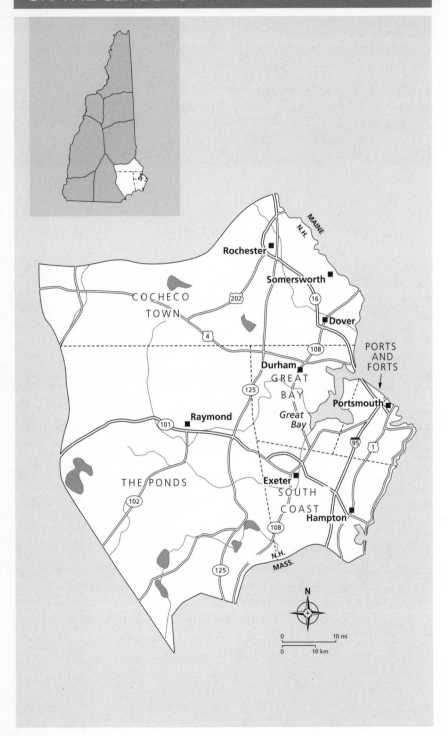

Although most visitors' views of the New Hampshire coast are the traffic and commercialism of Route 1, there are lovely and quiet backroads to enjoy even in this playground area. Portsmouth, too, has its surprises, tucked away amid its tangle of old lanes and paths that grew into streets. New Hampshire, as a colony, began in this seacoast area, and it's an appropriate place for us to begin exploring the state.

Portsmouth and the seacoast are accessible by air and bus, but if you are taking a bus, make sure it stops at Market Square, downtown. Some of the buses use the Pease International Tradeport, out of town, and there is no bus service to the city, so if you arrive by air or your bus lets you off there, you'll have to call a cab. This is an odd gap in otherwise excellent public transportation. C&J Trailways, www.ridecj.com, buses stop at the downtown Starbucks, 1 Market Square; tickets can be bought at The Victoria's Vegetarian Juice Bar, 512 Hanover St., opposite the downtown parking garage; (603) 430-1100, (800) 258-7111. Greyhound (www.greyhound.com) buses operate from Mainely Gourmet, 55 Hanover St.; (603) 433-3210.

You can travel throughout the seacoast area from Hampton through Portsmouth to Rochester and as far west as Exeter on the Coast transportation system. Its seven routes provide bus service from the Massachusetts border, all along the ocean and up the Maine border to Farmington and all the towns along Great Bay. The fare is $1, and kids five and under are free; half-fare for seniors (sixty-five and over) and those with disabilities. Exact change is required, so bring a supply of ones and quarters. A complete fare and route guide is available at the Portsmouth Chamber of Commerce, town and city halls, local businesses, and on the buses. For specific route or fare questions,

For Off-the-Beaten-Path Travelers

New Hampshire's state highway map, available free at most information offices, is an essential reference, of course, but those who like to know exactly where that interesting-looking road goes (or where it doesn't go) need the definitive set of road maps. DeLorme publishes a book of these large-format maps for nearly every state, and *The New Hampshire Atlas and Gazetteer* is required reading for explorers like us. Along with the roads, DeLorme maps show cemeteries, schools, streams, rail lines, and other landmarks to help you identify your whereabouts. Places of interest, such as parks, boat launches, campgrounds, covered bridges, waterfalls, and natural features, are shown by symbols and name. It's the natural companion for *New Hampshire Off the Beaten Path.* You'll find the maps in bookstores or you can order copies from DeLorme, 2 DeLorme Dr., P.O. Box 298, Yarmouth, Maine 04096; (800) 561-5105; www.delorme.com.

you can also call (603) 743-5777 from 6:30 a.m. to 10:30 p.m. Mon through Fri or 8 a.m. to 9:30 p.m. on Sat, or visit www.coastbus.org.

Seacoast Trolley Company has trolley service around Portsmouth and to Wallis Sands State Beach, Odiorne Point State Park, Rye Beach, New Castle Common, Strawbery Banke, and just about every place we mention in this section. Daily service is available from mid-June to Labor Day, 10 a.m. to 5 p.m. Trolleys leave Market Square on the hour, Strawbery Banke at fifty minutes past the hour, and other locations on a schedule available at tourist-information offices, their Web site, and on the trolley. Fares are $5.00 for adults and $2.50 for children (for the one-hour narrated tour), and reboarding is free with the tour ticket. For details call (603) 431-6975 or (800) 828-3762.

Ports and Forts

The link with the sea did not end with the sailing of the last clipper. Ships were built in Portsmouth for both world wars, and the forts that guarded the harbor in the Revolution still dot the coast.

New Castle, once called Great Island, was the first seat of government and even now looks like the tiny prosperous fishing and seafaring village of its colonial origins. Streets too narrow for sidewalks are lined with houses whose doorways open directly onto the roadway. The numbers on them are not addresses, but dates, most of them from the 1600s and 1700s.

Fort Constitution had its beginning in 1632 with the earthworks and four "great guns"; a blockhouse was built in 1666; and at the end of the century a breastwork was added to protect the military stores. It was named Fort William and Mary.

Paul Revere, the Boston silversmith and patriot, is best known for his ride on the night of April 18, 1775. But in New Hampshire, he's remembered for a ride almost four months earlier. On December 13, 1774, he brought a message that British troops were coming from Rhode Island to protect the garrison and secure it against the fractious Sons of Liberty. The next day, 400 of the latter converged on the fort and liberated one hundred barrels of gunpowder and some small arms, which they loaded on a gundalow (a type of boat built at Portsmouth and used to navigate tidal rivers) and sailed up the Oyster River to Durham. They hid the gunpowder in homes and under the pulpit of the meetinghouse until they could haul it by oxcart to Cambridge for use at Bunker Hill. On December 15, before the British could get reinforcements, another group helped itself to sixteen small cannons and whatever other military supplies could be carried off. It was the first active engagement of the Revolution.

EVENTS ON THE SEACOAST

Market Square Day,
Second Sat in June, Portsmouth
(603) 436-3988;
www.proportsmouth.org.

Jazz Weekend and Festival,
late June, Portsmouth
(603) 436-2848;
www.prescottpark.org.

Prescott Park Arts Festival,
July–Aug, Portsmouth
(603) 436-2848; www.prescottpark.org.

Seafood Festival and Sidewalk Sale,
early Sept, Hampton Beach
(603) 926-8717;
www.hamptonbeach.org.

Strawbery Banke Candlelight Stroll,
early Dec, Portsmouth
(603) 433-1100;
www.strawberybanke.org.

**Portsmouth Chamber of Commerce
Events Calendar,**
www.portcity.org.

Renamed Fort Constitution, it was used in 1812 and every other war until it was returned to the state of New Hampshire in 1961. Its walls and ramparts are a fine place for viewing the lighthouse, harbor, and Fort McClary, which guards the other side of this harbor entrance from Kittery Point, Maine. Visitors must observe the parking restrictions posted at the Coast Guard Station entrance now more than ever. For general information call (603) 436-1552.

For access to the rocks and sandy beach of the neighboring shore, go through **Great Island Common,** a park overlooking the harbor. From here you can see two lighthouses, islands, and Fort Constitution, as well as passing sailboats. Rocky tidal areas surround the park with pools to explore and a gentler tide than the one that crashes against the rocks along the ocean. While the beach isn't very long, it's set in a very attractive cove. The park provides picnic tables, a pavilion, and grills, as well as playgrounds, ballfields, and restrooms. There are no camping facilities. Open daily May to Sept, dawn until dusk. Admission is $3 per adult; seniors and children are free. No pets or boating are allowed.

Close to this park, look for the entrance to Wild Rose Lane, which ends at **Fort Stark.** It is another of the seven forts built to protect Portsmouth Harbor and the naval shipyard. Although it was the site of earthworks during the Revolution and the War of 1812 and of a later stone fort, the present batteries were built at the turn of the twentieth century and were used in both world wars. The huge steel doors of the magazines stand ajar, grass grows from the cement, and one round gun emplacement has begun to slide down the crumbling cliff. Interior access is closed due to vandalism. Open by appointment only; call (603) 436-1552.

Portsmouth brewing magnate Frank Jones bought a small hotel in New Castle at the end of the nineteenth century and rapidly expanded it into *Wentworth by the Sea,* a premier resort of the New England coast. In 1904 representatives of Japan and Russia negotiated an end to the Russo–Japanese War here, earning President Theodore Roosevelt the Nobel Peace Prize. By the 1970s, such grand hotels had lost their luster, and this one closed. After standing forlorn and empty for years, in 2003 this pride of the New Hampshire seacoast reopened its doors, its elegance regained in a multimillion-dollar restoration. Rooms have marble showers, leather-topped desks, and down pillows, and an in-house spa pampers guests. Reviving the dining traditions of the original Wentworth by the Sea, while improving on them significantly with a menu based on fresh local ingredients, the *Wentworth Dining Room* offers such main dishes as pan-seared chicken with forest mushrooms, herb-mustard crusted pork loin or pan-seared sea bass with black olive risotto and garlic-roasted Japanese eggplant. The pastry chef's signature is lemon curd tartlet with strawberry, almond, and honey tuile. The smaller waterside dining room, *Latitudes,* overlooks a marina of white boats bobbing in the waves, backed by the bay and a fringe of marsh grasses and trees on the opposite shore. The chef keeps diners' attention on the food with contemporary free-form china to frame a tempting selection of small dishes, possibly including crispy calamari with spicy peppers and toasted peanuts or a trio of bite-sized burgers, each different. Hearty salads and traditional entrees round out an appealing menu. Hotel rates are in the expensive range. The address is Wentworth Rd., P.O. Box 860, New Castle 03854; (603) 422-7322 or (866) 240-6313; www.wentworth.com.

Facing New Castle Island and Fort Stark is *Odiorne Point,* where the first Europeans in the state settled. Site of Fort Dearborn during World War II, the grass-covered hills are actually camouflaged casemates for gun emplacements and their support systems. The entire point is now a nature center, with diverse coastal habitats to explore. Along with the rocky shore and salt marsh, there are a freshwater marsh and coastal woods. A drowned forest of pine, birch, and hemlock stumps is firmly rooted about 2 feet below tide level at the south end. Throughout the natural habitat you can see signs of human habitation as well. Stone walls of old farmlands and a colony of summer cottages cross the area, and you may see the hardy remnants of some of the formal gardens of the long-gone cottages. Day use $4; children ages six to 12 $3 and ages zero to five $2; N.H. residents over age 65 free. Boat launch fee $5 to $8. No pets. Route 1A, Rye; (603) 436-7406; www.nhstateparks.com/odiorne.html.

Portsmouth is a lively city with warrens of back streets to explore. The path to its abundant historic homes is part of the *Portsmouth Harbour*

Read All about It

New Hampshire's history is a microcosm of American history, from the earliest settlements on the coast in the early 1600s. The book *It Happened in New Hampshire* (Globe Pequot Press) records thirty-one events and incidents that illustrate life and times from those early settlers to the twenty-first century. The stories are anecdotal, some serious, some humorous (such as how George Washington got a black eye during his presidential visit to Portsmouth). Some record little-known events, such as the secession of the Indian Stream Republic and the role of the Concord coach in winning the west. Others shed a new light on places: President Wilson's Summer White House in Cornish, a World War II prisoner-of-war camp in Stark, and the last of the great log drives in the north country.

Trail. A full-color map and thirty-two-page guide are available ($2) and provide a handy and excellent reference to historic buildings and sites and varied architectural styles along the way. The **Black Heritage Trail** *guide* also costs $2. Write or call Greater Portsmouth Chamber of Commerce, 500 Market St., P.O. Box 239, Portsmouth 03802-0239; (603) 436-1118; order online at www.portsmouthnh.com/harbourtrail/order.cfm; or go to the visitor kiosk at Market Square during the summer.

Most people are surprised to learn that slavery was a part of early colonial life in New Hampshire. In 1775, the eve of the Revolution, there were 656 slaves in the state. The story of their lives is told on the Portsmouth Black Heritage Trail. The twenty-four sites on the trail include Long Wharf, where slaves were unloaded and sold; the William Pitt Tavern at Strawbery Banke; the Governor John Langdon House; and the Portsmouth Children's Museum, which served as the state's first black church in the late nineteenth and early twentieth centuries. Copies of the *Portsmouth Black Heritage Trail* brochure, which describes the sites and contains a map, are available from the Portsmouth Black Heritage Trail, P.O. Box 5094, Portsmouth 03802; (603) 431-2768. For a list of sites and some excerpts from the booklet, visit www.seacoastNH.com/blackhistory; www.pbhtrail.org/.

Much of Portsmouth is best seen on foot, and the city has wisely provided a good parking garage right in the center of town on Hanover Street. It's very inexpensive and saves you the hassle of trying to find a legal space on the narrow streets of this ancient port town. It's just 1 block north of Market Square off Market Street.

The original name for the settlement here was *Strawbery Banke,* after the riverbanks reddened with the fruit in the late spring. A museum preserving nearly four centuries of this old waterfront neighborhood, saved from

blackheritage

Portsmouth has an intriguing black heritage. For more see *Black Portsmouth: Three Centuries of African-American Heritage,* Sammons & Cunningham, University of New Hampshire Press.

demolition in the 1950s, now uses the name Strawbery Banke. Thirty of the thirty-five historic homes here stand on their original foundations. The unusual feature of the restoration is that instead of returning the neighborhood to any single period and showing what things looked like then, the buildings and their furnishings show the evolution of homes, gardens, shops, and daily life throughout the entire period of its existence.

The most dramatic example of this whole-history approach is at the **Drisco House,** built in 1795. The house changed with the times, and when it was acquired, one side of the duplex was a "frozen-in-time" 1950s apartment. It has been saved as it stood, but the other half of the house has been restored to its origins as the store and home of an eighteenth-century mid-level tradesman. This, too, is unusual, for the homes that are usually saved and restored are those of wealthy and prominent citizens—homes far more elegant and ornate than the Drisco House. This one building, with its 1795 and 1955 halves, spans the history of the Puddle Dock neighborhood in Portsmouth.

The process of discovery and restoration is a continuing one, and visitors are invited to share in it through a number of exhibits showing cutaway walls and structural details. The **Joshua Jackson** and **Sherburne Houses** are dedicated entirely to old-house archaeology, showing not only how the homes were built but also how historians can detect the changes made over the centuries. To anyone restoring an older home, looking inside the mechanics of original and renovated construction is an invaluable lesson. To the more casual visitor, it's just plain interesting.

Thanks, Gov

Royal Governor John Wentworth unwittingly helped train and equip three regiments of New Hampshire soldiers for the Continental Army, which were ready from the first shots of the Revolution. Wentworth had vigorously supported these as a local militia to defend Portsmouth in case of attack from French or other enemies of the Crown; all they had to do was change their names and march off to Bunker Hill. These three regiments fought in nearly every major encounter and were credited with an important role in winning the war.

Portsmouth was a major shipyard during World War II, and life on the home front in a coastal city is illustrated at the ***Abbott Grocery Store,*** restored to its 1943 appearance and contents. The storekeeper's apartment next door and exhibits in the rear of the building all show how life on the home front changed during the war.

For more than fifty years the family of a New Hampshire governor of the Civil War era lived in the ***Goodwin Mansion,*** and his wife's detailed and spirited diaries provide information that has made it possible to restore not only the house but her remarkable gardens as well. At various times in summer and fall, Victorian teas are served in these gardens.

In keeping with the museum's philosophy, its newest restoration tells the story of a Russian Jewish family that settled in Puddle Dock at the turn of the twentieth century. ***Shapiro House*** celebrates the lives of the family of Abraham and Shiva Shapiro and is restored to the 1910 period. From the kosher kitchen to the bedrooms on the second floor, and even to family treasures and a boarder's room on the third floor, this is an immersion in the immigrant experience of adaptation to life in a new country. Holidays appropriate to the family are celebrated here.

Without major endowment, Strawbery Banke continues to grow as funds are available, usually from local donations or entry fees. It is exciting to watch the restorations take place, and each visit gives a dimension of being part of its progress. Even the gifts purchased at the museum shop help fund the restoration. It's like giving twice when you do your Christmas shopping there.

Speaking of Christmas, on the first two weekends of December, the village opens for a ***Candlelight Stroll.*** Candles light the windows as you wander through the streets with costumed carolers and musicians. The houses are decorated for the holidays and offer free refreshments to visitors. Craftspeople are at work, and you can shop for gifts in their workshops or in the museum store. Each year brings new features, and it's an occasion for local people to enjoy the uncrowded winter quiet of Strawbery Banke. The stroll takes place on four evenings only, from 4 to 9 p.m., and costs $18 for adults, $10 for children ages five to seventeen (age four and under are admitted free); packages are offered for families and groups.

The restored buildings are open May through Oct, daily 10 a.m. to 5 p.m., and Nov through Apr, Sat 10 a.m. to 2 p.m., and Sun noon to 2 p.m. Guided ninety-minute walking tours leave on each hour. Admission is $15 for adults, $10 for ages five to seventeen, and free for children under age five. Write Strawbery Banke, Marcy St., P.O. Box 300, Portsmouth 03802; call (603) 433-1100; or visit www.strawberybanke.org.

Gardeners should stop at **Prescott Park** across the street to see the All America Show Garden, where each year's All America selections are grown. Show gardens such as this are located in different parts of the country to demonstrate which flowers perform best in various climates. Northerners who spot boxwood at Strawbery Banke may wonder how it grows in New Hampshire.

holdyourtongue

As "witches" were being hanged in neighboring Massachusetts on no more than the testimony of children, Goody Walford of Portsmouth, described as an old crone and accused of witchcraft, brought a defamation suit against her accusers and was awarded damages by the court.

The answer is that Portsmouth and a tiny coastal strip are in a different gardening zone from the rest of the state, due to the moderating effect of the sea. In addition to the garden, the park has an active marina and hosts almost daily activities throughout the summer. The **Prescott Park Arts Festival** in July and August offers twilight and Sunday brunch concerts, theater, art shows, and craft shows. On the Saturday of Memorial Day weekend (or the first Saturday in June) area restaurants compete in a **Chowderfest** at the park, and on the Saturday of Columbus Day weekend they meet again for a **Chili Cook-Off** at midday. Check www.prescottpark.org.

Rich, creamy chowders made from scratch are a fine art that's been perfected at **Geno's Chowder Shop** (603-427-2070) near Prescott Park. Geno's daughter, Francesca Marconi, keeps up a tradition that Geno began in the 1960s, adding a changing selection of other savory soups and legendary meaty lobster rolls. Boat owners can tie up here to eat on Geno's deck or their own.

Another lively Portsmouth event is the annual **Market Square Day,** the second Saturday of June (603-431-4398). Music, food booths, activities, art exhibits, and crafts shows all end with fireworks. The city is ablaze with color, balloons, and throngs of people having fun. Check out www.proportsmouth.org/aboutusppi.cfm for more information. A **Jazz Weekend and Festival** takes place in June or early July. It features regional and local musicians in live performance at Harbour Place, near Memorial Bridge, and at Strawbery Banke. For information on specifics of these or other activities such as **First Night,** call the Greater Portsmouth Chamber of Commerce at (603) 436-1118.

St. John's Church on Chapel Street, just off Bow Street, is a masterpiece of colonial architecture with later trompe l'oeil painting decorating its galleried interior. The bell in the steeple, still used to summon worshippers each Sunday, was captured at the French fortress at Louisbourg, Nova Scotia, in 1745, brought to Portsmouth, and presented to this church. The bell fell during a fire in 1806 and was recast by Paul Revere. The church silver was given by Queen Anne, and the Brattle organ, built in England in 1662, is a pure baroque organ of the sort J. S. Bach played and the oldest operating pipe organ in America. E. Power Biggs made a recording on it for the 1976 bicentennial celebrations. The church also has a copy of the rare "Vinegar Bible." Royal Governor Benning Wentworth is buried in the adjacent churchyard. You can see all of these things with the help of a little brochure that you will find in the front of the church. We hope you'll leave a contribution for the building's upkeep and repair when you leave.

Built at the Portsmouth Naval Shipyard in 1953, the *USS* **Albacore,** now at the *Port of Portsmouth Maritime Museum,* never went to war. Its mission was an experimental one, as it was planned to be redesigned and adapted as the prototype for the submarine of the future. The teardrop hull design made the *Albacore* the fastest submarine ever put in the water. That and dive brakes, sonar systems, and other new theories tested onboard have become part of modern submarine design. The fascinating story of this experimental submarine and how its fifty-five-member crew lived in its 205-foot-by-27-foot confines during its nineteen years of commission is told during a ten-minute video and a half-hour tour of the vessel. Now sunk in a dry basin so you can see the entire hull, the USS *Albacore* looks a bit like a beached whale up close. It's the only one of its kind, so even if the sea and its ships don't interest you at all, don't pass up the chance to see it. Open daily Memorial Day to Columbus Day 9:30 a.m. to 5 p.m. Winter hours Thurs through Mon 9:30 a.m. to 4 p.m. Adults $5, children $3, family $10. You'll find the *Albacore* on the Market Street Extension, or Route 1 bypass, 600 Market St., Portsmouth; (603) 436-3680 or www.ussalbacore.org.

For entertainment in Portsmouth you can't do better than The *Music Hall.* This nicely restored theater is run by a local nonprofit organization and offers current movies, classic and foreign films, live theater, ballet, and music. Touring groups such as the Acting Company perform here on a regular basis. It's at 28 Chestnut St., Portsmouth; call (603) 436-2400, or call the twenty-four-hour film line at (603) 436-9900 for information; or visit www.themusichall.org. Movie admissions are $8, including a $1 preservation fee; live performance fees vary. *Seacoast Repertory Theatre,* a professional company, presents a full entertainment calendar (603-433-4472, www.seacoastrep.org). One night a month, Portsmouth's art galleries host Art Round Town gallery walks, with refreshments and artists on hand to discuss their work (603-436-7007).You might also want to check the "Spotlight" section of the *Portsmouth Herald,* a weekly supplement to the paper, which covers music, theater, and the visual arts throughout the seacoast area, with addresses and phone numbers of clubs.

Portsmouth has developed a reputation for some of the best dining in the state, with a range of styles to choose from. ***Ristorante Massimo*** has an elegant basement setting with lots of wood and etched glass, and the menu includes intriguing appetizers of duck, peekytoe crab, and rabbit; and entrees of rib eye steak finished with hedgehog mushroom-bordelaise, sweet potato-sage encrusted veal rib eye finished with a cognac and peppercorn demi-glace, and grilled Australian rack of lamb with a lavender-chestnut demi-glace. Pasta courses (all pasta is made on premises) run about $11 to 12 and Secondi entrees $22 to $34. Massimo is at 59 Penhallow St.; call (603) 436-4000 or visit www.ristorantemassimo.com.

The former chef at Lindbergh's Crossing, Evan Mallett, has opened his own restaurant at the same location. ***Black Trumpet Bistro*** has the same cozy atmosphere, retaining the low-beamed, brick dining room, and upstairs wine bar. An expert mycologist, Chef Mallet literally steps out his back door for ingredients, finding a garden of exotic mushrooms in the woods behind his home. He makes and cures the sausages he serves in the restaurant and works closely with local farmers to find wholesome, unusual, pesticide-free ingredients from which he creates a constantly changing seasonal menu. Mallet delights in interesting game dishes and in artistic presentations that are as enticing to the eye as to the palate. For example, elk rib eye is served with cherry-pepper coulis on a square plate, beside a tangerine shell filled with pistachio rice pudding. Quickly seared sashimi-quality yellowfin tuna might be fanned over a mound of shoestring blue-potato fries. Black Trumpet Bistro is at 29 Ceres St.; (603) 431-0887, www.blacktrumpetbistro.com.

At ***Dunaway Restaurant*** on Marcy Street, adjacent to Strawbery Banke, the chef has the pick of the Strawbery Banke gardens, where each season brings a largess of herbs, flowers, fruits, and vegetables, often heirloom varieties that grew in colonial times. This often brings to the menu vegetables and preparations that have been out of fashion for generations: salsify, braised radish, spring garlic, and celery root. But don't expect "old-fashioned Yankee cooking" at this stylish restaurant. The menu and the concept are twenty-first century, the service is highly professional, presentations are handsome, and the menu is filled with happy surprises. The meat is locally raised and the seafood menu emphasizes those harvested in local waters. Those fruits (four varieties of pears, heirloom apples) and vegetables that are not picked in the Strawbery Banke gardens are bought from local farms. But the proof is in what happens to them in the kitchen. To sample the latest creations, indulge in the Dunaway Celebration Menu, six courses of seasonal specialties that the chef designs each night. For a-la-carte starters consider the fois gras—you won't find a better preparation—and the succulent sea scallops, if they are on the menu. Servings are plentiful, but it's well worth saving some room to round out dinner with a cheese plate. The selection includes some rare varieties you'll not find easily. Reservations are almost essential. The Dunaway is at 66 Marcy St., Portsmouth; (603) 373-6112 or www.dunawayrestaurant.com.

For casual lunches with a lot more to offer than the usual burgers-with-chips menu, stop at *KNR's Wood Grill & Specialty Sandwiches,* operated by the chef/owner of the former (and popular) restaurant 43 Degrees North. Some of the menu items—the popular duck spring rolls for one—carry over from the previous restaurant, but the focus is on lunch and on the nuances of grilled-to-order specialties, from made-to-order hamburgers to the wood-grilled shrimps on the salads. KNR is open daily at 75 Pleasant St.; (603) 373-6330.

If there were a contest among Portsmouth chefs for the most tempting appetizers, *The Green Monkey* would be in the running with such tempting starters as Asian pear salad with goat cheese, honey-roasted macadamia nuts, and blueberry soy dressing; wontons filled with Fuji apple and pork; or mango-barbecued scallops. Entrees are interesting, too, with choices such as duck breast fanned over braised red cabbage with a blackberry reduction. The Green Monkey is at 86 Pleasant St.; (603) 427-1010 or www.thegreen monkey.net.

Pesce Blue has a menu almost entirely devoted to seafood, from the appetizer of tuna tartare to the signature Mediterranean Branzino (sea bass). The latter is roasted in two inches of salt, making the fish so buttery and flavorful that it doesn't even need the three choices of different oils served beside it. The chefs favor Italian influences with this and their other signature entree, a classic Griglia Mista. This is a mixed grill of five of the day's freshest fish, which might include salmon, halibut, haddock, sea bass, and tuna, served over mixed grilled vegetables. It may sound simple, but the flavors and textures give the seafood here remarkable complexity. Pesche Blue is at 103 Congress St.; (603) 430-7766 or www.pesceblue.com.

Muddy River Smokehouse is what it says it is, serving baby back ribs, chili, smoked chicken, pan-blackened catfish, jerk chicken—you get the idea. This is also a hot local venue for live blues and other styles, with frequent performances. Call or check their Web page at www.muddyriver.com. The restaurant's open every day, serving lunch and dinner, and the downstairs lounge is open evenings, Wed through Sat, at 21 Congress St.; (603) 430-9582, www.muddyriver.com.

Ceres Bakery, at 51 Penhallow St., bakes incomparable breads, cookies, tortes, and coffee cakes. Nowhere else will you find such generous slices of the last two served up for $1.00 to $1.50. Hearty thick soups are served with a slice of their daily bread, or you can choose quiches or salads. Lunch with dessert will be under $6. The bakery opens Mon through Fri: 7 a.m. to 5 p.m., Sat: 7 a.m. to 4 p.m. (603-436-6518 or www.ceresbakery.com).

Martin Hill Inn is the kind of place you create in your mind when you're traveling and tired, but you know you'll never find. Right downtown, within a few blocks of restaurants and shops, this engaging inn is country-quiet, with a large, shady garden where you can stroll amid periwinkles and tulips in May or peonies and lilies in the summer—or just relax with a book. Inside it's all antiques and elegance, but the kind you want to sink into instead of tiptoe through. Each room has its own character, colors, and style, and we like them all, especially the master bedroom, in shades of China blue and an Abigail Adams bedspread. Although the historic building is restored and decorated in antiques, modern conveniences abound: ample reading lights and brand-new plumbing and fixtures. Full breakfast is served in a lovely period room. The inn is at 404 Islington St., Portsmouth; (603) 436-2287; www.martinhillinn.com.

Within walking distance from Strawbery Banke and most of the other attractions of Portsmouth, the *Ale House Inn* occupies the top floor of a harborside building that once housed a brewery. Tastefully decorated rooms with queen-size brass beds frame views of the harbor. Restaurants and Market Square are close by. Rates are $139 to $199 in high season, about $40 lower in winter. The inn is at 121 Bow St., Portsmouth; (603) 431-7760; www.ale houseinn.com.

Out of town, where the Little Harbor Road ends at the water's edge, is the *Wentworth-Coolidge Mansion.* It is one of the very few residences of a royal governor virtually unchanged since the Revolution. The governor lived well. The home that he built in 1750 was originally even larger and was the most elegant of its day. It was not only his residence but the center of government as well. You can tour the original rooms and the Governor's Council Chamber, where he signed the charters for land grants and towns throughout New Hampshire and Vermont. Tours (forty-five minutes to one hour) are $3, free for those under eighteen and New Hampshire residents over age sixty-five. The grounds, where you are welcome to picnic, are planted with the first lilacs brought to the New World. They are the state flower, and if you visit New Hampshire in May you will see them blooming in dooryards and gardens and at the sites of long-deserted farms throughout the countryside. Although technically an "exotic" here, lilacs have a long history in the state and have been accepted as native. Open daily 10 a.m. to 5 p.m. from Memorial Day weekend to Labor Day. The Wentworth-Coolidge Mansion is on Little Harbor Road, off Route 1A in Portsmouth; (603) 436-6607.

South of Portsmouth, not far from Route 1, is the 150-acre property of the *Urban Forestry Center.* A beautiful place to visit for its gardens, woodland,

and salt-marsh landscapes, it is also an attractive demonstration area, the purpose of which is not only to protect this piece of land but to show others how they can protect and enhance their own property as well. Individuals, municipalities, developers, and conservation commissions all look to the center for inspiration and advice. Throughout the property are mailboxes where you will find extensive information on each project. Plant-by-plant descriptions are available at the perennial border, and a thorough booklet on herb culture and uses, prepared by Tanya Jackson (one of New England's leading herb experts), is free at the herb garden. The center sponsors lectures, field trips, and programs on natural history, wildlife, gardening, and New Hampshire forests. Most of the programs are on Thursday evenings and cost $5 to $15. Visit www.nhstateparks.org for more information.

A Garden for the Senses, created especially for the visually and physically impaired, emphasizes plants selected for flavor, fragrance, color, and texture, with wide paths and raised beds for easy access. An arboretum contains examples of trees for street plantings, cold-hardy trees, and those with unusual and interesting flowers, bark, or leaves. Several plantations and trails as well as ample space for watching birds that live in the marsh and shore areas add to the center's attractions. Free and open year-round, the trails are favorites of

Whodunit?

John and Maren Hontvet shared their cottage on Smuttynose, one of the Isles of Shoals, with John's brother, Maren's brother, and his beautiful wife, Anethe, all freshly arrived from Norway. Maren's sister, Karen, was visiting. A friend, Louis Wagner, lived in Portsmouth and was jobless. Thus the scene is set for the night of March 5, 1873.

The three men from Smuttynose decided to spend the night in Portsmouth, and they mentioned this to Louis, whom they met there. From here, the story has two distinctly different versions. The accepted one, based more on contemporary public opinion and sentiment than on the actual trial and testimony, is that Louis rowed a stolen dory 10 miles out to the island and, in an attempt to rob the house, hacked Anethe and Karen to death with an axe while Maren managed to escape and hide all night in the rocks along the shore. She identified him as the murderer, and he was caught, almost lynched by incited mobs, tried, and hanged.

While popular opinion of the era would not accept the idea of a family woman committing murder, the trial evidence points to Maren as the villain and shows no evidence that Wagner was even on the island that night. But anyone who knew the truth was dead, and Maren and John moved to Portsmouth, without either brother or the pretty sister-in-law. Smuttynose is uninhabited today.

cross-country skiers and snowshoe hikers (no motorized recreational vehicles). Hours are dawn to dusk daily. The office is open 8 a.m. to 4 p.m. Mon through Fri. The center is at 45 Elwyn Rd. (off Lafayette Road) in Portsmouth; call (603) 431-6774 or visit www.nhdfl.org/land-conservation/urban-forestry-center/ for more information.

Off the coast, shared with Maine but with access from New Hampshire, and visible only in clear weather, are the *Isles of Shoals.* Described by the writer and poet Celia Thaxter, who grew up there, they were painted by the impressionist artist Childe Hassam, who came to the summer arts colony that developed there. His work includes more than 400 paintings of the islands, many of which were done to illustrate Thaxter's *An Island Garden,* a classic of garden writing as fresh in its facsimile reprint as it was in its original printing at the turn of the twentieth century. These islands are as wrapped in tales of ship-wrecks, pirates, ghosts, and buried treasure as they are in fog. Craggy and bar-ren as they were when Captain John Smith called them "barren piles of rock," the islands still fascinate visitors. *The Isles of Shoals Steamship Company* at 315 Market St. will take passengers to Star Island for a three-hour shore visit on two sailings. Boats depart Mon through Fri at 9:25 a.m. and 1:25 p.m. Fare is $24 for adults. Contact (603) 431-5500, (800) 441-4620, or www.islesofshoals.com. *Whale-watching,* fishing, harbor, and Great Bay cruises from Portsmouth are also offered by Portsmouth Harbor Cruises at Ceres Street Dock, 64 Ceres St., Portsmouth; (603) 436-8084 or (800) 776-0915; www.portsmouthharbor.com. Between May and Oct they offer harbor, bay, and river cruises. You can also take cruises there from Rye Harbor (see next section).

The South Coast

The shoreline in Rye is less developed than elsewhere, with long stretches of open salt marsh (some of it a wildlife preserve) and rocky coast broken by beaches. *Atlantic Fishing Fleet* offers *deep-sea fishing* trips and whale-watches on board *Atlantic Queen II* from April through mid-October. You might catch flounder, mackerel, or, rarely, cod. The trip is fun, whatever the catch, and offers an education about the fishing industry. Atlantic Fishing Fleet can be found at 1870 Ocean Blvd., Rye. For a schedule call (603) 964-5220 or (800) 942-5364, or visit www.atlanticwhalewatch.com.

Island Cruises operates tours to the Isles of Shoals and lobster tours from Rye Harbor. The two-hour island tour is narrated with historical facts and tales of mysterious doings. On the one-hour lobster tour you learn all about the elusive crustaceans and how they are harvested, coming face to face with one when a trap is brought aboard. During July and Aug, they operate the island tour several times each day and the lobster tour Sat through Wed at 10 a.m. In June and Sept, they operate weekends only. Contact them at Rye Harbor State Marina, Route 1-A, Ocean Blvd., (603) 964-6446, or www.uncleoscar.com.

Overlooking the ocean is *Saunders at Rye Harbor,* a local institution for more than seventy years. The menu offers a wider range of dishes than you would expect in a restaurant best known for its lobster. Seafood-stuffed mushroom caps, herbed toasted pita points, Jamaican scampi, and five "healthy choices," including chicken Marsala, highlight the menu. Ben Saunders sold lobster from the dock in the 1920s, and it's his recipe they still use for the old-fashioned lobster stew. The restaurant was a favorite of poet Ogden Nash, but he never immortalized it in any of his verses. On Route 1A, 175 Harbor Rd., Rye; call (603) 964-6466.

For a shorebound excursion that gives you nature on one side and human nature on the other, walk or bicycle around *Little Boar's Head.* A 2-mile path goes along the ridge of a rocky promontory, with waves crashing on the rocks below. Inland stands a row of beach "cottages" built in the pre–income tax days, when wealthy city dwellers moved their families and household staffs to the shore for the summer. In the early summer wild roses bloom along the path.

Roses at *Fuller Gardens* are clearly not wild: 1,500 carefully tended rosebushes thrive in the sea air in an All America Rose Display Garden, once part of a fine old Boar's Head estate. Both roses and perennial beds are at their peak in June, but the gardens are filled with blooms all summer and late into the fall. Don't miss the gate in the hedge leading to the cool, cedar-shaded Japanese garden with its pool, bridge, and stone lantern. Marble walkways surround a terraced formal garden. Open 10 a.m. to 5:30 p.m. daily, mid-May through mid-Oct, the gardens are at 10 Willow Ave., which leaves Route 1A just north of its intersection with Route 101D in North Hampton. The telephone is (603) 964-5414. Admission is $7 for adults, $3 for children under twelve, and $6 for seniors. You may also visit www.fullergardens.org.

The town of Hampton lies inland, out of hearing distance of raucous Hampton Beach. Follow Park Avenue east from Route 1 to find the original settlement at Meetinghouse Green. The old common is now a memorial park to the first settlers, with a stone for each of the pioneer families put there by their descendants. Across the street is the *Tuck Museum,* operated by the Hampton Historical Society, a group of buildings that includes an old one-room schoolhouse, a museum of early farm implements, the Seacoast Fire Museum, and a variety of exhibits on the area's history. It isn't the Smithsonian, but it is a very approachable collection; most items are not in glass cases but right where you can see them. A playground on the shady lawn outside will amuse the children if your attention span exceeds theirs. Open 1 to 4 p.m. Wed, Fri, and Sun from mid-June to mid-Sept. Admission is free. The museum is at 40 Park Ave., Hampton; call (603) 929-0781 or visit www.hamptonhistorical society.org for news of special events.

There's not much off-the-beaten-path about Hampton Beach, but you might miss a tempting enclave of authentic Mexican dining at *La Chiquitas.* The chef/owner is from Rosa Rita, in the Mexicali region of Baja. His menu offers authentic fish tacos, on tortillas that are made here, fresh daily. Mexican cooking is more about flavor than about hot, and this chef concentrates on using the right chilis to bring out natural flavors. Look for La Chiquitas just north of A Street; (603) 926-1250.

The *Science and Nature Center* at Seabrook Station, the area's power station, explores various sources of energy and their effects on the environment. Hands-on exhibits, such as a bicycle-powered generator (how long can you keep the light burning?) and computerized quizzes, fill the science center, and an aquarium shows local marine life. The Owascoag Nature Trail winds through woods and marshlands, where markers explain the habitats, natural history, and plant life. Shorebirds abound, and muskrats, foxes, rabbits, and woodchucks may wander within sight if you are quiet. Such salt marshes are important sources of food and breeding grounds for wildlife, as well as filtration areas to keep groundwater pure. The Science & Nature Center and *Owascoag Nature Trail* are open to the public Mon through Thurs from 10 a.m. to 3 p.m.; free admission. Write Seabrook Station, Route 1, Seabrook 03874, or call (603) 474-9521 or (800) 338-7482; or visit www.fpl.com/environment/ nuclear/seabrook_science_and_nature_center.shtml.

Bordering Route 1 near the state line in Seabrook is the Hampton Harbor Marsh, New England's largest salt marsh, with over 5,000 acres of sea grass, mudflats, and sandbars. It's an important migratory stop for more than 21 species of shorebirds. Exeter, like Portsmouth, is a nice place for walking. Fine homes line its streets, and three of the finest Federal mansions face the bandstand in the center of town. The *Gilman Garrison House* was built of massive hewn logs in the late 1600s as a fortified garrison. In the mid-1700s the house was enlarged and remodeled, adding a wing and more formal rooms in which its owner felt more comfortable entertaining John Wentworth, the royal governor, during his visits to Exeter. These visits ended abruptly when the governor had to take refuge in Fort William and Mary and finally flee altogether at the outbreak of the Revolution. (Since Portsmouth was considered a hotbed of Toryism, the seat of the state's government moved to Exeter—making it the state's first capital.) Later, Daniel Webster boarded in this house while he was a student at Phillips Exeter Academy. Tours by appointment only. The Gilman

Garrison House is at the corner of Water and Clifford Streets in Exeter; call (603) 436-3205 for an appointment.

Also in the center of town is the ***American Independence Museum,*** a newly established combination of the Ladd-Gilman House (home of New Hampshire's governor during the Revolution) and the Folsom Tavern, with the archives of the Society of the Cincinnati. The collections in the two eighteenth-century buildings feature furnishings from the 1600s, two annotated drafts of the U.S. Constitution, and historic artifacts. Open mid-May through late Oct Mon through Fri 10 a.m. to 4 p.m. Escorted tours are given Wed through Sat (the last tour begins at 3 p.m.), May through Oct. Located at 1 Governor's Lane (off Center Street), Exeter; (603) 772-2622; www.independencemuseum.org.

Art deco enthusiasts should stop at the ***Ioka Theater*** in downtown Exeter, where the lobby has been restored to its 1915 origins, and includes a jukebox and an original soda fountain. This is also a venue for live performances; call for a schedule. Movies are $6, $4 for children and seniors; (603) 772-2222; www.iokaentertainment.com.

Known best to students, parents, and alumni of Phillips Exeter Academy, the ***Exeter Inn*** offers a wide variety of rooms that retain the charm of a historic hotel while providing modern and stylish lodgings. The spacious lobby sets the tone of unstuffy elegance. The inn's Epoch Restaurant gets high scores for fine dining and for favoring—and crediting on the menu—local producers, such as Sandwich Creamery's cheddar in the Dauphine Potatoes and North Country Smokehouse bacon in the corn fritters. Seafood gets the attention it deserves in dishes such as olive oil poached ahi tuna, served with asparagus risotto. A vegetarian dish is always offered, getting every bit as much attention to detail as the other entrees; perhaps orange-ginger tofu brochettes with

Where's the Beach?

New Hampshire's shoreline just can't seem to sit still. As glaciers melted away and raised the ocean level about 12,000 years ago, the tide line reached as far west as Route 125 in Barrington and Lee, with Stratham Hill as an offshore island. However, as glaciers continued to melt away, their weight stopped pressing down on the land behind, and it rose, pushing the shoreline farther east, until it reached the Isles of Shoals. Once the land stopped this process of readjustment, known as isostatic recovery, the shoreline settled into its present place.

But don't get complacent. Ocean levels are on the rise again, at the alarming rate of $\frac{1}{25}$ inch each year. That means a rise of about 3½ feet by the year 3000, so you'd better build that sand castle farther back.

roasted tomatillo quinoa, grilled pineapple, and toasted pepper coulis. The restaurant is busy during special events at the academy, so call ahead to be sure of a table. The inn is at the corner of Front and Pine Streets, Exeter; call (603) 772-5901 or (800) 782-8444, or visit www.theexeterinn.com.

Great Bay

Past Portsmouth Harbor, the Piscataqua River opens into Little Bay, which is fed by the Oyster River and **Great Bay.** At 5 miles long, Great Bay is the largest inland body of salt water in New England, but it's very hard to see since only one road, Route 4, passes within sight. Even that allows views of only the northern end. The towns that lie along the rivers feeding it are all far from its tidal shores.

The best way to see this area is from the water, on a **Piscataqua River Cruise,** a three-hour trip from Portsmouth to Durham, with a stop at the site of the Bickford Garrison to learn how it was defended in 1694 by one farmer who cleverly changed coats and voices to make the post seem well-manned. The tour includes a buffalo farm (see below) and a chance to sample a buffalo burger as well. Offered on weekends in the fall, when the foliage along the wooded shores is at its best, cruises are run by Isles of Shoals Steamship Company, 315 Market St., P.O. Box 311, Portsmouth 03802; call (603) 431-5500 or (800) 894-5509 in New Hampshire, (800) 441-4620 outside the state, or visit www.islesofshoals.com.

Another way to see this area from the water is to paddle your own canoe or kayak, putting in at **Hilton Park,** on Dover Point, on the north side of the big highway bridges. Paddlers should be aware that the current under the bridges is among the strongest on the East Coast, a place to avoid. But you're going the other way, north along the shore of Dover Neck and the Piscataqua River. You have two possible destinations from here: The Piscataqua is formed by the **Cocheco** and **Salmon Falls Rivers.** The first leads to Dover (about 6 miles) and the second to South Berwick, in Maine, about 7 miles. The shores of both are fairly undeveloped, so either makes a scenic trip.

The Little Bay Buffalo Company is a family-run farm on rolling meadows and woodlands extending to the waters of Little Bay. It is a habitat for a number of wildlife species and a migratory stop for waterfowl. The bison here are not for petting, but they are usually visible in the pasture, often at close range. Also at the farm are displays on the interrelationship between the bison and the Indians' way of life, as well as information on local Indians who camped here in the summer to fish and hunt. The Company Store sells buffalo meat, hides, and related products such as buffalo tooth necklaces. The clear message here, well stated by the Langley family, is that using resources requires responsibility. To reach the farm, take Durham Point Road from Route 108 and watch for the small sign on Langley Road to the left. Open daily mid-April through late Nov, 9 a.m. to 5 p.m.; observation area open until sunset. Contact the company at 50 Langley Rd., Durham 03824; (603) 868-3300 or (800) 380-3311.

Durham is best known for the *University of New Hampshire,* which dominates the town and brings it to life. Beside Thompson Hall on the campus is a lovely ravine filled in May with lilacs of every shade from white to dark purple. The Art Gallery at the University of New Hampshire is a little-known treasure trove of fine arts located in the Paul Creative Arts Center. The permanent collection includes 1,500 paintings, prints, drawings, and sculpture works, most from the nineteenth and twentieth centuries. Among these are works by Durer, Hogarth, Abbott Thayer, Corot, Frank Benson, Hiroshige, Daumier, Homer, Lotte Jacobi, Whistler, Miro, Roualt, Klimpt, Frank Shapleigh, and a host of other luminaries, as well as a major collection of Japanese woodcuts and historic works, including pre-Columbian and African art. Major exhibitions bring other works on a regular basis. The Art Gallery is at 30 College Rd.; (603) 862-3712.

Off Durham Point Road, on the way to Newmarket, is the *Great Bay Estuarine Research Reserve,* more than 4,000 acres of tidal waters, mud flats, salt marsh, tidal-creek woodlands, fields, and meadows on Adams Point. There is no nature center or organized visitor program here, but the habitat is filled with the flora and fauna peculiar to tidal estuaries. A boat put-in and parking area are reached by a stone-wall-bordered road that ends at the Jackson Laboratory, an estuarine research center. Park there to reach the viewing platform (wheelchair accessible) overlooking rolling meadows with the bay in the background. The air is filled with the trill of birds. For information on the Great Bay Reserve, call New Hampshire Fish and Game at (603) 868-1095, or contact the preserve at (603) 431-7511; www.greatbay.org.

The bay is a kayaker's heaven, with protected waters formed by an almost endless supply of rivers. Their tidal estuaries meander through grassy marshlands rich in bird life and past forested shores that turn gold and crimson in the fall.

From Adams Point, you can canoe or kayak along the shore and up the *Squamscott River* to Exeter (use NOAA map #13285 1:20000). Look for the chained gate to Adams Point (open 4 a.m. to 10 p.m.) to find the put-in. Paddle along the shore to your right, watching for birds and other wildlife on this undeveloped shore where bald eagles winter. High tide is best; tides are fairly

high here, and at low tide you'll see vast expanses of mud. The first big chan-
nel you come to is the Lamprey River, which you can follow to Newmarket for
a shorter trip. Past that is the Squamscott River; if you go all the way to Exeter,
it is about a 10-mile paddle one way.

Emery Farm was established in 1655, which, eleven generations later,
makes it high on the list of the nation's oldest family farms. Here you can pick
your own strawberries, blueberries, or raspberries. Juicy, tree-ripened peaches
and garden produce, as well as local maple syrup, honey, and fresh home-
baked breads, are sold; New Hampshire crafts and pottery add to the unique
farmstand. In the spring they sell herb plants and garden flats from their greenhouse. The farm is open every day, Easter through Christmas Eve (they also
sell Christmas trees) from 9 a.m. to 6 p.m. Emery Farm is on Route 4, 2 miles
east of Durham (603-742-8495 or www.emeryfarm.com).

The elegant *Three Chimneys Inn,* overlooking the mill pond in Durham, serves memorable meals in its dining room, or more casual and less
expensive—but good—dinners in its tavern. In the silver-set dining room,
expect the likes of pork tenderloin wrapped in bacon with raisin-apple-onion
compote and sweet potato–leek hash, finished with bacon sherry vinaigrette,
or tenderloin of beef stuffed with smoked gouda, roasted red pepper, and
basil, wrapped in applewood smoked bacon and accompanied by cognac
Dijon sauce. It's open for lunch Tues through Sat; dinner is served daily. Deep-
hued guest rooms have the air of an English estate, with ornate, hand-carved
beds and rich tapestries, set in Durham's oldest house, which dates from 1649.
Rooms are upwards of $220 with breakfast and dinner for two, but out of the
ordinary in terms of decor, with the original fireplaces restored and working,
whirlpool tubs, and several thoughtful details. The Three Chimneys is at 17
Newmarket Rd., Durham; call (603) 868-7800 or (888) 399-9777 outside of New
Hampshire, or visit www.threechimneysinn.com.

Just west of Durham, the village of Lee was once covered in farmland.
Many of the fields have been reclaimed by forest, but one of the old family
farms has taken on a new life as *Flag Hill Winery.* Unlike many northern wineries that buy in the juice, Frank Rheinholt has planted French hybrid grapes,
producing several fine wines literally from the ground up. Flag Hill also makes
wine from plums, apples, and raspberries. After the success of their wines, they
became New Hampshire's first distillery, producing General John Stark Vodka
in 2004. Flag Hill Chef Ted McCormack holds tasting dinners deeply rooted in
the philosophy of locally grown foods. Localvore Menus feature ingredients
from nearby farms, and Friday evening cooking classes offer hands-on food
experiences. You can visit the vineyards, learn about the process, and taste the
wines, which are also served at better local restaurants. Flag Hill is on Route

Wine and Cheese

Vineyards and cheese dairies are both relative newcomers to the state's agricultural landscape. Although dairy farms have long been part of the New Hampshire scenery, only recently have they turned their attention to cheesemaking. In 2008, the wineries and dairies joined with a cider maker to create the *New Hampshire's Wine & Cheese Trails,* in conjunction with New Hampshire Made. Their brochure is available at state tourist information centers and on the Web site www.visitnh.gov. When planning travels to smaller farms and vineyards, it is always a good idea to call first to be sure they will be open.

155, near the Route 125 intersection, and is open for tours and tastings Wed through Sun 11 a.m. to 5 p.m.; call (603) 659-2949 for information or visit www .flaghill.com.

On leaving the winery, go right, following Route 155 north through Lee. In the town cemetery, opposite the schoolhouse, look for a large boulder near the center, with plaque marking it as the grave of Sherwood (Woody) Sherburn. He was so incensed at vandals knocking over cemetery stones that he vowed he'd find one they couldn't budge. He seems to have succeeded.

The historic towns of Greenland and Stratham lie along the southern shore of Great Bay, whose ecosystem and history are explored at *Sandy Point Discovery Center.* Interactive displays inside show the importance of tidal estuaries as habitat and how they cleanse polluted waters. A look at the bay's history shows fishing and salt-hay harvesting. Trails lead to various ecosystems along the shore and estuary, and nature pamphlets help you identify the birds and other wildlife you'll meet there. The center is open May through Oct, Wed through Sun 10 a.m. to 4 p.m.; admission is free. To find the center, which is signposted from Route 33, take Depot Road and turn left at the T; (603) 778-0015.

After such a fine dinner, you needn't drive far to be home for the night. *Ayers Homestead B&B* is in the village, a cluster of pre-revolutionary and colonial buildings tucked out of earshot of Route 33. The Thomas Ayers House was built in 1737 and enlarged in 1775, then carefully restored by its present owners and filled with antiques. Guests start the day with a full breakfast served in front of the huge fireplace in the original kitchen. Rooms are $80 to $110 including breakfast, among the most modestly priced in the seacoast region. It's at 47 Park Ave., Greenland; (603) 436-5992.

Cocheco Town

Dover was the scene of repeated Indian attacks during the early years of the settlement, so nearly all of its garrison houses were destroyed. The only one still surviving is the 1765 **Damm Garrison,** which is protected by a roofed lattice portico between two brick buildings of the **Woodman Institute.** In original condition, this heavy log structure houses a collection of early furnishings and implements. To learn the story of the Dover Massacre, which this garrison house survived, read *It Happened in New Hampshire,* an anecdotal history of the state with thirty-one incidents that tell its story from the first settlements to the fall of the Old Man of the Mountain in 2003.

The two exhibition buildings of the Woodman Institute are a tribute to the inquiring minds of the Victorians who assembled their contents. The collection of mounted animals contains specimens of most of the mammals native to the state and many, such as an 8-foot-tall polar bear, that are not. In addition to an extensive collection of rocks, minerals, and butterflies, the museum displays fine examples of Sioux beadwork. President Lincoln's saddle, used in his last review of troops and inherited by his aide Colonel Daniel Hall after the assassination, highlights the Civil War collection on the third floor. The Hale House contains fine antique furniture and a variety of collections from the nineteenth century. Open Wed through Sun 12:30 to 4:30 p.m. Limited winter hours. Admission charged. The Woodman Institute, 182 Central Ave., Dover; call (603) 742-1038 or visit www.woodmaninstitutemuseum.com.

Kids and their parents love the **Children's Museum of New Hampshire,** just off the Lower Square on the banks of the Cocheco River. The 2009 facility explores the river in a multifaceted Cochecosystem exhibit that looks at both natural and industrial history. Visitors can see the river from a beaver's perspective as it builds its lodge, or learn how Native Americans fished for alewives. Kids can also board a Piscataqua River gundalow to help load and unload cargo or "navigate" the boat down the river. A human-sized kaleidoscope fascinates everyone, as they see themselves reflected in every direction, but the museum's piece de resistance is "Build It, Fly It." This aerodynamics exhibit teaches by doing, as budding engineers design their own flying machine from interlocking foam pieces in different shapes, then crank it up to the ceiling for a test flight. If it flops, the exhibit helps them redesign it until it flies. The museum is open Tues through Sat 10 a.m. to 5 p.m. and Sun from noon until 5 p.m., and on Mon from 10 a.m. to 5 p.m. during the summer, school vacations, and some holidays. Children's Museum of NH, 6 Washington St., Dover; call (603) 742-2002 or visit www.childrens-museum.org.

Along the Cocheco River in the center of Dover's downtown is an impressive complex of brick mill buildings, and facing these across Central Avenue are rows of classic mercantile buildings. Views and reminiscences of old Dover are posted along the sidewalk at various points, noting stores that were once there, and other historical anecdotes. A walking path follows the river through a park. On Central Avenue, near the Lower Square is a local institution that has provided generations with wedding and birthday cakes for more than half a century, run by the same family. *Harvey's Bakery* now has a coffee shop, so you can enjoy their famous maple bars with a cup of coffee at a booth, or have a more filling breakfast or lunch, Mon through Sat 5:30 a.m. to 3:30 p.m. The bakery is open Mon through Fri 6 a.m. to 5:30 p.m. and Sat 6 a.m. to 5:30 p.m. Harvey's Bakery is at 376 Central Ave., Dover; call (603) 742-6029 or visit www.harveysbakery.com.

Salmon Falls Stoneware is a potters' studio where they make salt-glazed stoneware and decorate it by hand with traditional designs. It is open Mon through Sat 8 a.m. to 5 p.m., and Sun 9 a.m. to 5 p.m. You can find Salmon Falls Stoneware in the old Boston and Maine Engine House on Oak Street in Dover; (603) 749-1467, (800) 621-2030 or www.salmonfalls.com.

Dover is a good place to use as a base while visiting the seacoast area. Quieter than Portsmouth or the beach towns, it is easier to find lodging here, especially in the summer. *Highland Farm* is a gracious bed-and-breakfast in a large mid-nineteenth-century brick home set on seventy-five acres of riverside meadow. Rooms are bright and large with either queen-size or double beds and are reached from a broad central hallway and an elegant double staircase. Breakfast, served in a formal dining room, features fresh fruit and homemade muffins or scones in addition to the main dish. The setting is so quiet and lovely that it's tempting to forget sightseeing entirely and enjoy the walking or cross-country ski trails along the river, the gardens, badminton and lawn games, or the hammock on the wide porch shaded by the mulberry tree full of birds. Highland Farm is open June through mid Nov as a B&B. Rates are about $130 per night double. Write Highland Farm, 148 County Farm Rd., Dover 03820, or call (603) 743-3399.

North of Dover is Rochester, where the *Rochester Opera House* has a tipping floor that rises on one end to provide better views of the stage and lowers to make a flat dance floor. By 1996, when the second effort to restore the magnificent 1908 theater began, no one remembered how the unique floor mechanism worked, and it seemed unlikely that it could be restored to working order. But the UNH engineering school began investigating and discovered its secret—a large screw, well hidden inside a column at the back of the auditorium. The mechanism has been restored and the floor once again rises and falls. The Opera House is at 31 Wakefield St. in Rochester; (603) 335-1992, www.rochesteroperahouse.com. Route 6 of the COAST bus stops at the city hall; check www.coastbus.org.

Off Routes 4/202, west of Northwood, is **Northwood Meadows State Park.** This undeveloped parkland along the Lamprey River has several walking trails and fishing platforms, which are accessible to wheelchairs; call (603) 436-1552 for information.

The Ponds

Rides in fine restored carriages, sleighs, and wagons at **Point of View Farm** are more than transportation; they are, as owner Tyke Frost puts it, an "attempt to recapture some of the elegance that was part of the nineteenth century." For a romantic evening Sue Frost prepares a full-course dinner after the carriage ride (with the coachman in top hat and tails) and serves it on antique china in a private Victorian dining room. Brunch combined with a surrey ride is about $50 per couple. The Gathering Room is designed for birthday parties and other groups to have cake and ice cream after a hay or sleigh ride. Open year-round, reservations are required for special programs and are appreciated

Missing: A 48-Foot White Rock

You will notice that we are fond of glacial erratics, those giant boulders the glaciers picked up in their travels and left off someplace else. But what promises to be one of the most striking of these seemed to have disappeared. A WPA guidebook written in the 1930s refers to one in Raymond as follows: "South of the railroad station is an erratic boulder of white quartz that was transported several hundred feet. It is 48 feet long, 39 feet wide, and from 24 to 30 feet high. Two pine trees have found lodgement in crevices." We've looked for it, and everyone we've asked there is stumped. That's a pretty hefty rock to carry off, unless you're a glacier, so it must either be there (perhaps now covered in moss and pine needles) or have been a figment of someone's imagination. Many of these erratics were quarried, but quartz is an unlikely building stone. We asked readers to share any information with us, and a Raymond man, Bob Hart, took up the challenge. He began, as we had, with the WPA guide that mentions the rock, but he extended his search in other directions. We had combed the area north of the railway station, as described in that 1930s book, but the stone is actually south of the station. Unfortunately for our readers it's in someone's back yard, surrounded by trees and quite covered in lichen, so it no longer stands out as a white beacon and we cannot send readers to visit it. But it is there, and our curiosity is satisfied.

Mast Tree Riot

In 1734, more than four decades before Lexington and Concord, rebellious colonists in Fremont instigated an event known as the Mast Tree Riot. At that time, white pine trees over a certain girth (perfect for masts for the Royal Navy's ships) were the property of the king of England, and colonists were forbidden from cutting any of these. When the king's surveyor came to inspect some illegally cut trees in Fremont, locals threatened his life. He wisely retreated, but when he returned with reinforcements, they were attacked by a band of "Indians," a handy, if politically incorrect disguise. It was one of the earliest armed encounters between colonists and representatives of the Crown.

for individual and family visits. The farm is at 160 South Rd., Deerfield; (603) 463-7974, www.pointofviewfarm.com.

Pawtuckaway State Park has both boat and canoe launch areas on the lake, two campgrounds with tent sites, a beach, and several hiking trails. One of these leads to the *Pawtuckaway Boulders,* a forest filled with huge glacial erratics that were broken from the cliffs on the three small mountains nearby and carried by the glacier to their present location a few thousand feet away in a valley to the east. The boulders vary in size, with some as long as 60 feet and over 30 feet high. Paths also lead to the summits of the three small mountains, two of which offer open views to the south. The campgrounds are open from mid-June to Labor Day, with camping through Oct. Write Pawtuckaway State Park, RFD #1, 128 Mountain Rd., Raymond 03077; call (603) 895-3031 or (603) 271-3628 for reservations.

Until recently, the town of *Fremont* was home to a relic of early Americana, which, sadly, closed a few years ago. Spaulding & Frost Cooperage had made white pine barrels since 1874. It was the oldest and largest cooperage in the world, and you can still see their building, marked by yet another state historic marker. This is not far from the old gunsmith shop, where John and Andrew Brown, prominent New Hampshire gunsmiths, had their shop from 1845 to 1907. Their shop served as the recruiting office where local men could enlist to serve in the Civil War. Route 107 crosses Route 101 near Raymond, east of Manchester, and Fremont is just to the south.

The small town of Fremont, where you will see an abundance of state historic markers, was a hotbed of historical happenings, one of which was the Mast Tree Riot in the mid-1700s, when locals, in the oft-used guise of Indians, attacked an agent of the king who came to investigate reports of locals cutting mast trees reserved for the Royal Navy. The 1800 *Fremont Meeting House* is one of only two in the United States with twin-ended porches and stairwells. Note also its high pulpit and box pews, typical of such early meetinghouses. The Fremont Meeting House is open by appointment and for the town's lively Old Home Days, the third Sunday in August (603-895-4032 or 603-887-6100).

The **Sandown Depot Railroad Museum** is housed in a restored 1873 railroad station. It is thought to have been the busiest single-line railroad line in the country, with eighteen freight and sixteen passenger trains passing through Sandown each day. Most of the original railroad equipment is still in place, including the telegraph office. Open Memorial Day through Labor Day, Sun 1 to 5 p.m. Admission is free. The museum is on Route 121A in Sandown. Call (603) 887-6100 or visit http://www.sandown.us/historical_society/Historical HomePage.htm.

Inquire at the museum to see if the **Sandown Meeting House** on Fremont Road is open to visitors. Built in 1773 and 1774, it is the finest and best-preserved church structure in the state. It still has its original hand-wrought hinges and latches on the paneled doors, as well as the square pews and slave gallery. (It surprises many to learn that owning slaves was a fairly common practice among wealthier New England families—although never to the extent it was in the South.) The pulpit is goblet-shaped, with a canopy that acts as a sounding board. If you are interested in early construction techniques, ask to see the loft, reached by a ladder from the gallery. Crossbeams are staggered, and mortised joints are held by wooden keys. According to a local tale the church took longer to construct than was anticipated, and the rum supply ran out. The workmen refused to continue until the supply was replenished. Just down Route 121A from the depot is **Zorvino Winery,** where they produce wines from grapes grown on the 80-acre property, and where the vintner offers complimentary tastings Tues through Sat noon to 5 p.m. from Apr through Sept. At tasting dinners, the chef pairs their wines with various food styles, including Asian and Caribbean. Zorvino Vineyards is at 226 Main St., Sandown; call (603) 887-8463 or visit www.zorvino.com.

The **Chester Village Cemetery** dates from 1751 and contains monuments by a number of colonial master stone carvers. Look especially at the faces of the angels, a common motif on tombstones of the period. The story is that stoneworker Abel Webster, who lived in Chester in the 1700s, had a running theological quarrel with the townspeople, and to get even with them he put frowns on the faces of all the angels on the tombstones. The cemetery is located at the crossroads of Routes 121 and 102 in Chester.

Route 121 leads from Chester to Auburn, past Lake Massabesic, where the Audubon Society has created a center for education and wildlife viewing. The **Massabesic Audubon Center** has miles of trails through fields and forests

ALSO WORTH SEEING ON THE SEACOAST

**John Paul Jones House,
43 Middle St., Portsmouth;**
(603) 436-8420.
The 1758 house where Captain "Don't
Give up the Ship" lived when he was in
Portsmouth.

**New Hampshire's coast has several
beaches,** the best of which is Jenness
State Beach in Rye. Larger and more
crowded, with a perpetual carnival
atmosphere, is Hampton Beach; (800)
GET–A–TAN.

Northwood,
on Routes 4/202, west of Dover, is an
antiques center, with more than a dozen
shops and group antiques markets lining
the road.

on a 135-acre point of land surrounded by water. Nature exhibits at the center include birds of prey, reptiles, and a garden to attract birds and butterflies. Frequent programs feature a variety of nature experiences and include day camps for children in the summer. From Route 101, follow Bypass 28 to Spofford Road, following signs to the center, which is at 26 Audubon Way, Auburn; (603) 668-2045; www.nhaudubon.org.

Bed-and-breakfast accommodation is surprisingly rare in this part of the state, so visitors are happy to discover *Stillmeadow B&B,* one of several well-restored mid-nineteenth-century homes on Route 121 in Hampstead. Rooms are moderately priced from $65 to $100, and are warm and welcoming, with private baths, nicely chosen color schemes, and pleasant views. Breakfast is served with elegance in the dining room and features home-baked breads and muffins. Write to P.O. Box 565, Hampstead 03841, or call (603) 329-8381 or visit www.mv.com/ipusers/stillmeadow/. Reservations are required.

TO LEARN MORE ABOUT THE SEACOAST

Portsmouth Chamber of Commerce,
Market St.; (603) 436-1118.

More Places to Stay on the Seacoast

DOVER

Silver Fountain Inn
103 Silver St.
(603) 743-3000
In a former private mansion, replete with fine details—Austrian crystal doorknobs, imported stone fireplaces, hand-painted wall coverings—at moderate to high rates.

DURHAM

Hickory Pond Inn
1 Stagecoach Rd.
(603) 659-2227 or (800) 658-0065
www.hickorypondinn.com
Adjoining its own golf course, the inn has a homey feel, despite its motel-like rooms. There is cross-country skiing and a skating rink in the winter. Rooms include continental breakfast. Moderate rates.

HAMPTON

Lamie's Inn
490 Lafayette Rd.
(603) 926-0330
www.oldsaltnh.com
An inn in a 1740 home with a well-thought-of restaurant, and thirty-two rooms. Rates high-moderate.

HAMPTON BEACH

The Seascape Inn at Plaice Cove
955 Ocean Blvd.
(603) 926-1750
www.seascapeinnhampton.com
Motel style, nineteen rooms. Doubles moderate, lower off-season.

PORTSMOUTH

The Inn at Christian Shore
335 Maplewood Ave.
(603) 431-6770
www.innatchristianshore.com
Bed-and-breakfast; six rooms, four with private baths. Doubles moderate, special weekends excepted; including full breakfast.

The Inn at Strawbery Banke
314 Court St.
(603) 436-7242 or (800) 428-3933
www.innatstrawberybanke.com
From Market Square, go 2 blocks east to Court Street, then north on Court Street. Bed-and-breakfast in a heritage home; seven rooms, all with private baths, air-conditioned. Rates high; include full breakfast.

The Sise Inn
40 Court St.
(603) 433-1200 or (877) 747-3466
www.siseinn.com
Elegant bed-and-breakfast inn in an 1881 home, all private baths. High.

ROCHESTER

Governor's Inn
78 Wakefield St.
(603) 332-0107
www.governorsinn.com
Suites in an elegant mansion in downtown Rochester.
Prices moderate.
(For additional dining and lodging, remember that Portsmouth is only 12 miles away.)

More Places to Eat on the Seacoast

CANDIA

Pasquale's Ristorante
145 Raymond Rd. (Birchwood Plaza)
(603) 483-5005
www.pasqualeincandia.com
The Italian chef/owner studied with the great chefs of Naples, and it shows in his preference for seafood and in his fondness for Neopolitan classics, such as Caprese salad (using fresh-made mozzarella), minestrone, and *pasta ai fagioli*. Moderate.

CENTER BARNSTEAD

The Crystal Quail
Pitman Rd.
(603) 269-4151
www.crystalquail.com
Game meats are a favorite of chef/owner Harold Huckaby, who describes the three choices on the prix fixe menu to guests. Expect to hear about dishes such as rabbit in a mushroom cream sauce inside delicate crepes, pheasant breast sauced with red wine, or pheasant ravioli with wild boar bacon. Dinner by reservation only. Expensive.

DOVER

Orchard Street Chop Shop
Orchard St.
(603) 749-0006
www.orchardstreetchop shop.com
The much-admired local chef/owner Chris (Koz) Kozlowski insists on the best ingredients, from prime cuts of meat to locally grown vegetables for his menu of comfort foods with class. High-moderate.

EXETER

11 Water Street
11 Water St.
(603) 773-5930
www.11waterstreet.com
The lunch and dinner menus offer a good variety, from mainstream to chicken saltimbocca and rosemary-smoked pork tenderloin. Moderate.

Loaf and Ladle Deli and Bakery
9 Water St.
(603) 778-8955
Town and gown meet in this cafeteria-style classic over whole-grain sandwiches, hearty soups, and chili. Inexpensive.

HAMPTON

The Old Salt
490 Lafayette Rd.
(603) 926-8322
www.oldsaltnh.com
Chicken pot pie to prime rib, in a colonial setting. The chef insists on native clams and shrimp, and schrod from local waters, as well as using as much locally grown produce as possible. Inexpensive to moderate.

NEWINGTON

New Asia
99 River Rd.
(just off Routes 4/16)
(603) 431-2240
Serves a fairly standard Chinese menu, but very well prepared and with an exceptionally cordial atmosphere. The Sunday buffet (11:30 a.m. to 3 p.m., $6.95) is bountiful and includes many of their specialties. Newington borders Portsmouth on the north, just across the bridge from Dover Point. Inexpensive.

PORTSMOUTH

Jumpin' Jay's Fish Cafe
150 Congress St.
(603) 766-3474
www.jumpinjays.com
Innovative approaches to fish and seafood, such as sole roulades and haddock piccata. Up to seven varieties of fish are on the catch-of-the-day list, with a choice of sauces, such as lobster veloute. Open daily, reservations suggested. Moderate.

THE MERRIMACK VALLEY

While the seaport provided the early links that built Portsmouth and Exeter, the size and force of the Merrimack River as it gathered waters from rivers and mountain streams in the north provided power for manufacturing that built the valley cities. Towns sprang up around the mills, and they continued to grow together. Manchester, the state's largest city, grew with the largest cotton-mill complex ever built. Even today, long after the mighty Amoskeag Mills closed their doors, the remaining mill buildings continue to dominate the city's riverbank.

This swath up the center of the state is flatter than the land to the north or the west and is characterized by rolling hills, small lakes, and a surprising amount of open space, especially north of Manchester.

The Merrimack Valley has never been tourist country. Most visitors pass through it on their way to the pleasures of the lakes and mountains farther north. Concord is occasionally visited for its historical sites, but Manchester's rich ethnic cultures are largely unnoticed.

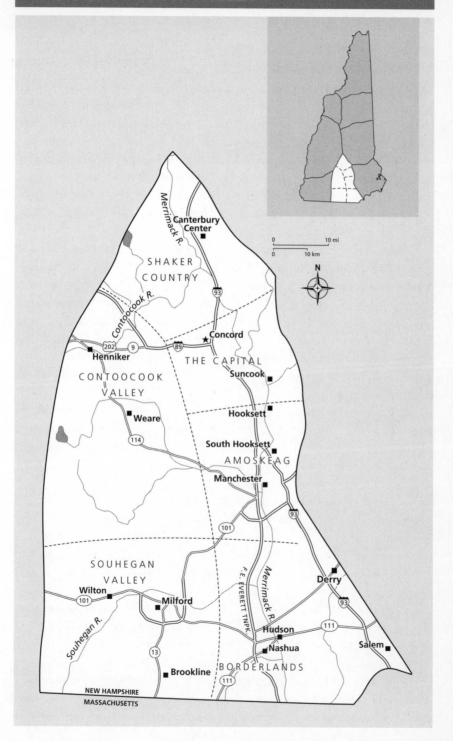

Canterbury
Center

SHAKER
COUNTRY

Merrimack R.

Contoocook R.

93

Concord

202   9   89
Henniker

THE CAPITAL

Suncook

CONTOOCOOK
VALLEY

Weare

Hooksett

114

South Hooksett

AMOSKEAG

Manchester

101

93

SOUHEGAN
VALLEY

Wilton

101

Milford

F.E. EVERETT TNPK.

Merrimack R.

Derry

93

13

Souhegan R.

Hudson

111

Salem

Nashua

Brookline

111

BORDERLANDS

NEW HAMPSHIRE
MASSACHUSETTS

0   10 mi
0   10 km

N

Borderlands

Although it is the state's second-largest city, Nashua is as rarely explored as the backroads that surround it. An early manufacturing city, it retains much of its mill yard area and the canal that provided the 36-foot vertical drop needed to run the machinery. This history, as well as life in Nashua during the industrial era, is well illustrated in the museum of the **Nashua Historical Society.** Changing exhibits feature subjects ranging from the role of Nashua in wars since the Civil War (arranged with interpretive and background information, as well as artifacts) to the interior of a local dry-goods store. Children will enjoy the schoolroom and the player piano. Open year-round, Tues, Wed, and Thurs 10 a.m. to 4 p.m., subject to guide availability. The museum is at 5 Abbott St., just off Route 101A (Amherst Street), Nashua; (603) 883-0015.

Next door, and also owned by the historical society, is the elegant **Abbot-Spaulding House,** a Federal-style home built by the "Father of Nashua," Daniel Abbot. Both Daniel Webster and Franklin Pierce were frequent guests here; the furnishings were collected by the later owners and include several originals by designer Dexter Spaulding, as well as the family's collection of Sandwich glass. Although the Spauldings added some decorative details that were not there when the Abbots owned it, these are historically correct to the period and style of a leading family of the time. Open by appointment; call (603) 883-0015.

For a view of Nashua's canal, walk along the **Mine Falls Park Heritage Trail.** The path borders the river and canal, forming a loop that can be reached from Riverside Street, where there is ample parking. A put-in on Mill Pond gives canoes and small boats access to the canal. You can also reach the trail from the mill yard in downtown Nashua.

A bright urban bistro, **Michael Timothy's** is upscale and casual in its atmosphere but not casual about its food. Presentation is attractive, and the dishes are a nice blend of innovation and tradition. They also have a celebrated wine list, with tastings on Tuesdays. Open Tues through Sat 3 to 5 p.m. and from 5 p.m. for dinner, Sun brunch 10 a.m. to 2 p.m. Located at 212 Main St., Nashua; (603) 595-9334; www.michaeltimothys.com. Prices are moderate. Just down the street the same chef operates Surf, specializing, as you might suspect, in the freshest of seafood, artfully prepared and presented. Open Tues to Thurs 4:30 to 9:30 p.m., Fri and Sat until 10 p.m. Moderate pricing.

Another good choice for eating out, and a bit less formal, is **Martha's Exchange** at 185 Main St.. Martha's has been there for a long time and offers good, well-prepared food in an informal atmosphere. They also have their own mini-brewery and music and dancing Friday and Saturday nights. Open every day at 11 a.m. for lunch and dinner, closing Mon through Wed and Sun at 9 p.m., Thurs at 9:30 p.m., Fri and Sat at 10 p.m. Prices are moderate.

The *Seedling Cafe* offers a warm and friendly atmosphere where you can get fresh, seasonal, organic foods prepared to order. Much of the produce in season is from the owners' organic gardens. The menu is heavy on wraps, but not those filled with the same old ingredients. Innovative sandwiches, such as honey-roasted turkey with tomatoes, red onions, cheddar cheese, applewood-smoked bacon, and fresh avocado on a whole wheat tortilla are finished on the grill. Salads feature equally interesting flavor combinations. Organic and local beer and wines are also served. The Seedling Cafe is open Mon through Fri 8:30 a.m. until 3 p.m. and Sat 11 a.m. until 3 p.m., at 9 Water St.; (603) 594-4002, www.theseedlingcafe.com.

You don't have to be Portuguese to appreciate Portuguese fried dough, traditional, slightly sweet Portuguese bread dough dropped in sizzling oil to cook and served piping hot. You'll find it on Saturday morning only at *Lucia's Portuguese Bakery,* 12 Scripture St. in Nashua; (603) 882-3099.

One of the best known of New Hampshire's food products is made at *Stonyfield Farm Yogurt Works* in Londonderry, just west of Derry. If you've ever been curious about how milk becomes raspberry yogurt, take the tour of their factory. Because of construction in 2009, tours have been temporarily suspended but call or check the Web site to find out when they are renewed. It's open Tues through Sat 10 a.m. to 4 p.m., or call for off-season times. It's at 10 Burton Rd., Londonderry; (603) 437-4040 or (800) PRO–COWS; www.stonyfield.com.

The *Robert Frost Homestead* on Route 28 was the home of the poet for the first decade of the twentieth century. Frost credited the years that he spent at this Derry farm with shaping his future by providing him with time and seclusion. The simple 1880s farmhouse, the barn, the brook, orchards, and stone walls mentioned in his poems are all here, much as they were during his time. A nature trail labeled with lines of his poetry winds through meadow and forest. Open daily mid-June to Labor Day and weekends only Memorial Day to mid-June and Labor Day to Columbus Day. It's at 122 Rockingham Rd., Derry; (603) 432-3091.

Although sawmills are not rare in New Hampshire, the *Taylor Up and Down Sawmill* is the only up-and-down mill still operating. It is water-powered, with gears made of wood. The mill runs two Saturdays a month, May through Sept 10 a.m. to 3 p.m.; ask for dates if you are interested in seeing it. Write Ballard State Forest, Island Pond Rd., Derry 03038, or call (603) 431-6774.

EVENTS IN THE MERRIMACK VALLEY

High Hopes Hot Air Balloon Festival,
Father's Day Weekend,
Hillsboro
(603) 429-1010 or (800) 639-6804.

Hillsboro County Agricultural Fair,
early Sept, New Boston
(603) 673-2510.

Spring Farming Day,
early May, Beaverbrook Farm, Hollis
(603) 465-7787; www.beaverbrook.org.

On the first floor of the old fire station on West Broadway is the **Derry Fire Department Museum,** with old photos, vintage lifesaving and firefighting equipment, and an old industrial pumper from a local mill. Look for the poem Robert Frost wrote for the Derry Fire Department after he lost control of a grass fire on his farm. Across the street at 29 West Broadway (603-434-1247), collections of the **Derry Historical Society** cover subjects ranging from the local witch hazel, shoe, and egg industries to native son and astronaut Allan Shepard. Robert Frost is, of course, featured here. The museum is open Thurs through Sun from 1 to 4 p.m.

The village of East Derry, a short detour on the way to the Taylor Sawmill, was the original settlement in 1719; today several fine old buildings, including the village hall, make up the **Upper Village National Historic District.** A catalog of the buildings is available at the library, across from the village hall. A marker notes that the first white Irish potato in America was planted in the adjacent "common field."

The brunch buffet at **The Bedford Village Inn** has been voted the best in the state by *New Hampshire Magazine* readers, and it may be the biggest, too. Chef's stations prepare made-to-order omelets, waffles, and carved meats, and the buffet may include citrus-poached shrimp, maki rolls, steamed dumplings, or cheese blintzes with fruit compotes. The dinner menu is equally interesting, depending on fresh seasonal ingredients. In the fall, for example, look for such dishes as grilled quail with red lentils and chorizo, or roasted heirloom beets mixed with horseradish, citrus aioli, and marinated cucumber. Desserts are a specialty: Consider hot chocolate pot pie with White Russian ice cream and black currants. The Bedford Village Inn is at 2 Village Lane, just off Route 101 in Bedford; (603) 472-2001 or (800) 852-1166, www.bedford villageinn.com.

Amoskeag

Scouts and leaders will want to stop on the way into **Manchester** at one of the finest collections of Boy Scout memorabilia and books in the United States. The **Lawrence L. Lee Scouting Museum** is located at the headquarters of the Daniel Webster Council, where there are also picnic tables and camping facilities. Covering more than 3,000 feet of floor space, the museum houses more than 95 percent of all scout books written in the United States, as well as historic uniforms, worldwide postage stamps commemorating scouting, and the original paintings used for covers of *Boy's Life*. Open 10 a.m. to 4 p.m. daily in July and Aug, Sat only in Sept through June, on Bodwell Road in Manchester; call (603) 669-8919 for more information or visit www.scoutingmuseum.org.

For more than a century, the **Manchester Historic Association** has preserved the history of this city. At one time the association's collection was shown in their 129 Amherst St. headquarters, but now that facility is used for research and special exhibits and the museum collections are housed in the **Millyard Museum,** located in Mill #3 at the corner of Pleasant and Commercial Streets in Manchester (contact 603-622-7531 or www.manchesterhistoric .org). The building housing the museum was once part of the huge Amoskeag Mill complex. The exhibit Woven in Time: 1,000 Years at Amoskeag Falls tells the story of human life around the river and falls, beginning with paleo-Indians and ending with the mills and the people who manned the machines that made millions of yards of fabric. Another exhibit serves as the orientation center for the Amoskeag Millyard Scenic and Cultural Byway and includes large photomurals of the mills when they were in operation. In addition to the permanent exhibits, special exhibits are mounted frequently. The museum is open Wed through Sat from 10 a.m. to 4 p.m. While there, be sure to take the kids upstairs to the **Science Center** (603-699-0400; www.see-sciencecenter .org), where interactive exhibits allow kids to walk on the moon and experience weightlessness, explore momentum, and even delve into chemical reactions in a real chemistry lab. Open Mon to Fri 10a.m. to 4 p.m., Sat and Sun 10 a.m. to 5 p.m.

Z Food and Drink has made a big splash in Manchester, although the minimalist white-and-wood restaurant is not a very big. Chef/Owner Tom Puskarich is passionate about using fresh, local, seasonal, and, whenever possible, organic ingredients. The goat cheese in his croquettes is local, as are the field greens he serves them on. Chef Puskarich divides the menu into "simple" and "signature" entrees, but the veal stew with baby carrots and Swiss chard in a Madeira–wild-mushroom demi-glace, served with Yukon mashed potatoes, is anything but simple. Even more complex are the flavors of duck meatballs, with porcini mushrooms, melted baby leeks, smoked tomato sauce, and crispy Asiago, served over pappardelle pasta. Lunch salads get the same careful attention, as in Chinese Chicken, a mélange of romaine, sesame chicken, somen noodles, blood oranges, snow peas, water chestnuts, and cashews with miso vinaigrette. The genial service is attentive without hovering, and the espresso piping hot—a testimony to a well-trained and alert waitstaff. Z is open for lunch Mon through Fri 11:30 a.m. to 2:30 p.m. and for dinner Mon through Thurs 4 until 9:30 p.m., Fri and Sat 4 to 10 p.m., at 860 Elm St., Manchester; call (603) 629-9383 or visit www.zfoodanddrink.com.

For a no-frills meal, walk a block off Elm Street to the **Red Arrow Diner.** It will be open, whatever the time of day; it has been since 1922. Well, almost always; it does close for eight hours on Christmas Eve. The menu includes pork pie, baked beans (baked right there), chicken pot pie, liver and onions, and meat loaf—you get the idea. Most entrees are priced under $6. Breakfasts are as generous as dinner and just as inexpensive. Open twenty-four hours, seven days a week, all year, at 61 Lowell St. (between Chestnut and Elm Streets) in Manchester; (603) 626-1118.

An intimate atmosphere and a smashing menu combine to make **Richard's Bistro** a favorite for dinner in Manchester. Its chic Euro look sets the stage, with white linens and small drop spotlights over each table. Much of the kitchen is open and visible. While Richard has brought in an exciting young chef, he is often around to greet diners and share his experience. The menu is out of the ordinary, innovative in its unique blendings of unexpected flavors, but without the crazy combinations by chefs who work too hard at being different. The breads that begin each dinner might include an artichoke and sundried tomato baguette with an anchovy (just a touch) olive oil on the top. The menu offers such entrees as lamb rack dusted with ginger and cumin, served with quinoa, dried apricots, baby fennel, and confit lamb shoulder, or grilled braciola of flank steak stuffed with blue cheese and roasted red peppers with new potatoes and spinach. Richard's Bistro has a dessert list that makes choosing nearly impossible, ranging from chocolate walnut pecan pie served warm with ice cream to a refreshing mango sorbet laced with red wine. Prices are moderate to expensive. The bistro is open for lunch Mon to Sat and dinner 4 to 10 p.m. daily, with Sun brunch 10 a.m. to 2 p.m. Richard's Bistro is located at 36 Lowell St., Manchester; (603) 644-1180 or visit www.richardsbistro.com.

Manchester has a lot of little places to eat, many of them ethnic restaurants run by people who came from the country whose cuisine is featured. **The Athens,** on Central Street (603-623-9317), is good for hearty portions of Greek food. A French-Canadian flavor is found at **Chez Vachon** at 136

Kelley St. (603-625-9660). Even if you never had a Quebecois *memere* (grand-mother), you could grow nostalgic over a big piece of *tourtiere* (pork pie) or the savory cretons on hot buttered toast. Locals even dip into Quebec-style *poutine,* fries topped with chicken gravy and fresh grated cheese. The atmosphere isn't fancy, nor is the food, but it's authentic, hearty, and tasty. Open for breakfast and lunch Mon through Fri 6 a.m. to 1:30 p.m., Sat and Sun 6 a.m. to 2 p.m.

The atmosphere is hardly intimate at this cavernous seafood palace, but it's the impeccably fresh seafood and the lively scene at the bar that brings the crowds to **Commercial Street Fishery.** The menu is not long or complex, but the combinations are well-considered and designed to highlight the quality of the star ingredients. Opt for a traditional New England lobster bake with corn on the cob, or grilled Atlantic salmon served with lobster mashed potatoes, arugula and shiitake mushrooms, or if you can't choose between the sea critters, get them all in a savory cioppino made with shrimp, haddock, mussels, and scallops. Always listen carefully to the specials to get the chef's latest takes on the daily catch. Commercial Street Fishery is open for dinner Mon through Sat, and usually on Sun, at 33 South Commercial St., Manchester; call (603) 296-0706 or visit www.csfishery.com. Show them your Palace Theater tickets for a 20% discount the night of the show. To the best of our knowledge, you'll only find one Nepalese restaurant in New Hampshire (maybe only one in New England), **Cafe Momo.** Try the *momo,* from which the name derives, a popular Nepalese appetizer of steamed dumpling similar to the Chinese dim sum, but filled with meat or vegetables seasoned with ginger, chilis, and cumin. There's a good selection of vegetarian dishes served, but meats, including goat kebabs, are also on the menu. Cafe Momo is well outside the downtown, at 1065 Hanover St.; (603) 623-3733, http://cafemomonh.com.

The French-Canadian influence is still strong in Manchester, with a daily French-language newspaper and the **Association Canado-Americaine** at 52 Concord St. (603-625-8577), whose library of more than 4,000 volumes centers on the development of French culture in North America. An art exhibit features French American artists' work, with regularly changing exhibits, open 8 a.m. to 4:30 p.m. weekdays. The west side of town, across the river, was the French-Canadian neighborhood, dominated by the impressive **Sainte Marie's Church.** The architecture is

somethingto beefabout

Before it became Manchester, the settlement of a few hardy souls at the falls of the Merrimack River was called Derryfield, and its residents subsisted largely on a diet of river eels, which became known as Derryfield beef.

distinctive, and the stone interior is reminiscent of the cathedrals of Quebec and Montreal.

Known for the breadth and depth of its collections, which include more than 11,000 works, the *Currier Gallery of Art* lacked space to show most of it, until the opening of 33,000 square feet of new space in 2009. Several first-floor galleries are reserved for changing exhibitions, bringing to view hundreds of items that had long languished in storage. The second floor is devoted to American art from the eighteenth and nineteenth centuries, highlighting the works of romantic artists such as Albert Bierstadt and Thomas Cole, along with works of Benjamin Champney and other artists who worked in the White Mountains. American Impressionists include Childe Hassam and William Metcalf.

The museum's European collection—featuring works by Tiepolo, van Ruisdeal, Constable, and Monet—shares galleries with works dating from the late Middle Ages. Twentieth-century art occupies five galleries that include paintings by Matisse, Picasso, Rouault, and Georgia O'Keefe. An immense collection of paperweights is in a gallery devoted entirely to glass and ceramics. Tours of the *Zimmerman House,* designed by Frank Lloyd Wright, begin at the museum, by reservation only. Open hours are Sun, Mon, and Wed through Fri 11 a.m. to 5 p.m., Sat 10 a.m. to 5 p.m., and the first Thurs of each month from 11 a.m. to 8 p.m. Admission is $10 for adults, $9 for seniors and children. The Currier is located at 150 Ash St., Manchester; (603) 669-6144; www.currier.org.

On Hanover Street between Chestnut and Pine Streets, is a nicely designed and executed *wall mural* depicting the mill heritage that built Manchester. Continue up Hanover Street, away from the center of the city, to see some excellent examples of Victorian architecture lining both sides of the street.

The Merrimack River, whose power once operated machinery of the Amoskeag Mills, now produces electricity at the Amoskeag Hydro Station. When salmon were restored to the river, a fish ladder was built to permit the fish to return to their spawning grounds. The Merrimack River basin can support an adult salmon population of about 3,000, and visitors to the *Amoskeag Fishway* can watch the fish make their way up a series of stepped pools in late May. Large viewing windows allow visitors to observe fish at eye level. The fish ladder is open from May to mid-June, with displays, programs, and films that illuminate the history, ecology, and wildlife of the river and of Manchester. Admission is free, and the area is wheelchair accessible. Enter from Fletcher Street, behind the TraveLodge at the Amoskeag Bridge. The exhibit hall is open Mon through Sat 9 a.m. to 5 p.m. year-round. Contact (603) 626-FISH; www.amoskeagfishways.org.

While hotels are plentiful in the city, B&B accommodations are rare. Travelers who prefer the surroundings of a finely kept home should call **Derryfield Bed & Breakfast.** Located in a quiet residential neighborhood with quick access to I-93, Derryfield has surprisingly low rates. Breakfast is served overlooking the pool and surrounding woods on a table set with fine china and crystal. Rooms must be reserved in advance at this small and very personal hostelry. The owner will meet guests at the airport, an unusual and welcome service. The B&B is at 1081 Bridge St. Extension, Manchester; call (603) 627-2082 for reservations.

The only public archery ranges in New Hampshire are at **Bear Brook State Park,** northeast of Manchester. Maintained by the Fish and Game Department, each consists of fifteen targets. An additional four-target practice range is wheelchair accessible. The park includes several ponds, two marshes, and a wildlife refuge and offers swimming, tent camping, and fishing as well. Hiking trails, many of which become cross-country ski trails in the winter, cover the area.

One of the very few Civilian Conservation Corps (CCC) camps left in the northeast is in Bear Brook State Park. The buildings house a **CCC museum,** a **snowmobile museum,** a nature center, and the **Museum of Family Camping** (603-485-3782; www.ucampnh.com/museum). This unusual museum was the dream of Richmond campground owner Roy Heise, whose own collection formed the nucleus. Here you will see camping equipment from the sport's earliest years—tents, stoves, lanterns, and cooking utensils that show how camping evolved from a relatively rare means of travel to one of America's most popular summer pastimes. All buildings are open daily Memorial Day through Labor Day 10 a.m. to 4 p.m. and some weekends during spring and fall. Much of the parkland itself was part of the CCC camp during the 1930s, and many of the picnic sites, hiking trails, recreation buildings, and roads you will enjoy on New Hampshire's public lands were built by the CCC. Write Bear Brook State Park, 157 Deerfield Rd., Allenstown 03275, or call (603) 485-9874.

The park is also home to the **New Hampshire Snowmobile Museum,** again, housed in a former CCC building. The collection is rather extensive and begins with one of the very first snow-traveling machines, an early '20s Model T Ford adapted by Virgil White of Ossipee. In addition to the well-known brands Arctic Cat and Bombardier, the collections include Lombard, Eliason, and Bolens, among others. Also at the museum is a 1992 Arctic Cat driven on a 10,252-mile trip from Alaska to Nova Scotia in 1992. The museum is open Jan through Mar 1 to 3 p.m. and from Memorial Day to Columbus Day daily but they suggest you call to make sure a volunteer is there. Call George Burdick at (603) 648-2304.

The *Fitts Museum* in nearby Candia is a two-story house with a low hipped roof. Two rooms are the original 1820 dwelling, with later Federal additions. Along with its antiques-filled rooms, it has a special event each Saturday afternoon in the summer—the only time it's open. Children's Day, herbs, spinning and weaving, or classic cars may be the subject; you're bound to find an interesting activity at this free community museum. Open July and Aug on Sat, 1 to 4 p.m., Route 27, Candia. Appointments for viewing can be made by contact through www.fittsmuseum.org.

A couple of miles west of the museum and also on Route 27, *Charmingfare Farm* offers hay rides and sleigh rides through their forest wildlife park, where you'll see native New Hampshire animals. Smaller sleighs and carriages for a couple or a family can be reserved ahead. In the winter, bring marshmallows to roast at the campfire, where the sleigh stops for a warm-up. In the *Oakhurst Dairy Discovery Barn,* you can see miniature sheep and goats, as well as baby animals that children can feed and pat in this hands-on environment. Call (603) 483-5623 or visit www.charmingfare.com.

The Capital

Although it is important as the center of government for the state, *Concord* is not a large city. (Incidentally, if you want to immediately label yourself as an outlander, pronounce Concord as you would the usual noun. In New England, it's pronounced "conquered.") Its manufacturing remained small, and it retains even now the appearance of a stately turn-of-the-twentieth-century city, with its brick business blocks and government buildings of gray granite.

Blending into these buildings that surround the statehouse is the *New Hampshire Historical Society.* The sculpture above the columned granite façade is the work of Daniel Chester French, creator of the Minuteman statue in Concord, Massachusetts, and the seated Lincoln in Washington, D.C.

Most of the society's collections are in the nearby *Museum of New Hampshire History,* opposite the front of the State House, on Main Street. You'll find the museum tucked into a little plaza, behind an unusual iron gate. As the state historical society's museum, it has collections far too vast to be displayed in their entirety, but modern gallery space allows the museum to mount special exhibits that last for a few months to a year, interpreting events, trends, and periods in the state's history. Whether the historical society is examining the works of the White Mountain artists during the era of the grand hotels or taking a closer look at the Shakers, the exhibits are arresting and informative.

Special exhibits mounted by the museum have centered on the Old Man of the Mountain, the work of prominent seacoast photographer Lewis Hine, the

Baseball in New Hampshire

The national pastime is as popular in the state as elsewhere. Nashua has its own independent minor league team named *American Defenders,* which plays at the city's historic Holman Stadium on Amherst Street. A few former major league players, including Jose Canseco, are on their roster, and in 2000 they won the Atlantic League title. Call (603) 883-2255, or buy tickets online at www.americandefenders.us. The summer games of the *New England Collegiate Baseball League* are another way to see great ball and watch future major league players. The league season is from the first week of June to the first week of August. Players from colleges all over the nation join teams in the league, living, working, and playing ball in their host communities.

The *Concord Quarry Dogs* are the newest (2001) of the two teams in the state and draw their name from the granite quarries on the north end of that city. They play at Memorial Field in Concord, off Clinton Street on South Fruit Street, easily reached from I-93. Tickets are available at the stadium or by calling (603) 225-1111 (for groups only). Visit their Web site at www.quarrydogs.com.

Keene is hometown to the *Keene Swamp Bats,* a clever play on words involving the little creatures that fly high over their Alumni Field home on Arch Street. In 2000 and 2003 they won the New England Conference title and in 2001 they ended the season in second place. They are known to baseball fans for an exciting ball game and their lovable mascot, Ribby. From Central Square take West Street about 1.75 miles and turn left onto Arch Street. Tickets at the stadium cost $3; call (603) 352-5120 or go to their Web site at www.swampbats.com.

historic New Hampshire primary, and "Treasures of New Hampshire History." Included among the treasures are letters from George Washington, Thomas Jefferson, and Walt Whitman, a 1583 bible rescued from pirates, and the New Hampshire Constitution, which was printed six months before the Declaration of Independence.

A focal point is an original *Concord coach.* Splendid in decorative detail, these coaches were as strong and as well constructed as they were beautiful. They were, in fact, so perfect in their design that from the 1820s to the early 1900s, during which time more than 3,000 of them were built in Concord, almost no changes were made in their construction. It was the most perfect traveling vehicle known to its time, often called "the coach that won the West."

The small museum shop in the historical society is an excellent source of publications on New Hampshire and its history. Many of these are privately printed and hard to find elsewhere.

The admission charge is $5.50 for adults, $4.50 for seniors, and $3.00 for children ages six to eighteen (or a family maximum of $17.00); it's free

ifitain'tbroke don'tfixit

Built of New Hampshire granite (is there any other kind?), the State House in Concord is the oldest state capitol building in the nation where the legislature still meets in its original chamber. It was first occupied in 1819.

on Thurs from 5 to 8:30 p.m., the only day it has evening hours. It's open Tues through Sat 9:30 a.m. to 5 p.m., Sun noon to 5 p.m. Open Mon July 1 through Oct 15 and in Dec. Just off I-93 at exit 14, Eagle Square, Concord; (603) 226-3189; www.NHHistory.org.

House of India is a good downtown dining choice, with a varied menu of well-prepared dishes from the Indian subcontinent. From the tandoor oven comes fresh-baked *nan, poori,* and *chapatti* as well as tandoori chicken and shrimp and chicken *tikkas.* Flavors vary from delicate and mild to a chicken vindaloo that will curl your hair. If you're not familiar with Indian foods, ask for one of the combination dishes or the mixed grill from the tandoor. House of India is just off South Main Street, at 6 Pleasant St.; (603) 227-5266.

Concord's arts calendar is enriched by the **Concord Community Music School,** which brings recitals, lunch-hour concerts, free outdoor summer concerts, children's programs, and a variety of other classical and jazz performances to the area. For a complete schedule, write to the school at 23 Wall St., Concord 03301; call (603) 228-1196 or visit www.ccmusicschool.org.

The **McAuliffe-Shepard Discovery Center** opened in 2009, replacing the former Christa McAuliffe Planetarium, built to honor the New Hampshire teacher who died along with six other astronauts in the Challenger disaster. The air and space science center covers space exploration and allied sciences in interactive exhibits and a twenty-first-century planetarium. Visitors can try landing a space capsule on the moon, or use a flight simulator to land an airplane. Kids are engaged by Brain-Bites, short videos illustrating cool facts about space suits, using an electric screwdriver in a weightless environment, and how astronauts train to overcome motion sickness. State-of-the-art projection shows are scheduled daily, among them Dawn of the Space Age, Tonight's Sky, Oasis in Space, Black Holes, and Ice Worlds. Exhibits appeal to all ages; many are more complex and explain astronomical phenomena and the challenges of space on an adult level. The Countdown Café serves fresh-built sandwiches, salads, and snacks. The McAuliffe-Shepard Discovery Center is at 2 Institute Dr., Concord, and is open daily 10 a.m. to 5 p.m. Admission is $9, seniors $8, children three to twelve $6; planetarium shows $3 per person. For information call (603) 271-7827 or visit www.starhop.com.

Birth of the Concord Coach

Lewis Downing and Steven Abbot built an industry that made Concord the Detroit of its time. Downing started making carriages in the early nineteenth century and by the Civil War was shipping hundreds annually, most to the American West. These were the famed stagecoaches used by Wells Fargo and other companies. Buffalo Bill spread their fame, using one in his Wild West Show.

Visitors today can see these transportation heroes at the Concord Group Insurance Companies on Bouton Street in Concord, the Museum of New Hampshire History at 6 Eagle Sq., the Concord Monitor at 1 Monitor Dr., and Canterbury Shaker Village at 288 Shaker Road in Canterbury.

Elsewhere in the state they can be found at the general store in Moultonborough, the Flume in Franconia Notch, Six Gun City in Jefferson, at the base of the Mount Washington Auto Road in Glen, and at Old Home Days and other local events when those owned by historical societies and private residents are rolled out to be admired.

More information on the coaches is available from the Concord Coach Society, 18 Park St. in Concord, or visit http://theconcordcoach.tripod.com.

At the north end of Concord is the ***Silk Farm Wildlife Sanctuary*** and the headquarters of the New Hampshire Audubon Society. Trails traverse the forests and wetlands along the edge of Great Turkey Pond and cross orchards, hedgerows, and fields where visitors can see rare wildflowers as well as birds and small animals. Audubon House provides a year-round bird blind, an excellent wildlife library, and a shop featuring a variety of nature guides and gifts with a wildlife theme. It is open Mon through Sat 9 a.m. to 5 p.m. The library is open Thurs 10 a.m. to 4 p.m. The New Hampshire Audubon Society is at 3 Silk Farm Rd. (off Clinton Street) in Concord, easily reached from exit 2 off I-89. Call (603) 224-9909 for more information.

Silk Farm Road leads into the back entrance of ***St. Paul's School,*** whose chapel has a finely executed fresco in the oratory to the left of its entrance, a replica of Lorenzetti's great fresco at Assisi. Two mobiles by Alexander Calder are also on the campus; one is suspended from the ceiling in the lobby of Memorial Hall, and the other is on the grounds nearby. The outdoor mobile is stored from November through March to protect it from the harsh winter weather.

Across the river to the east, in Concord Heights, the ***Society for the Protection of New Hampshire Forests's Conservation Center*** maintains several buildings powered by alternative energy sources, as well as nature trails. This organization is responsible for the preservation of huge tracts of

land throughout the state by either outright ownership, purchase of development rights, or helping private and governmental bodies in their efforts to save
important lands and forests. You can tour their passive-solar building Mon
through Fri 9 a.m. to 4 p.m., free of charge. There is also a gift shop featuring
environmental gifts and publications. Take East Side Drive (Route 132) north
from Bridge Street (Route 9) to a left turn onto Portsmouth Street (you will
pass the other end of this street going to the right shortly before the turn you
want). The address is 54 Portsmouth St. (603-224-9945).

The **Merrimack River Watershed Council** sponsors free canoe trips on
rivers in all parts of the state; you can bring your own canoe or rent one. For
a schedule of trips, write to them at 54 Portsmouth St., Concord 03301; call
(978) 275-0120 or visit www.merrimack.org.

Shaker Country

East Side Drive becomes Mountain Road, still Route 132, which leads to **Canterbury** and the beautifully maintained **Shaker Village.** Set on a hill among
rolling meadows, this was once a thriving 4,000-acre farm where 300 Shakers
lived and worshiped in an atmosphere of common ownership, celibacy, and
a strong work ethic. In the twenty-two buildings of the village, you will see
original examples of Shaker crafts in the furnishings of the houses. Skilled
craftspeople are at work with wood, fiber, and plants creating baskets, boxes,
brooms, and herbal crafts. Authentic lunches and dinners are re-created in
the Creamery, where they use herbs from the village's garden. Guided tours
begin on the hour and take about ninety minutes. A gift shop features Shaker
reproductions and New Hampshire crafts. Thomas Merton once observed,
"The peculiar grace of a Shaker chair is due to the fact that it was built by

Anybody Seen a Boulder around Here?

We were in Salisbury one Sunday afternoon with friends, searching for the Salisbury
Boulder, of which we had a description and vague directions written in the 1930s,
when roads were a bit different. We went over one of these nearly abandoned
routes, climbing Oak Hill on little more than a track edging around the washouts
and expecting the road to end at any point. When we finally came out onto a paved
road—much to the surprise of the man who lived in the farmhouse at the corner—
we asked him if he knew where we'd find the Salisbury Boulder. His eyes swept his
rock-strewn pasture, where at least a dozen rocks were as tall as we were, and he
repeated, "THE Salisbury Boulder?"

someone capable of believing that an angel might come and sit on it." Both that grace and its spiritual origins are evident throughout the village. Open daily May through Oct, 10 a.m. to 5 p.m., weekends 10 a.m. to 4 p.m., Apr, Nov, and Dec. For information write to Canterbury Shaker Village, 288 Shaker Rd., Canterbury 03224; call (603) 783-9511 or visit www.shakers.org.

The Shaker Table is a fine dining restaurant at the village, open for lunch and dinner Fri and Sat, and for Sun brunch. Reserve at (603) 783-4238 or visit www.theshakertable.com.

One of the things we love most about New Hampshire's backroads is the little surprise around the next corner, and one of these is about 4 miles north of the Shaker Village, where you'll find **Fox Country Smoke House.** That's a treat, since they sell a boggling variety of their own smoked products, from garlic kielbasa and beef jerky to smoked almonds, duck, Irish bacon, rainbow trout, smoked cheeses, and even dog treats. What's more, you (and Rover) can enjoy a picnic including any of these at a table in their own picnic area in the woods. The shop is open Tues through Sat from 10 a.m. to 4 p.m. and Sun from noon to 4 p.m. They are also open on Mon from Sept though Dec and on holidays. To find Fox Country, follow signs from I-93 to Shaker Village, then continue north about 2.5 miles and go left, following Smoke House signs for another 1.5 miles; (603) 783-4405 or (800) 339-4409, www.oldehouse smokehouse.com.

The town of **Tilton** is inextricably linked with the Tilton family, the generous benefactors of much of the town's artistic heritage. Charles Tilton, like many cultured men of his times, believed in the importance of public statuary and began to set about ornamenting his hometown. Overlooking the town from a steep hillside on the opposite side of the river is the **Tilton Arch,** an exact replica of the Arch of Titus in Rome. Built of Concord granite, it rises 55 feet from its base, upon which lies a red granite lion. It is actually in the town of Northfield, and you can get there via the bridge at the monument on Main Street, turning left on the far side and going uphill to the Northfield Town Hall. Beside the town hall, a dirt road leads to the top of the hill and the monument.

Five of Charles Tilton's statues remain. A marble allegorical statue of America—depicted as an Indian princess—stands on Main Street, as do statues symbolizing Europe and Asia. A zinc statue of Chief Squantum now stands in a parking lot. An iron footbridge connects the town with an island, once the site of the Tilton summerhouse and now a shaded park.

Fine mansions still grace Tilton, and one of them, on West Main Street, is of particular interest. The **Black Swan** bed-and-breakfast is a beautifully preserved Victorian, filled with period architectural and decorative detail.

Original wall stenciling has been uncovered during renovation. One guest room includes a huge semicircular sitting room alcove with stained-glass panels over each of its seven windows. Each room has some distinctive antique feature or furnishing, and the dining room is fully paneled in oak with built-in china cupboards and a fireplace. The gardens and lawns sweep down to the riverbanks, overhung by shade trees. It's a thoroughly enjoyable resting place at moderate prices. Write the Black Swan at 354 West Main St., Tilton 03276; (603) 286-4524.

A number of fine craftspeople have studios in or near Tilton. The *Country Braid House* is both workshop and showroom for hand-braided wool rugs. Visitors are welcome to tour the workshop and learn about rug braiding. Those who would like to try their hand at it will find rug-braiding kits for sale. Open Mon through Fri 9 a.m. to 5 p.m., and Sat 9 a.m. to 4 p.m.; at 462 Main St. in Tilton; (603) 286-4511 or www.countrybraidhouse.com.

Affectionately called T-HOP by locals, *Tilton House of Pizza* doubles as a family restaurant and community center, thanks to the good food and friendly owners. Pizza is only the beginning of the menu, which includes Italian and Greek dishes (including baklava), as well as seafood plates. Meatball subs just don't get any better. From I-93 exit 20, head west on Route 3, which becomes the main street of downtown Tilton. Tilton House of Pizza is at 298 Main St., Tilton; call (603) 286-7181.

The sign with the happy cow will make you smile, but the fried clams will make the smile even wider at *Dipsy Doodle Dairy Bar,* just over the line into Northfield. Their big, fat, juicy clams taste like the sea—and are cooked just right, so they are tender and juicy inside, crisp outside, and never greasy. Warning: Once you've eaten their hot lobster roll with butter, you may never be satisfied with ho-hum mayo lobster rolls again. And of course, there is the ice cream, served in giant scoops. To find them from Route 3 in Tilton, turn south at the railway station, at the west end of the business district—that's Park Street. Open May through Oct. Dipsy Doodle Dairy Bar, 143 Park St., Northfield, just north of I-93 exit 19; call (603) 286-2100 or visit www.dipsy doodle.biz.

Contoocook Valley

West of Concord lies an area of rolling farmlands and attractive villages. Hopkinton's wide Main Street is lined with trees and a number of homes of the colonial era. In the center of town on Main Street, the *New Hampshire Antiquarian Society* features a museum of early items including journals, diaries, maps, and a collection of music scores. The building, which is on the

National Register of Historic Places, also houses a library for genealogical and historical research. Open Thurs and Fri 9 a.m. to 4 p.m., Sat 9 a.m. to 1 p.m.; (603) 746-3825; www.nhantiquarian.org.

St. Andrew's Episcopal Church, in the village center, has particularly fine stained-glass windows and, unlike most churches, has a thorough printed history of them, researched and written by retired St. Paul's teacher John Archer. The latest of these windows to be added is by Tiffany, a cross-and-lilies design much simpler than most Tiffany windows. You can get a copy of Archer's book and a key to the church from the office on weekdays.

Meet farm animals up close, ride in a horse-drawn wagon to choose your own pumpkin from the field, get lost in a corn maze, or just buy a big ice cream cone and enjoy it at the picnic tables on the front lawn of *Beech Hill Farm* in Hopkinton. Now in the ninth generation of the Kimball family, this diverse farm also has a garden center, a small museum of antique farm tools, and a bakery, all open May through Oct. Beech Hill Rd., Hopkinton; call (603) 233-0828 or visit www.beechhillfarm.com.

A turn off Route 9/202 onto Route 127 in West Hopkinton takes you across the Hopkinton Dam, with its Art Deco–style control building. At the foot of the hill on the other side is Rowell's Covered Bridge. The road parallels a pretty stretch of the Contoocook River and leads past *Elm Brook Park,* with a beach, playgrounds, walking trails, a shaded picnic grove, and launch for

Paddlers' Alert

The Merrimack River between Franklin, where the river is formed by the confluence of the Pemigewasset and the Winnipesaukee, and Concord offers gentle paddling for kayakers and canoeists, with a few stretches reaching class II. The put-in in Franklin is below the high school, where the water can be fast moving, but below that the river slows and swings in great snake-like curves through Boscowan until it reaches a dam a little over 3 miles below the bridge where Route 4 crosses the river in Penacook.

The prettiest stretch is between Northfield, south of Franklin, and a take-out just downstream from the point where the Contoocook River joins from the west (left). In this stretch you'll see hardly any sign of humans as you paddle a very lazy river, sometimes beneath 50-foot banks. Don't expect much help from the current in the summer, when the surface is almost lakelike.

You can paddle farther, taking out above the Sewalls Falls Dam in West Concord. Or you can run a stretch of rapids below the dam and continue about 7 miles farther, past sand bluffs to a take-out south of the bridge where U.S. 202/I-393 crosses the river.

kayaking and canoeing on one of the several lakes of the dam impoundment. At the far end, airplanes often circle above the park's radio-controlled model airplane flying field. The park is open mid-May through the second weekend in Sept from 9 a.m. to 8 p.m. May through Aug and 9 a.m. to 7 p.m. in Sept. A fee of $1 per person is charged, with a maximum of $4 per car. Call (603) 746-3601 or visit www.nhstateparks.com. The only *Henniker* on earth was named for a London merchant who was a friend of Royal Governor Benning Wentworth. New England College is in the center of town and gives it a lively air. The college offers a series of cross-country ski trails named for Marx Brothers movies. The toughest, which goes over a small mountain, is called You Bet Your Life.

Skiing is not a new pastime in Henniker. For more than thirty years, the Patnaude family has operated one of New Hampshire's southernmost ski areas, *Pats Peak.* It's not easy keeping a mountain skiable in southern New Hampshire, but when it is brown everywhere Pat's manages to keep the trails white. Some of the most modern snowmaking equipment in the east covers 100 percent of the trails and fires up whenever the temperature allows; that is good enough to keep skiers happy and on the slopes. About half of the twenty-two trails are rated as novice, whereas the balance are split between advanced and expert—and when they say expert, they mean it. The food in the base lodge is homemade, and it's the kind of family ski area where you don't mind your kids skiing alone. Ski school, nursery, rentals, and other facilities are offered, and ticket sales are limited to the number of people that the lifts can comfortably handle without overcrowding. Write Pats Peak, Route 114, Henniker 03242; call (603) 428-3245 or (888) PATS–PEAK, or visit www.patspeak.com.

Fine dining and lodging are only a bit out of town at the *Colby Hill Inn,* a rambling New England hostelry that has been updated and renovated without

Is It the Ghost of Ocean-Born Mary?

On Gulf Road off Route 114 in Henniker stands a house that was home to "Ocean-Born Mary." Shortly after her birth on the high seas in 1710, the ship was attacked by pirates, but their leader, on seeing the infant, promised to leave the ship unharmed if the mother would name the child Mary, after his mother. The pirate left a bolt of silk for Mary's wedding dress. Mary lived to a ripe old age in her Henniker house. After her death and until fairly recently, owners and neighbors have reported seeing a black carriage drive up to the house at night and stop, while a veiled figure descended and walked (or floated) to the well, where it appeared to drop in a parcel before leaving in the ghostly carriage. You can find Mary's tombstone, labeled "Widow Mary Wallace," in the Quaker Cemetery on Quaker Meeting House Road.

losing its country-inn flavor. The sixteen guest rooms, each with a private bath and two with working fireplaces, are decorated with antiques. Details of decor and hospitality are all here—elegant bed linens, a full cookie jar, plenty of public rooms, and spontaneous and gregarious hosts. The location is perfect, surrounded by meadows and a backyard where you can watch pheasants as you sit in the perennial garden. In the winter, part of the backyard becomes a skating rink for guests. This is a full-service inn, so its prices are higher than those of a typical bed-and-breakfast, beginning at $110 for a double, including a full country breakfast.

The dining room at Colby Hill Inn serves dinner to the public as well as to inn guests—and a fine dinner, too, with a frequently changing menu. Chicken breast stuffed with lobster is the signature dish. The salmon is cooked to perfection. Dinner prices are in the upper-moderate range. The dining room is open nightly 5:30 to 8:30 p.m., year-round. Sun brunch 11 a.m. to 3 p.m. Write Colby Hill Inn, the Oaks, Henniker 03242; call (603) 428-3281, outside New Hampshire (800) 531-0330, or visit www.colbyhillinn.com.

The entire Contoocook Valley abounds with antiques shops, and the **Fiber Studio** features hand-dyed yarns, beads, and supplies for spinning, weaving, and knitting as well as handwoven fabrics and sheep-related gifts. It's at 161 Foster Hill Rd. off Routes 202 and 9 in Henniker; (603) 428-7830; www.fiberstudio.com.

The Souhegan Valley

Zahn's Alpine Guest House, on Route 13, will bring back immediate fond memories to anyone who has traveled in Bavaria, Austria, or Switzerland. It looks and feels exactly like those warm, hospitable mountain chalets that welcome travelers throughout the Alps. A big tile stove fills one corner of the Stube, which doubles as breakfast room and guest lounge. The pine post-and-beam construction with deeply overhung roof provides each of the guest rooms with a sheltered balcony—rimmed with window boxes full of bright flowers in the summer. Alpine antiques, multicolored rag rugs, big feather pillows, and wrought-iron fixtures complete the scene, but Zahn's has not fallen prey to the temptation to make it "Ye olde Alpine cute." It's the real thing, as is the hospitality; rates are below our moderate range at $70 per room, single or double occupancy. In the winter, kids can go for dogsled rides at the adjacent Christmas Tree Farm while parents cut their own tree. To reserve a room, write to Zahn's at P.O. Box 75, Milford 03055; call (603) 673-2334 or (888) 745-0051, fax (603) 673-8415, or check www.intercon design.com/zahns.

The owners of Zahn's have been asked so often for directions to area antiques shops that they've printed a little map for their guests showing twenty-two different shops.

Union Square, known to everyone as "The Oval," is lined with shops, among them the eclectic **Moonstone Antiques** (603-673-0303), with a quirky assortment that ranges from vintage hats to furniture and china. If a stop at Moonstone puts you in the mood for serious antiquing, continue on 101A (now Elm St.) to number 323, and the easy-to-spot **New Hampshire Antique Co-Op.** The 200-plus dealers occupy 20,000 square feet of galleries and display area, some of it in room settings. For the best bargains, investigate the Discovery Barn, or raise your sights in galleries devoted to 19th- and 20th-century fine art paintings. Call (603) 673-8499 or visit www.nhantiquecoop .com.If you're within reach of the Milford area in late September, you're sure to see brightly colored balloons decorating the sky. They are from the High Hopes Foundation's annual **High Hopes Balloon Festival** It opens at 5 p.m. Fri and continues on through Sunday evening, ending with a 6 p.m. balloon flight. In addition to popular hot-air balloon rides, the event has hay rides, skydivers, helicopter rides, live entertainment, a craft show, and food booths. The proceeds go to the foundation, which is dedicated to granting the wishes of seriously ill New Hampshire children. Contact them at High Hopes Foundation, 416 Daniel Webster Hwy., Unit K, Merrimack 03054; (603) 429-1010 or (800) 639-6804; or www.HighHopesNH.org.

A very handy (and very good) stop on Route 101 for breakfast, lunch, or teatime is the **Black Forest Cafe** in Amherst. Classical music, the morning papers, giant scones, and huge cups of coffee make for a good way to start a day. Lunch brings grilled chicken on a bed of greens, crab cakes, or unique sandwiches at moderate prices. The bakery (with cafe tables) is open 8 a.m. to 6:30 p.m. (to 5 p.m. on Sun). The dining room serves from Mon for lunch only 11 a.m. to 3 p.m., Tues through Sat 11 a.m. until 8 p.m., and Sun brunch 8 a.m. to 2:30 p.m.; (603) 672-0500 or www.theblackforestcafe.com.

Sausage is the specialty of **The Dog House,** also beside Route 101 a bit farther west in Wilton. Choose a traditional long hot dog ($1 with drink) or bratwurst on a *brochen* with sauerkraut and a side of tasty German potato salad. The House scoops up generous ice cream cones; you can eat at the picnic tables in the tidy yard.

Almost next door is **Santos Dumont Coffee and Ice Cream,** named for the famed Brazilian aviation pioneer, serving coffees they roast themselves and their own pastries, plus sandwiches and premium ice cream. Open Mon through Thurs 6 a.m. to 10 p.m., Fri 6 a.m. to 11 p.m., and Sat and Sun 7 a.m. to 10 p.m. The address is 770 Elm St. (Route 101), Milford; 603-672-5464.

Water power was central to New Hampshire industry from the earliest days, and *Frye's Measure Mill* is still operated by an upright turbine driven by water from two ponds. Actively engaged in the making of fine round and oval wooden boxes, just as the first ones were made here in 1858, the mill also operates ninety-minute tours on Sat starting at 2 p.m., June through Oct. The mill shop sells the boxes made here as well as other early crafts. The mill is located at 12 Frye Mill Rd., at the junction of Davisville Road and Burton Highway in Wilton; call (603) 654-6581 for more information or visit www .fryesmeasuremill.com.

Not far from Frye's, on a winding country road that briefly becomes the main street of Wilton Center, *Stepping Stones Bed & Breakfast* stands among lovely terraced gardens. The gardens seem to move inside with you as you enter the sunny, plant-filled breakfast room, which overlooks the terrace through a solid wall of windows. Down comforters, wicker furniture, and vintage pieced coverlets make this lodging memorable, as does breakfast, which may feature corn quiche, an almond omelet, or stuffed French toast as its main course. Pets and children are welcome here, but smoking is not. Stepping Stones, 6 Bennington Battle Trail, Wilton Center; (603) 654-9048 or (888) 654-9048; www.steppingstonesbb.com.

Six-tenths of a mile from Stepping Stones (follow the road toward Frye's, turning right and then right again), you come to a stream. Park just before the bridge and follow the old road on foot to a pond, beyond which there is a lovely cascade on the left.

Andy's Summer Playhouse, also in Wilton, gives children stage experience and adults enjoyable summer-theater productions, June through Aug. Tickets $9, children $6; (603) 654-2613; www.andyssummerplayhouse.org/.

The rambling *Birchwood Inn* is as much a part of the town of Temple as the neighboring white-spired church. Its low-ceilinged dining room is decorated with murals believed to be by Rufus Porter, an itinerant nineteenth-century painter. Now owned by a trio of Brits, there is an emphasis on things British such as a full English breakfast and British specialties in the dining room. Look for the likes of steak and ale pie, bangers and mash, and shepherd's pie in addition to the daily specials. The emphasis in the kitchen is the use of fresh locally grown products when available. On Route 45, a few miles off Route 101, in Temple, the inn is open year-round and serves dinner Wed through Sat evenings from 4:30 to 9: 30 p.m.; (603) 878-3285 or www .thebirchwoodinn.com.

Along the border west of Nashua are the quiet country towns of Hollis, Brookline, and Mason, where roads wind among fields and through forests that sometimes meet overhead. *Silver Lake State Park* is here, with a good

The Early Bird Gets the Surprise

It's not unusual for flea-market dealers to arrive the night before and camp in trucks so they can set up early in the morning, but Gerald St. Louis probably won't do it again, at least not at Hollis Flea Market. He and two boys who were helping him were startled one night in 1977 by an 8-foot furry creature, which left footprints over 16 inches long. Mr. St. Louis didn't wait to measure the prints; he jumped in his truck and left with the boys. Two other dealers, unaware of St. Louis's experience, described having their truck shaken by big furry hands, and they left pretty quickly, too. The tracks found by their truck matched the others.

horseshoe-shaped shallow beach that is nearly empty on weekdays (but can get very crowded on summer weekends); admission is $2.50, with kids under eleven and seniors free. The adjacent **Wallace's Grove** also has a beach and a picnic grove in the pines. **Silver Lake Flea Market** is nearby, a huge area that on weekends is covered with dealers and locals cleaning their barns and attics. There's no predicting what you'll find there; call (603) 465-7677 for information and dates.

On Route 123 in the town of Mason, watch for a sign on the south side of the road that announces **Uncle Sam's House,** a little red cape farmhouse that Samuel Wilson helped his father build. It was about 1780 when the family moved there in order to get away from British troops in Menotomy, Massachusetts, now Arlington Center. Sam lived in the farm in Mason from the time he was fourteen until he left at the age of twenty-three, in 1789, to establish his career in Troy, New York. Sam and his brother first established a brick kiln and then branched out into meat packing, providing food for the U.S. Army. Sam returned to Mason in 1797 to marry his sweetheart, Betsey Mann, and tradition says he won out over Johnny "Appleseed" Chapman for her hand.

A popular man, Sam was called Uncle by everyone who knew him. The Army required him to brand the letters u.s. on those barrels of meat destined for government use, and when a steamboat passenger asked one of his employees what the u.s. branded onto the barrels meant, the employee responded "Those are Uncle Sam's initials; he's feeding the whole Army!" The notion stuck and word spread.

Seen as a joke, within a year everything marked with u.s. came to be known as "Uncle Sam's," from beef to rifles and ships. Sam himself enjoyed the notoriety and rode in Fourth of July parades wearing a top hat. By 1813 a recruiting poster stated IF UNCLE SAM NEEDS, I'LL BE GLAD TO ASSIST HIM. The theme was later used in James Montgomery Flagg's well-known "I Want You" poster for the U.S. Army in 1938. The figure of Uncle Sam we know today came from a costume first worn by George Buchanan at a parade in Amesbury, Massachusetts, in 1851. A *Leslie's Illustrated New York News* correspondent saw him, and a picture of Buchanan in costume was in the next issue. The image grabbed the public's fancy and soon it appeared everywhere. The house in Mason, which is not open to the public, stands much as Uncle Sam and his family built it.

If you love herbs or perennial flowers, or just enjoy lovely gardens, follow the signs from Mason to **Pickety Place.** It's so far off the beaten path that you'll be sure you're lost long before you get there. Persevere and you will find, along with gardens, the cottage used by Elizabeth Orton Jones for Grandmother's House in her classic illustrations of *Little Red Riding Hood* and a shop brimming with handmade and herbal gifts. You can have an herbal luncheon in the cottage, which is open daily, but be sure to call for reservations, since a lot of people manage to find their way here. Pickety Place, 248 Nutting Hill Rd., Mason; (603) 878-1151. When you leave Pickety Place, you can go on to New Ipswich instead of backtracking—or you can approach Pickety Place by following signs from Route 31 in Greenville.

Lucia's Tavola combines an improbable size (only seven tables) with an unlikely location (a tiny shopping plaza on a back road in a town few have heard of), and her success shows the power of good food. Perhaps, in addition to her own exuberant personality, it's because she eschews both the trendy Northern Italian and the drowned-in-red-sauce Sicilian-American for her own native Roman cuisine, rarely found in American restaurants. Lucia serves classics such as hearty oxtail stew, and an appetizer rare even on Rome menus: Suppli al Telefono. Delectable balls of risotto conceal a morsel of sweet mozzarella, then are rolled in crumbs and deep fried until the creamy rice warms through and the cheese melts, forming long strings as you bite into it (the telephone wires in the name). True to Roman custom, you can order sides of roasted vegetables or baby peas with red onions and proscuitto, dishes that highlight the veggies in their own right. Desserts include more Roman favorites, Zuppa Inglese and a crispy crostata served with light tangy lemon cream. Open Tues through Thurs 4:30 to 8 p.m., Fri and Sat 4:30 to 9 p.m.; express lunch Tues through Fri noon until 2 p.m. Find Lucia's Tavola in Stoney Ledge Plaza, 181 Route 13, Brookline; call (603) 249-9134 (no advance reservations, but call a half hour ahead for seating) or visit http://luciastavola.com.

The **Barrett House** in New Ipswich, one of the state's most outstanding federal mansions, remained in the Barrett family from its construction in 1800 until it was given to the Society for the Preservation of New England Antiquities in 1948. Ornamented with pilasters and a central pediment, it is said to have been built as a wedding present to Charles Barrett Jr. from his father. Furnished with the best that each generation of the family could afford, including imported china and even a glass harmonica, the house interprets the life of a wealthy New England textile manufacturer and farming family over the course of several generations. Teas with guest lecturers are held throughout the summer, and special events such as a late-May antiques show highlight the schedule. It is open June through Oct 15 on the second and fourth Sat of the month, with house tours hourly from 11 a.m. to 4 p.m. Admission is $4, with special rates for seniors and children. Take Route 124 to New Ipswich, then Route 123A. You can write them at Main Street, New Ipswich 03071, or call (860) 928-4074 or visit www.historicnewengland.org/visit/homes/barrett.htm.

In the same town there is another house filled with antiques, but these are all for sale. ***Estelle M. Glavey Antiques*** fills an entire home, not with showrooms, but with fully furnished rooms of museum-quality antiques. This is no jumble of merchandise. Everything, from the oriental rug on the floor to the china on the table and the flame-stitched wing chair by the fire, is just as it would be in a home—but all for sale and clearly tagged with a price, not a code. The surprise is that the pieces are very reasonably priced, considering their quality and condition. Open all year daily except Monday on Route 124; (603) 878-1200.

Windblown Ski Touring Center keeps 25 miles of trails well groomed for cross-country skiers. Along with their waxing shed and restaurant, the center offers a warming hut with "sleeping-bag accommodations." The views are spectacular. It's at 1180 Turnpike Rd., Routes 123 & 124, 3 miles west of the town of New Ipswich; call (603) 878-2869 for more information or visit www.windblownxc.com.

More Places to Stay in the Merrimack Valley

In Nashua–Manchester areas, most of the major chains have hotels, but for inns or bed-and-breakfast lodgings, you'll need to look a little farther north or west.

BEDFORD

Bedford Village Inn
2 Village Inn Lane (off Route 101)
(603) 472-2001
www.bedfordvillageinn.com
In a converted barn behind the farmhouse, stylish rooms with all the comforts. Expensive.

CONCORD

Holiday Inn
172 North Main St.
(603) 224-9534 or
(888) 465-4329
Not the ordinary chain hotel, this hotel is stylish and immaculately maintained. Moderate rates.

HENNIKER

Don't plan to stay near Henniker on Mother's Day weekend; it's graduation at the local college, and rooms are booked two years in advance.

Henniker House Bed and Breakfast

2 Ramsdell Rd.
(603) 428-3198 or
(866) 428-3198
www.hennikerhouse.com
A Victorian house, with king and twin rooms. Full-course breakfasts in the solarium overlooking the river. Moderate.

LOUDON

Lovejoy Farm B&B

268 Lovejoy Rd.
(603) 545-2016
www.lovejoy-inn.com
In a 1700s colonial close to the Shaker Village, the rooms all have private baths; hearty breakfasts. Moderate.

The Wyman Farm Bed and Breakfast

22 Wyman Rd.
(603) 783-4467
Three guest rooms with private baths and sitting areas, full breakfast (from a menu selected the night before) and afternoon tea tray. Moderate.

MANCHESTER

Ash Street Inn

118 Ash St.
(603) 668-9908
www.ashstreetinn.com
The well-kept Victorian house with a wraparound

porch offers guest rooms furnished in antiques and is known for its afternoon teas, served at 2 p.m. on Tues, Thurs, or Sat. Tea is also served to nonguests by reservation. High-moderate, includes a full breakfast.

TEMPLE

The Birchwood Inn

Route 45
(603) 878-3285
Breakfast included. Moderate. See text for description of dining room.

More Places to Eat in the Merrimack Valley

BEDFORD

Bedford Village Inn

2 Village Inn Lane (off Route 101)
(603) 472-2001
www.bedfordvillageinn.com
Choose between the old New England farmhouse dining rooms or the bright, airy sunporch; the menu puts a new spin on old favorites. Expensive.

CANDIA

Pasquale's

Birchwood Plaza
Route 27 (2.5 miles from the Route 43 intersection)
(603) 483-5005
www.pasqualeincandia.com

Authentic Italian dishes served at lunch Fri through Sun, and dinner Tues through Sun.

CONCORD

The Barley House

132 North Main St.
(603) 228-6363
www.thebarleyhouse.com
Across the street from the State House, this lively restaurant serves hearty soups and stews and an internationally inspired list of sturdy entrees that range from Irish Whiskey Steak and Cuban Mojito Double Chop to jambalaya and bratwurst braised in beer. A variety of bands and solo artists perform Monday through Saturday nights.

Caffenio

84 North Main St.
(603) 229-0020
Good for lunches and coffees, if you don't mind balancing them on the saucer-size tables. Open 7 a.m. to 5 p.m. Mon through Sat.

Common Man

25 Water St.
(603) 228-3463
www.thecman.com
A popular and solid choice for meals on the road. Seafood, prime rib, sandwiches, or a lighter menu. Breakfast, lunch, and dinner.

Hermano's Cocina Mexicana

11 Hills Ave.
(1 block off Main Street)
(603) 224-5669

A wide choice of beers—
Mexican and otherwise—
accompany traditional
South-of-the-Border dishes
and some unusual ones.
Lunch Mon through Sat,
dinner every night.

DEERFIELD

The Lazy Lion café
4 North Rd. (Route 43)
(603) 463-7374
www.thelioncafe.com
Casual dining with a varied
menu, from blackened
salmon to meatloaf. Open
for lunch and dinner Mon
through Sat, Breakfast on
Sat and Sun. Baked goods
are served in the café all
day, along with an impressive selection of teas and
Fair Trade coffees.

HENNIKER

**Daniel's Restaurant and
Pub**
Main St.
(603) 428-7621
Sandwiches, pastas, and
light and full-size entrees
in a pub atmosphere over-
looking the river. Moderate.

HUDSON

Mia's Place
203 Central St.
(603) 595-2251
Open Tues through Sun 7
a.m. until 2 p.m. Soul food
from both New England
and the south fills the menu
of this cheery breakfast-
and-lunch cafe. Look for
jambalaya and biscuits with
gravy, along with meatloaf

and lighter dishes, such
as a chicken salad with
cranberries and walnuts.
Inexpensive.

Que Pasa Restaurant
Route 114
(603) 428-8226
Mexican food, as you probably guessed, at moderate
prices.

MANCHESTER

Cotton
75 Arms Dr. (in part of the
old mill off Bridge Street)
(603) 622-5488
American bistro theme,
specializing in fresh wood-
grilled fish. Moderate dinner
entrees, weekend reserva-
tions recommended.

**Fratello's Ristorante
Italiano**
155 Down St. (in the
Amoskeag Mills complex)
(603) 624-2022
www.fratellos.com
Moderately priced porto-
bella pannini or chicken
Capri are favorites at lunch,
and a delicious combo
of chicken and sausage
crema rosa or seafood
Sophia is a good choice
for dinner. Open weekdays
for lunch and dinner, dinner
only on weekends. Wheel-
chair accessible.

Wild Rover
21 Kosciuszko St.
(603) 669-7722
www.WildRoverPub.com
Irish music plays in a traditional (almost—it's smoke-
free) pub setting every Wed

and Thurs evening, but
the menu is more interna-
tional, with quesadillas and
Bourbon Street Beef Tips
alongside the lamb and
Irish sausage stew.

MASON

Parker's Maple Barn
1316 Brookline Rd.
(603) 878-2308
www.parkersmaplebarn
.com/index.php
Maple-sugar house with a
rustic country restaurant
that serves breakfast and
lunch.

MILFORD

Elisha's Restaurant
437 Nashua St. (Route
101A)
(603) 673-8764
www.elishasrestaurant.net
Charbroiled meats, barbe-
cue, and seafood, $8 and
up. Lunch and dinner.

The Mile Away
52 Federal Hill Rd.
(603) 673-3904
www.mileawayrestaurant
.com
The continental menu
includes a wide variety of
entrees, with rack of lamb,
fish, chicken, and several
veal specialties from veal
Marsala and picatta to
schnitzels. At least one
vegetarian dish is always
on the menu. All entree
prices ($16 to $26) include
a full four-course meal.

TILTON

The Olive Branch Tavern
255 Main St.
(603) 286-7774
Although the menu may
seem to be same-old Italian
and traditional New Eng-
land fare, the dishes served
are more interesting than
they sound on paper.

Upper Crust Pizzeria
65 Laconia Rd.
(east of I-93 exit 20)
(603) 286-3191
The independently owned
pizza shop is almost
hidden behind the tangle
of malls and superstores,
but it's worth looking for.
Take out or eat in; Italian
entrees, including chicken
Marsala, join excellent pizza
and pasta dishes.

THE MONADNOCK REGION

Word has it that **Mount Monadnock** is no longer the second-most-climbed mountain in the world. With motorized access to Fujiyama's summit, fewer people are climbing it, so Monadnock may now be number one. Whichever, its rocky ledge summit on a fine summer day is definitely not off the beaten path. But its broad-shouldered cone standing alone with no other mountains for company is the focal point for an entire region. Views of it provide the backdrop for towns miles away, from Jaffrey, where most of the mountain lies, to Keene. On clear days you can see as far away as Boston and the Green Mountains of Vermont.

Geologically, the mountain is the definitive monadnock, a mass of rock more durable, hence more resistant to erosion and glacial action, than the land around it. It is this mountain for which the geological phenomenon was named. The rest of the land of this southwest corner of New Hampshire is rolling, accented with small mountains and lakes. Only one city, Keene, is located in the entire area. It and Peterborough provide the cultural and business centers, but the smaller towns are surprisingly active, with their own museums, concert series, and theater groups. The bandstands that decorate

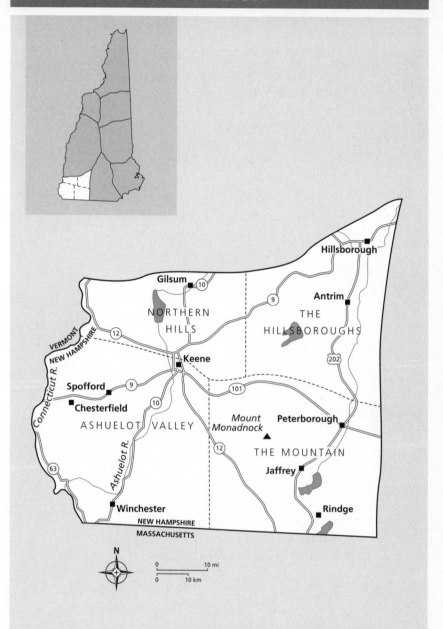

the commons of Monadnock's towns are not there to be photographed only. Painters, writers, and musicians have found a haven in this area for a century, giving it a rich tradition in the arts.

The Hillsboroughs

Visitors from outside New England often comment on the apparent lack of originality displayed in the naming of towns here. In one area will be found town after town with the same name prefixed by the four points of the compass or by "Center," "Upper," or "Lower," or suffixed by "Falls," "Mills," "Junction," "Street," or "Depot." The reason has to do with the town system of government, which was often based upon the original land grants. Large parcels of land were settled with several villages springing up within the boundaries of a town. Hillsborough is a good example. Within the limits of the town are Hillsborough, Hillsborough Center, Hillsborough Upper Village, and Hillsborough Lower Village.

Now bypassed by a new limited-access highway, the town of **Hillsborough** should not be bypassed by travelers. Take old Route 9-A at either end of town to 5 West Main St. and **German John's** (603-464-5079), a bakery featuring fine European breads and pastries. The raspberry cheese Danish, like the other berry-based treats, is made with fresh berries. Pick up some bread and German meats to make your own sandwiches, or enjoy the homemade soups from Jan through Apr. The soft pretzels are legendary. Open Tues through Sat.

The town offices and library on School Street (603-464-3595) are in the former Governor John B. Smith Mansion, a composite colonial revival and Queen Anne–style building that features exquisite woodwork and ornate gold arabesque ornamentation on its ceilings. It's open weekday business hours. Continuing on School Street, you will eventually come to Hillsborough Center. The road itself is worth the drive, passing well-tended countryside, old homes and farms, and some of the finest stone walls in the state.

Fox Research and Demonstration Forest is a 1,448-acre area of managed forest that contains plantations of exotics (trees that do not grow here naturally) and some unusual protected natural areas as well. One of these is a black gum, or tupelo, swamp. This tree is common to the South but rarely found in New England. A ravine of mature hemlock and one of the state's rare stands of virgin forest are here, as well as a true sphagnum bog formed by a floating mat of moss filled with rare wild plants. More than 20 miles of hiking trails wind through the forest; cross-country skiers are welcome on the trails in the winter, but there are no other recreation facilities here, since this is a forest, not a park. No motorized recreational vehicles are allowed in the forest. You are welcome to picnic on the grounds (they have a few tables) as long as you respect the "carry-in, carry-out" policy. Open year-round from dawn to dusk. Look in the display box at the kiosk beside the parking lot for a trail guide. Write *Fox State Forest,* Hillsborough Center Rd., P.O. Box 1175, Hillsborough 03244, or call (603) 464-3453 for more information, or visit www .nhdfl.org.

Hillsborough Center is among New Hampshire's loveliest towns, its houses set around a circular road on a slight slope, with two churches. The entire center of the village is webbed with stone walls, testament to the number of rocks that northern New Englanders have had to pull out of their farmlands over the centuries. A well-preserved town pound, built to keep stray animals out of neighbors' gardens, completes this almost perfect village scene. Just outside of town, rows of nearly perfect double stone fences border the fields of two exceptionally beautiful hillside farms.

Near the town pound and the old schoolhouse, the father-and-son team of *Raymond and Jonathan Gibson* produce heritage-quality, lead-free pewter in contemporary and traditional designs. Some of their work is in the Boston Museum of Fine Arts—in the museum displays, not just the gift shop. In addition to plates, bowls, tankards, and chalices, they produce candlesticks and collector-quality spoons. Their studio is open Mon through Sat 10 a.m. to 4 p.m. To inquire about the repair of old pewter, write them at 18 East Washington Rd., Hillsborough Center 03244; (603) 464-3410.

If you continue out East Washington Road, you will come to *Sage Knoll Herbs and Perennials,* a labor of love for Joan Phipps, who has collected many old herb and perennial varieties from cellar holes and roadsides, as well as by tracking them down in heritage gardens. Her plant list has more than 165 perennials and herbs for sale. She doesn't ship, so you'll just have to visit with this fascinating horticulturist between mid-May and the end of Oct, Tues through Sat 9 a.m. to 5 p.m. at 955 East Washington Rd.; (603) 478-5461.

EVENTS IN THE MONADNOCK REGION

Cheshire Fair,
early Aug, Keene
(603) 357-4740, (603) 271-3588

Pumpkin Festival,
late Oct, Keene
(603) 358-5344

Festival of Fireworks,
late Aug, Jaffrey
(603) 532-4549

Monadnock Music Craft Fair,
late Nov, Peterborough
(603) 924-7610

In East Washington, follow the road around to the right along the shore of the millpond, left at the meetinghouse, and up the hill. A few miles up the road, *Eccardt Farm* in East Washington is a real, operating dairy farm, where you can watch the milking and see an amazing collection of live birds including peacocks and exotic chickens and ducks, as well as sheep, goats, and rabbits. Milking times are 2:30 and 7 p.m. In the spring, you can help them turn sap into syrup. They also have a fascinating collection of old farming equipment including tractors and tools. This is a multigenerational farm, a real place without glitz and a great experience for kids. The farm is open all year; (603) 495-3157.

While you are passing the millpond in East Washington, it would be a shame not to visit two places that are less than a mile away, just over the line into neighboring Bradford and much easier to find from here. Follow Springs Road from the three corners by the forlorn little tumble-down building, and in less than a mile you will see a sign on your right at the entrance to *Bradford Bog.* It's a fine one, an Atlantic white-cedar swamp, its floor formed by an eerie tangle of sphagnum-covered cedar roots. A boardwalk provides a safe foothold over impossibly uneven "ground," and a profusion of seclusion-loving wild plants grow beside the trail. Continue into the open bog to an observation tower, which gives an overview of this flat bog ringed by low hills. You'll see tamarack, mountain holly, heather, and black spruce, along with bog rosemary and laurel. A leisurely exploration takes about half an hour.

Less than half a mile past the bog entrance, look for a lane into a grassy clearing and a sign for the site of *Bradford Springs.* New Hampshire had very few of these mineral springs, which were fashionable health spas in the late 1800s. But, like the White Mountain Mineral Springs (see the Eastern White Mountains chapter), this one had a rather grand hotel for guests who came to take the waters. The hotel's foundation of large granite stones is beside the road, and if you look in the woods behind it, shortly past the sign reading BRADFORD SPRINGS, you'll find the round stone-lined spring—or former spring. Over it once stood an octagonal springhouse, which you can now see, along with an engraving of the hotel itself, at Muster Field Farm Museum in North Sutton (see the Dartmouth-Sunapee Region chapter).

Just west of Hillsborough on Route 31 North is the boyhood *home of Franklin Pierce,* New Hampshire's only native son to become president of the United States. The mansion is a more elegant residence than was common in rural New Hampshire when it was built in 1804, and its interior has some surprises in store for those who think of New England decor as having been in somber puritan colors. The stenciling and decorative painting, which have been restored from remaining paint samples, are in vivid reds; the original

Balfour mural wallpaper in the parlor is among the finest examples in any restored home. Hillsborough's active historical society, which maintains and staffs the house, also holds monthly programs, with speakers who explore some facet of New Hampshire history. These are usually held at the Pierce Homestead on the fourth Monday of the month at 7 p.m. You can call the house for a schedule. Open Sat and Sun 10 a.m. to 4 p.m. late May to late June and early Sept to mid-Oct, daily July through Aug, the last tour is at 3:30 p.m. Free for New Hampshire residents; adults $7, ages six to eleven $3. It's at the intersection of Routes 9 and 31; (603) 478-3165.

This was Pierce's boyhood home; to see the house where he took his new bride (not open to the public), turn left from the driveway and cross Route 9. Begin counting houses at the corner, and the Pierce house is the fourth on the right. Continue on down that road, passing a small cluster of homes with a little church at Union Village, where the pavement ends. Just beyond, on the unpaved road, you'll cross a fine pair of stone arches, which you can see best from the little road that goes off to the right just after you cross them. A brochure with a self-guided walking tour of the Franklin Pierce neighborhood is available at the mansion. The walk is about a mile in length, and the brochure describes the lives, times, and structures that surrounded the future president as he grew up.

Hillsborough has five fine *stone-arch bridges.* One is bypassed by the new US 202 at its intersection with Route 9 just west of the town of Hillsborough. Another is at the intersection of Shedd Jones and Beard Roads. This one stands in the open, where you can get a good view of it from both directions. From the Pierce house, turn right, then right again down the hill onto Shedd Jones Road. Follow it until you come to the intersection with Beard Road, and you'll see the double-arched bridge right ahead of you. If you turn right, Beard Road will take you back to Route 9, passing a riverside *swimming hole* maintained by the town, but without lifeguards.

If, however, you go left on Beard Road, you will cross another stone bridge, this one spanning *Gleason's Falls,* which you can best see by following the path downstream a few yards. The river continues to cascade from pool to pool through a jumble of moss-covered boulders for a little way below the falls; notice the long groove the water has carved in the ledge. Be careful above the upper pools, since the pine-needle floor of the forest is very slippery and the drop a substantial one. If you continue on Beard Road a very short way and turn right onto Gleason Falls Road, you'll come out just above Hillsborough Center, on the road to East Washington. A left turn onto Gleason Falls Road does not take you back to Route 31 where you began, even though maps show it. Trust us on this one.

As you go west on Route 9, look for a double stone-arch bridge beside the road. It's worth a stop here to walk around to the upstream side for a better picture of what it looked like in the nineteenth century.

If you follow Route 31 instead of going right onto Shedd Jones Road, after leaving the Pierce Homestead, you will come to Windsor Road on your left, which leads to **Stonewall Farm Bed & Breakfast.** This 1785 farmhouse is well restored, furnished with antiques and fine reproductions, and situated on five-plus acres of gardens and meadow. More than one hundred varieties of hybrid lilacs form a rare arboretum and extend the lilac-blossom time by at least a month. They are simply spectacular at their height in late May. Rooms are priced from $120 and up in high season and include a full breakfast. They are located at 235 Windsor Rd., Hillsborough; (603) 478-1947; www.stonewall farmbandb.com.

The Mountain

The white-spired meetinghouse in **Hancock** is said to be the most photographed church in the state, although it is hard to understand how such a statistic is determined. The entire town of Hancock invites photography with its neat rows of fine old buildings along the main street. The **Hancock Inn** has been welcoming travelers for more than 200 years. One of its guest rooms has wall murals painted by the itinerant artist Rufus Porter. It is at 33 Main St., Hancock; (603) 525-3318 or (800) 525-1789; www.hancockinn.com.

On Saturdays from May to October, the carriage sheds behind the church house a farmers' market. Between 9 a.m. and 2 p.m., herbs and vegetables, baked goods, honey, handcrafts, and other locally produced goods are sold in a friendly small-town atmosphere. For details call (603) 525-3788.

Davis Brook Farm is a joy to behold in the summer, when its rolling acres are covered with the brilliant yellows, oranges, creams, and reds—and every shade in between—of blooming daylilies. Hundreds of varieties are for sale, but you are welcome to just come and enjoy the view. Open late June to mid-Aug, Thurs through Sat 9 a.m. to 4 p.m. and Sun 10 a.m. to 3 p.m. at 106 Bonds Corner Rd. (Route 127), Antrim; (603) 525-4728.

The **Harris Center,** located in Hancock, is dedicated to educating the public about environmental and conservation issues, and it sponsors a full calendar of activities, field trips, outings, and workshops throughout the year. At least one hike or program is held each weekend. Some of these activities are at the conservation center, while others show participants little-known places of natural interest throughout the area. The center's own property of about 7,000 acres in Hancock includes two small mountains and is traversed

Leaf Peeping on Two Wheels

New Hampshire has hundreds of good venues for bicycling in the summer, and nearly every one of them is partially bordered by hardwoods that provide an entirely different experience in autumn. In contrast to the pine-scented rides of summer, fall's own strong earthy scents are reason enough to get out onto the road. But the visual show is even better when the foliage of the state's mixed hardwood forests bursts into red, yellow, and orange flame.

The secret to fall riding is to layer your clothing so that as you, and the day, warm up you can eliminate a layer and control the evaporation of perspiration. For long trips, begin with a wicking T-shirt and add several layers of light clothing. Also, be sure to wear a cycling helmet.

Pick a road that is not heavily traveled. We like those around Bennington, Mont Vernon, Greenfield, and Francestown—or look for any road that circles a pond or lake. Remember that although backroads are less traveled than highways, they are used by cars and trucks. Stay to the right and do not ride down the middle or side-by-side with others in a group. A hazard to watch for in autumn is fallen leaves and pine needles. Pine needles act like hundreds of ball bearings under your tires, and leaves—especially when they are wet—can make the road seem greased. So beware and go gingerly when you hit a patch of either.

by about 7 miles of trails that lead to their summits, woods-surrounded ponds, and boulder trains. You can walk, ski, or snowshoe there, or join one of their guided walks that usually have a theme. In early November of each year, they welcome volunteers to join them for a Saturday of trail maintenance, which is a good way to repay the free use of the trails and free programs. To get to the Harris Center, follow Route 123 (King's Highway) west from the village of Hancock for about 2.5 miles, turning left at the signs. To find out what programs are scheduled, call (603) 525-3394 or visit www.harriscenter.org. Trail maps and schedules of all events and programs are found just inside the door.

Only a short way past the entrance to the Harris Center, on the opposite (north) side of Route 123, is the road to one of New Hampshire's most pristine lakes, where you may see loons, wood ducks, or herons. Set inside the *dePierrefeu-Willard Pond Wildlife Sanctuary,* an Audubon Society property, the pond has a nice sandy put-in for canoes, kayaks, and non-gasoline-engine boats. A series of hikes ranging from fifteen minutes to two and a half hours parallel the shore and climb to a fine view of the area from the ledges on Bald Mountain. Boulders left by retreating glaciers line the shore and tumble into the clear waters, visible below the pond's glassy surface. The pond is splendid for kayaks and canoes, with a totally undeveloped shoreline.

From Route 9 in Stoddard, west of Hillsborough, turn south onto Route 123, signposted HANCOCK, and turn left shortly after you pass a pond alongside the road. From Hancock, take Route 123 for 3.7 miles and turn right.

Greenfield State Park reserves one sandy beach just for campers who have settled into its spacious, wooded tent sites and has another one for day visitors and picnickers. This is one of the rare places where you can rent a boat either for the fishing or to enjoy the quiet of Otter Lake. One of the smaller of New Hampshire's state parks and one of the least known, it is a perfect retreat for nature lovers, swimmers, and those who seek a place to paddle their canoes in peace. Write the park at P.O. Box 203, Route 136, Greenfield 03047, or call (603) 547-3497. For reservations call (603) 271-3628 or visit www .nhstateparks.org/state-parks/.

Only a few years ago New Hampshire regained a ski area everyone though was lost forever, and the skill and energy that the new owners brought to the mountain has quickly made it a top choice for skiers and boarders. *Crotched Mountain,* in Bennington, has come back to life, and with snowmaking and grooming added to its short distance from the Nashua-Manchester-Concord corridor, it draws skiers who only a short while ago were traveling to Vermont. The vertical drop is 875 feet, but the terrain is interesting and challenging. In fact that is the fun of the place, that each trail has a little something extra. The all-new, fan-gun snowmaking can produce up to 2 feet of snow in twenty-four hours and it covers 100 percent of the trails. And the groomers know what to do with it, producing some of the best-groomed trails in the east. Even the lodge is new, big, bright, and friendly. The ski rental shop also has boards and the ski school is as good as the grooming. Crotched Mountain has taken night skiing to new levels, with Friday and Saturday night lighted trails open until 3 a.m. Follow Route 101 to Peterborough, then Route 202 north to Bennington and Route 47 to Crotched Mountain. The address is 615 Francestown Rd. (Route 47), Bennington; call (603) 588-3668 or visit www .crotchedmountain.com.

Historical societies perform several valuable services to their towns, such as storing and preserving records of long-closed schools and businesses; providing a safe home for old photographs, maps, and books that would otherwise be lost; and offering a clearinghouse for historical and genealogical information. A few maintain museums based on purchases or gifts of local artifacts, furnishings, and property.

The *Peterborough Historical Society Museum* is one of the finest historical museums of any society in the state. Along with exhibition rooms featuring early tools and antiques, they have in the several buildings of their complex a complete Victorian parlor, a replica of a country store, a colonial-era kitchen, and a restored mill house. You can get a walking tour map of Peterborough here, too. Open year-round, Mon through Fri 10 a.m. to 4 p.m. Admission is $3 for adults. Tours are available in July and Aug; the cost is $1. The museum is at 19 Grove St. (P.O. Box 58), Peterborough; (603) 924-3235, www.peterboroughhistory.org/.

The **Mariposa Museum** is a colorful celebration of the world's variety of cultures. Costumes, toys, musical instruments, puppets, and artifacts are used to present differences and similarities of life around the planet. Many exhibits are hands-on, including musical instruments, puppets, and a costume corner for kids. There are frequent presentations of dance, food, and music, designed for all ages, and a large library of children's books provides stories set in cultures all over the world. Call or see the Web site for current hours. Admission is $5 adults, $3 children, and the museum is wheelchair accessible. The location is 29 Main St., Peterborough; (603) 924-4555; www.mariposamuseum.org.

Peterborough has maintained a lively downtown, whose specialty shops and eateries cluster just off Main Street on Depot Square. Here you will find the upbeat food center called **Twelve Pine,** where you can have lunch in the cafe, buy a full-blown picnic, or stock up on locally produced specialty foods. It is open 8 a.m. to 7 p.m. weekdays, 9 a.m. to 5 p.m. Sat, and 9 a.m. to 4 p.m. Sun. Although you might expect it to be at 12 Pine St., it's actually at 11 School St.; (603) 924-6140; www.twelvepine.com.

Just opposite, in the Toadstool Bookshop, is **Aesop's Tables,** a lively café open Mon through Fri from 7:30 a.m. to 4 p.m., and Sat 9 a.m. to 4 p.m. for sandwiches, soups, muffins, and cappuccino; (603) 924-1612. Across School Street is **Joseph's Coat,** with quality folk art and clothing; (603) 924-6683. Behind Twelve Pine, art glass and other handwork by local artists is shown and sold at the **Sharon Arts Center** shop, open Mon through Thurs 10 a.m. to 5 p.m., Fri and Sat 10 a.m. to 6 p.m., and Sun 11 a.m. to 4 p.m.; (603) 924-(2787), www.sharonarts.org.

Peterborough's community tradition as a center for the arts shows also in the **First Friday** evenings of music, open shops, and galleries and other free programs. Various town groups, including the MacDowell Colony and the Peterborough Folk Music Society, participate in this celebration on the first Friday of each month.

Overlooking the Contoocook River, you'll find the stylish **Aqua Bistro,** with a constantly changing seasonal menu. Start with a salad, served in prodigious portions, of fresh greens, goat cheese, and oranges or with Maytag blue cheese and toasted pine nuts. Entrees include dishes such as beef sirloin seared in an iron skillet and served with roasted shallots and potatoes mashed with roasted garlic. Or perhaps veal with porcini, highlighted by a delicate Bolognese sauce.

Five pizzas are on the regular menu, with frequent daily specials of the thin-crusted pizzas whose toppings are inspired by seasonal produce. Portobello Pizza is topped with meaty mushrooms, prosciutto, a sauce of garlic and cream, and fontina cheese; a daily special pizza might combine smoked duck, caramelized onions, and sweet peppers with a pesto Alfredo sauce. Prices are moderate to expensive. Open Tues through Sun 4 to 10 p.m. and for Sun brunch from 11 a.m. to 10 p.m. at Depot Square, Peterborough; (603) 924-9905, www.acquabistro.com.

thethirteenthwife

Joseph Smith, founder and leader of the Church of Jesus Christ of Latter-Day Saints, died suddenly in the 1840s, while Brigham Young was conducting a revival meeting in Peterborough. While still in Peterborough, Young was chosen to replace him as the Mormons' leader, and when he left for Utah, some time later, 136 "leading citizens" of the town followed him, including one young woman who became his thirteenth wife.

The chef at Aqua Bistro gets most of his vegetables from one of the state's largest organic farms, **Rosaly's Garden.** The farm is worth visiting for its produce stand and for the herb gardens, which include a tea garden and water garden. A full acre is bright with flowers you can pick yourself, and in each season are pick-your-own berries. More than 120 varieties of organic vegetables are grown here and sold at the farmstand, which is open every day from 9 a.m. to 6 p.m., mid-May until Columbus Day. Rosaly's Garden and Farmstand, Route 123 (just south of Route 101), Peterborough.; call (603) 924-3303 or visit www.rosalysgarden.com. Also on the road to Sharon, Route 123, which leaves Peterborough from Route 101 just as 101 begins the long climb over Temple Mountain, you'll pass **Apple Gate Bed and Breakfast.** Rooms, each named for an apple variety, are nicely decorated. We like Granny Smith, an airy corner room in pale green, but Crispin has a view over the neighboring apple orchard and would be our choice in the spring, when the trees are a cloud of white blossoms. Full breakfasts are bountiful and always feature one apple dish—perhaps muffins or baked apples. Even the inn's friendly dog is named McIntosh, but the apple theme isn't carried to the point of being tiresome. Rates are inexpensive to moderate, and the inn is not suitable for children under twelve. It is on the corner of Route 123 at 199 Upland Farm Rd., Peterborough; (603) 924-6543, www.applegatenh.com/.

The **Sheiling Forest** provides pleasant walking through fields and forests, following stone walls built by farmers of long ago trying to clear their fields of the oversupply of granite boulders with which New Hampshire was blessed.

These are easy, level walks. On Saturday there are programs for small-woodlot owners on the care and management of woodlands. Open daily dawn to dusk year-round on Old Street Road in Peterborough.

Peterborough residents evidently have a taste for good food, since there are a number of culinary havens in town. The ***Kernel Bakery*** was making flaky croissants for Monadnock-region breakfast tables long before croissant became a household word. And they are half the price of inferior products elsewhere. Their doughnuts, Danishes, cookies, Eccles cakes, and breads are just as good. You can get a cup of coffee here to go with your breakfast pastry but, alas, not a cup of tea. Open Mon, Wed, and Fri from 7 a.m. to 1 p.m. You'll find the Kernel Bakery on Jaffrey Road (Route 202) in Peterborough; call (603) 924-7930.

Although not as well known as its sister mountain, ***Pack Monadnock*** in Miller State Park offers easy access to mountaintop views extending from Boston to the White Mountains and Vermont. A fee is charged for use of the auto road to the summit, or you can climb it on foot by any of three hiking trails, each about 1.5 miles long. Picnic areas and an observation tower are at the open summit. The entrance is on Route 101 as the highway crests the hill. Only a few miles from Peterborough on Route 202, Jaffrey is a fine old mill town with its attractive nineteenth-century mill complex still intact and in good repair. Route 124, in front of the mill, leads to Jaffrey Center, a beautiful collection of nineteenth- and early-twentieth-century homes set around a common. The ***Melville Academy Museum*** (www.jcvis.org/museum/museum.php) is housed in a building that was a private academy from 1833 to 1857 and then a town school until World War I. Nicely restored, it has a local history museum on its first floor and the original classroom on the top floor. The classroom will make you acutely aware of how far education has come. Downstairs are reminders of life in small rural communities: kitchen implements, tools, straw hats, and handwork. What makes it particularly appealing, however, is the large collection of Hannah Davis hatboxes. This nineteenth-century woman established her own industry making boxes from especially thin-sawn boards. Once assembled, they were covered in attractive printed paper and sold from her wagon all over New England. The boxes have become highly collectable, and the Smithsonian covets this collection. The museum is open Sat and Sun from 2 to 4 p.m. in, July and Aug. Melville Academy is one of several historic buildings in Jaffrey Center's Historic District, which also features an outstanding church and a one-room schoolhouse, along with the burying ground. Near the wooded edge of the cemetery is the gravestone of the author Willa Cather, who first visited Jaffrey in 1917 and returned to rent rooms at the old Shattuck Inn for two summers and in the fall of the following years. She wrote in

And Then There Were None

Looking at the rocky peak today, it is hard to believe that Mount Monadnock was once covered to its top in forest. The entire summit and its ledges, except for Bald Rock, are described by early accounts as covered in red spruce. However, farmers clearing land on the lower slopes often set fires to make their work easier and faster. These fires spread quickly, fanned by the winds to which mountains are exposed, and spread unchecked to consume forests on the upper slopes and summit. In 1800 one of these blazes continued unchecked for two weeks as a ground fire burned the thick layer of needles and organic soil in which the trees were rooted. Giant spruces toppled, leaving a massive tangle that was made even more impenetrable by further blowdown from storms.

This entanglement provided a safe refuge for wolves between their forays into sheep pastures and pens on the lower-slope farms, so farmers banded together to burn it. Of course, the fire got away from them, and in two weeks of burning it consumed everything that was left growing on the top of the mountain. Contemporary reports describe a fire so hot that it caused rocks to split and explode.

a tent, pitched in a meadow behind a friend's summer home, and it was here that much of *My Antonia* was written. She left instructions to be buried in the Old Burying Ground.

The *Inn at Jaffrey Center* sits opposite the academy, across the wide village green, anchoring the idyllic village scene. Its rooms are individually decorated, many with antiques and each with a pleasant flair all its own. Although it has plenty of country inn warmth and charm, don't expect a same-old "ye olde country inne" menu in the dining room. Instead look for a creative menu of dishes such as pan-seared duck breast with dried plums soaked in Cassis or chicken rubbed in lavender and fennel seed, as well as new takes on traditional New England ingredients such as sweet potatoes, green apples, cranberries, and cider. These may be interpreted in styles borrowed from Venice, Japan, Provence, California, or Jamaica to create dishes that are like nothing that ever came out of grandma's kitchen. If you're lucky, the chef's signature Savory Sweet Potato Flan will appear on the appetizer menu—a surprising non-dessert twist, with soy sauce added to the maple glaze. Chicken and fig sausage is another specialty, and pork roast may be encrusted in almonds and sauced with Amaretto. Most entrees are under $20.

The Sunday brunch is served from the menu, not the ubiquitous buffet, and is divided into "The Breakfast Side" and "The Lunch Side." On the breakfast list are not only eggs Benedict, but also the chef's own variations between the English muffin and the egg/hollandaise layer: Eggs Atlantis (smoked salmon and sliced tomato with capers) and Eggs Godiva (baked ham, spinach, Swiss cheese, and cream), plus steak-and-eggs, a breakfast club, and the usual French toast and egg dishes. The other side of the menu offers Asiago Tortellini Carbonara among the lunch dishes. The dining room is open Mon through Sat for dinner and for brunch on Sun. The Inn at Jaffrey Center is on Route 124, 2 miles west of downtown Jaffrey; (603) 532-7800, www.theinnat jaffreycenter.com.

The space at 21 Main St. in Jaffrey once occupied by Aylmer's Grill is now filled by **Sunflower Café.** This welcoming place spices the flavors of fresh seasonal dishes with music—smooth jazz piano sounds on Sunday evening and a changing program of country, bluegrass, acoustic folk, jazz improv, and folk rock on Friday evenings. The bright dining room provides an easy, comfortable place for lunch or a light dinner—or one of chef/owner Carolyn Edwards's sumptuous desserts. Cakes are her specialty; they were always the hit of all the local parties she catered before opening the restaurant. Chef Edwards shares the secrets of these and other specialties in her cooking classes. The Café is open Tues through Sun for breakfast and lunch and serves dinner until 9 p.m.

Alice Blue Antiques is well worth a stop for a nostalgic bauble or perhaps a romantic bit of fine antique European needlework or French lace. Among the antique textiles (one of the owners travels to France frequently in search of outstanding examples), the shop mixes stylish modern designer wear, a combination that makes the shop even more appealing. It is open Mon through Sat 10 a.m. to 5 p.m., Sun 11 a.m. to 4 p.m. Alice Blue Antiques, 27 Main St., Jaffrey; call 603-532-7015.

Del Rossi's Trattoria does a good job with the unlikely combination of a real Italian restaurant and a first-rate folk, world, and jazz music venue. Neither is ever compromised for the other. Get their schedule and reserve early for big names, or go on a weeknight just for the food, which includes fettuccine with shiitake mushrooms, peas, and Marsala, or a breast of chicken stuffed with basil and fresh tomatoes in a Gorgonzola sauce. About twenty entree choices tempt you. The wine list is also excellent. It's open for dinner only, Wed through Sun, on Route 137 in Dublin, just north of Route 101; (603) 563-7195.

The **Friendly Farm** sits at the edge of the woods near Dublin Lake, where kids and adults can meet, pet, and get to know farm animals. Baby animals predominate and love to be fed. Wander about the tree-shaded farm and have close encounters of the good kind with baby chickens, hens, roosters, ducks, and geese. In one building are some of the strangest-looking fowl you have ever met. Also at the farm are sheep, goats, piglets, rabbits, and even a baby cow or two. Handy dispensers, like the old-time peanut machines, let you buy feed so kids (of any age) can get up close and personal. Open 10 a.m. to 5 p.m. daily from late Apr through Labor Day and weekends until mid-Oct, weather permitting. Half a mile west of the lake, Main St. (Route 101), Dublin; (603) 563-8444; www.friendlyfarm.com.

Across Dublin Lake, just east of The Friendly Farm, is a beautiful view of Mt. Monadnock. It's worth circling the lakeshore for a look at some of the fine homes that are more visible when the leaves are off the trees. Dublin was home to the **Dublin Art Colony** (www.dublinartcolony.org), a group that included Abbott Thayer, Frank Benson, George de Forest Brush, and Rockwell Kent. These and writers including Mark Twain, Rudyard Kipling, and Amy Lowell were frequent visitors at these lakeside "cottages."

The beautiful little brick village of **Harrisville** clusters at the head of its millpond, north of Dublin and Route 101. It is a rare nineteenth-century textile town that remains almost unchanged. Original small, brick mill buildings are in good repair and are still used by **Harrisville Designs,** where textile arts thrive in the Weaving Center. Knitting and weaving supplies sold there include high-quality yarns, original patterns, and looms. Weeklong (and occasionally shorter) workshops, taught by leading textile artists, concentrate on basic instruction and specific skills, such as Navajo weaving, rag rugs, or Estonian knitting. These take place June through Oct, with student housing provided in the 1850 Cheshire Mills Boarding House. The yarns sold in the shop are spun at the adjacent spinning mills. The shop is open Tues through Sat from 10 a.m. to 5 p.m., in Center Village, Harrisville; (603) 827-3996, www.harrisville.com.

West of Jaffrey, in Rindge, **Cathedral of the Pines** is an outdoor church as well as a national memorial to those who lost their lives in wartime military service. Services are held here by people of all faiths, using the various altars and wooded "chapels." The Memorial Tower holds a peal of Sheffield bells and a set of four Norman Rockwell bas-reliefs in memory of women who served in the military. Even when Cathedral of the Pines is not open for services, you can walk through the grounds, a forest of tall pines atop a hillside, with views of Monadnock, Kearsarge, and southern Vermont. Off Routes 202 and 119 in Rindge; call (603) 899-3300 for more information or visit www.cathedralpines.com.

Those with fond memories of the **Woodbound Inn** or of Aylmer's Grille, the popular Jaffrey restaurant, will be happy to hear that the two have been united. The newly renovated inn has a variety of rooms, some with double tubs. One- and two-bedroom cabins along the shores of Lake Contoocook have sitting areas, fireplaces, and refrigerators. In the winter guests can relax by the inn's fireplace after cross-country skiing through the inn's snow-covered meadows and woods. The inn is now the home of *Aylmer's Grille,* with a creative American menu that changes seasonally. Expect to find entrees such as "pan-kissed" pepper-crusted tuna, coated in fresh-crushed peppercorns, with a buttery sashimi interior. Aylmer shines at grilling fish, which he often serves with a salsa over micro-greens. Roasted tomato tart is a favorite starter, or begin with an example of his playful combinations of cuisines, the Cajun chowder. Perhaps end the meal with profiteroles with their own fudge sauce. Aylmer's Grille at Woodbound Inn, 247 Woodbound Rd., Rindge; call (603) 532-4949 or visit www.woodbound.com.

While other towns may be "postcard towns," Fitzwilliam is a "Christmas-card town." Its white town hall and stately homes set around the snow-covered common make it a favorite for artists and photographers creating greeting cards. One building on the common is the *Amos J. Blake House,* a museum maintained by the Fitzwilliam Historical Society. Built in 1837, this was the home and law office of a well-respected community leader. His law office is intact, and other rooms are furnished in period antiques. A kitchen, parlor, music room, and reconstructed schoolroom are part of the museum, as are displays of military and firefighting memorabilia. A small shop, filled with local crafts, New England food specialties, soaps, and gifts, uses original country-store counters, furnishings, and cash register. Admission is free. Open Sat late May to late Oct 1 to 4 p.m. and Thurs 9 to 11 a.m. Write the Blake House, On the Common (P.O. Box 87), Fitzwilliam 03447; or visit www.fitzhistoricalsociety .org/. Fitzwilliam has a number of antiques shops, several of them gathered picturesquely around the village green. *MacReay Landy Antiques* (603-585-9581, www.maclandy.com; open Thurs through Mon 10 a.m. to 5:30 p.m.) and Bloomin' Antiques (603-585-6688, open Thurs through Sat 10 a.m. to 5 p.m., Sun noon to 5 p.m.) face each other at one end of the green; a few steps away, behind the Fitzwilliam Inn, is *Brian Luddy American Country Antiques* (603-585-9180; open Wed through Sun 10 a.m. to 4 p.m.).

One of the largest stands of wild rhododendron north of the Allegheny Mountains is in Fitzwilliam at *Rhododendron State Park.* The fifteen acres of large shrubs bloom by mid-July in a riot of huge flower clusters against glossy, deep-green leaves. At any time of year, the trails through this park are bordered by masses of broad evergreen leaves and the thick tangle of trunks and branches that support them. An adjoining wildflower trail was created by the Fitzwilliam Garden Club. Native plants are labeled in the open woodland that borders the path. It is a lovely, quiet, and cool spot, with 1 mile of easy walking. Follow the signs off Route 119.

A back road that branches off Route 12, not far north of the rock ledges south of Keene, gives more views of Monadnock as well as a stone bridge. It brings you to Route 124 and into Marlborough. At the intersection with Route 101 is the **Homestead Bookshop.** Strong in local history, they have several shelves of long-out-of-print books on New Hampshire, as well as a travel section well stocked with the works of explorers and adventurers. In addition to finding nearly 50,000 used books, you will meet the nicest people there. Their book search service ferrets out books for customers in all parts of the country. Open Mon through Sat 9 a.m. to 5 p.m. and Sun 9 a.m. to 4:30 p.m. Call (603) 876-4213 for more information.

Unbridled Chocolates is no ordinary candy shop. Think of it as an art gallery, where the artist, Chocolatier Alan Crofut, works in an edible medium. Known for his unique combinations of natural and organic flavors, Crofut creates recipes not just for candy, but for cakes, pastries, hot drinks, and other delicacies. In addition to more than two dozen varieties of truffles and filled chocolates (don't say we didn't warn you about the addictive qualities of the raspberry cream filling) and his non-traditional ginger-laced cashew turtles, called Tortugies, he creates desserts like Cheshire Cream Pie, seven layers of chocolate mousse and vanilla custard. Stop in the shop for a cup of Single Origin Hot Chocolate, maybe a smooth Santo Domingo or an attention-grabbing Peruvian with cayenne. The hot cocoa mixes are for sale in the shop. Unbridled Chocolates, 135 Main St., Marlborough; call (603) 876-9111 or visit www.unbridledchocolates.com.

Ashuelot Valley

Keene's main street is lined for several blocks by beautifully cared-for private residences covering all architectural periods since the mid-eighteenth century. In the 1750s the founders of **Keene** laid out all of the main lots so that the buildings would be set well back from the center of the highway. That decision set the tone for the development of downtown. At the north end of Main Street stands a large white church with a wedding-cake spire. This is one of the most beautiful of New England's churches, and its location at the head of Central Square gives it a commanding presence.

On the west side of Main Street is the ochre-colored, eighteenth-century **Wyman Tavern.** It was from this tavern that a contingent of Keene minutemen departed to join in the Revolution on April 23, 1775, four days after the battle at Concord, Massachusetts. Prior to that, the first trustees' meeting of Dartmouth College was held here. The tavern is now a museum, furnished in the 1770-1820 period. It is open June 1 to Labor Day and admission is $2. Contact the Historical Society of Cheshire County up the street at 246 Main St. for hours or see their Web site at www.hsccnh.org. You'll find the Wyman Tavern at 339 Main St. in Keene (603-357-3855, summer only).

Keene was the home to the nationally known muralist and artist Barry Faulkner, whose works decorate public buildings in Washington D.C. and elsewhere. Several sites in Keene display individual pieces, and there are two full-scale murals. Elliot Hall, at Keene State College, is a large brick mansion near the corner of Main Street and Wyman Way that serves as the admissions office for the college. In the front hallway a large *Faulkner mural* depicting Central Square fills the winding staircase. In the main hall of Fleet Bank at the head of Central Square, his mural series *Men of Monadnock* fills the back wall, and at the Keene Public Library on nearby Winter Street a number of sketches he did for murals elsewhere are exhibited.

The *Archive Center of the Historical Society of Cheshire County* has a number of Faulkner works in its Barry Faulkner Room, to the left of the main entry. On display are an oil self-portrait, a rare 1930s lithograph of work done on the National Archives, and several drawings and sketches done over his lifetime. The newest accession is a full-color painting of the mosaic mural that Faulkner did for Radio City Music Hall in 1939.

Other exhibit rooms in the society's headquarters highlight the prominent role of local glass and pottery manufacture, with large collections on display. The society has acquired all of the metal toy collection of the Kingsbury Corporation dating back to the nineteenth century. Consisting of more than 250 items, the collection is a boon for antique toy lovers and includes cast iron and sheet metal items. Horse and wagon, fire engine, classic auto, zeppelin, and race car forms are among the toys included. Items of historical interest from the society's collection are also exhibited, with special exhibits mounted several times each year showcasing particular aspects of local history. The reference library contains extensive genealogical material and histories of the region and the state. The archive is open Tues through Fri from 9 a.m. to 4 p.m. and Sat from 9 a.m. to noon at 246 Main St., Keene; (603) 352-1895; www .hsccnh.org.

The *Arboretum and Gardens* at Keene State College are well described in a brochure that you can get free at the Mason Library on Apian Way, the pedestrian street that cuts through the center of the campus from Main Street. For some years tree plantings have been planned to create a collection of specimen trees, and it now includes a wide variety of exotics, several of which are at the far northern edge of their range. The booklet includes a map of the campus and silhouettes of leaf shapes to help you identify the species you'll see on a tour of the campus. For more information about the arboretum, call the Plant Sciences Department at (603) 358-2544.

Also on the Keene State College campus, the free *Thorne-Sagendorph Memorial Art Gallery* shows traveling exhibits and an impressive

Parrish the Thought

As you drive around Central Square in Keene, you may notice an advertisement for Parrish Shoes painted on the side of a brick building and featuring a picture of an old-fashioned shoe. It's all that's left of the sets for *Jumanji*, starring Robin Williams, which was filmed in Keene. For the movie, the brick business buildings surrounding the leafy park were transformed back to their appearance of many years ago, then trashed for the later scenes—their signs hanging, their paint peeling, and their façades unkempt. After filming, Keene was restored to its 1990s appearance, with only this painted sign as a reminder of Robin's time travels there.

permanent collection of well-known nineteenth-century artists who painted in the shadow of Mount Monadnock. The gallery is open June through Aug, Wed through Sun from noon to 4 p.m., Sept through May Sat through Wed from noon to 4 p.m., Thurs and Fri noon to 7 p.m. Thorne-Sagendorph Memorial Art Gallery, Wyman Way (off Main Street), Keene; call (603) 358-2720 or visit www.keene.edu. One of the state's most unusual "old house" museums is in this same neighborhood, next to St. Bernard's Church on Main Street. The **Horatio Colony House Museum** is not a home restored to one particular period, but the residence of a twentieth-century heir to a fortune that allowed him to live the life of a nineteenth-century gentleman of leisure. He traveled all over the world, collecting as he went, with a fine eye and highly cultivated tastes. The oriental art he brought back with him is at home in the 1806 federal mansion, amid fine eighteenth- and nineteenth-century furnishings. Some of his collections are in glass cases in the ell, while other items are displayed as he lived with them. You will leave feeling that you have known this well-read, well-traveled, and generous gentleman who left his estate for others to enjoy. Open May 1 to Oct 15, Wed through Sun 11 a.m. to 4 p.m., and in winter by appointment. Admission is free; park behind the church. The address is 199 Main St. in Keene; (603) 352-0460; www.horatio colonymuseum.org.

Locals were quick to approve of the newcomer, **Blue Trout Grill,** to a location across the street from the Horatio Colony House that had for years been occupied by the popular pub, 176 Main. The inviting interior, with low upholstered banquettes facing cherry-wood tables sets the right tone for the menu—stylish without being over-the-top or pretentious. Pan-seared sea scallops with coriander arrive sauced in lemongrass cream, and pecan-crusted rainbow trout in buerre blanc is laced with orange and served with an herbed risotto cake, a nice counterpoint to the delicate fish. Servings are generous, and chocolate desserts are a specialty of chef/co-owner Amy Miller. The restaurant is open every day, 11:30 a.m. to 2 p.m. and 5 to 9 p.m. Blue Trout Grill, 176 Main St., Keene; call (603) 357-0087 or visit http://bluetroutgrill.com.

Observe life farther up Main Street at the big windows of ***Thai Garden*** while dining on some of the best and most authentic Thai dishes in the state. The bright and pleasant dining room is staffed by helpful family members, who know the menu. Dishes marked with hot pepper symbols will curl your hair; others are delicate blends of exotic and fresh local ingredients. The restaurant is open daily for lunch 11:30 a.m. to 3 p.m. and for dinner 5 to 10 p.m. It is located at 118 Main St., Keene; (603) 357-4567.

On Main Street, just below Central Square, look for ***Hannah Grimes Marketplace,*** an excellent craft boutique carrying works of many local craftspersons. The crafts and locally made food products you'll find there include pottery, candles, fiberwork, woodenware, herbal sachets and cooking blends, jams, jellies, and even New Hampshire–made muffin mixes and stone-ground flours. We never know what new items will be on their shelves. They also carry stained glass, fine prints by local artists, photography, and cards. You can buy a cup of herbal or China tea there to drink as you browse, or you can sit down to drink it with a fresh scone or cookies from their bakery shelf. Hannah Grimes Marketplace is at 46 Main St., Keene; (603) 352-6862; www .hannahgrimesmarketplace.com.

Just up the street is the new ***E. F. Lane Hotel.*** Keene had not had a down-town hotel for decades, which makes this attractive place especially welcome. An air of calm and comfort begins in the lobby, with its stylish tones of tan and cream with dark green carpeting. Each room is decorated with quality classic and contemporary furniture. Some have king or queen beds, some offer whirl-pool tubs, and all rooms have desks with computer and high-speed Internet hookups. The creators of the inn have used detail work in the door facings and elsewhere that brings back the nineteenth-century flavor of this converted downtown office and commercial space. Rooms vary from the very large and high-ceilinged Classic room to the super-large Executive and a two-floor Chair-man's Suite, all of them handsome and comfortable. Rates for double occu-pancy are high-moderate, and special rates for a two-night stay are available for college graduation, parents, and homecoming weekends and for foliage and Pumpkin Festival weekends. Rates include a light breakfast. The hotel's dining room, the ***Chase Tavern,*** named for the nineteenth-century Supreme Court jurist who was educated in Keene, is a good place for casual dining. Lunch offerings run from soups and salads to burgers, Reubens, and quesadil-las, all moderately priced. The E. F. Lane Hotel is at 30 Main St., Keene; (603) 357-7070, (888) 300-5056, fax (603) 357-7075; www.eflane.com.

On the opposite side of the street is the ***Colonial Theatre.*** Thornton Wilder read his plays, Amelia Earhart lectured, and a Metropolitan opera star once sang four encores of *O Sole Mio* in this theater, opened in 1924 as a state-of-the-art stage and movie house. Its interior had deteriorated badly by 1991, when its restoration began. Today it retains part of its original art deco frieze and its other elegant details have been restored. It also hosts art films and traveling performers (Joan Baez and The Kingston Trio have performed here since its restoration). Watch the marquis at 95 Main St. or contact the box office at (603) 352-2033; www.thecolonial.org.

Next to the theater is ***Brewbakers,*** a coffeehouse with a laid-back atmosphere. Grab a paper or one of their many novels and curl up with a cup of coffee and a homemade scone or muffin. There is a booth, too, and ice cream tables; in the summer a few tables spill out onto Main Street. In addition to coffees and biscotti, they also have a lunch menu. Located at 97 Main St., Keene; (603) 355-4844.

Celebrating Food

While some states have a trademark food product or dish—such as Maine lobster, Vermont cheddar, or Rhode Island jonnycakes—New Hampshire has a little of everything. Its boats harvest lobsters and fish from the sea, and its farms and orchards produce an abundance of apples, berries, and field-fresh vegetables. In the spring its hillsides run with sap that is boiled into maple syrup.

Although it produces an abundance of native foods, from farm cheeses to pumpkins, no one harvest is its trademark. However, the state does celebrate each season with a splendid cornucopia of food festivals. In the southwest corner (the Monadnock region) alone are a strawberry festival in Fitzwilliam, an apple festival in Walpole, and a gingerbread festival in Charlestown.

The granddaddy of them all is Keene's Pumpkin Festival, held just before Halloween each October. In 2003 the tree-canopied square and main street were lined with 28,952 jack-o'-lanterns, each with a lighted candle inside. Keene holds the Guinness World Record for the most carved pumpkins in one place, a category it originated and defends with an increasing number each year. All day Saturday you can see the collection grow while you feast on harvest goodies, including cider and homemade pumpkin pies and cookies; www.centerstagenh.com.

A week earlier, in nearby Winchester, is one of our favorite local homegrown celebrations: the Pickle Festival. In 1999 more than 4,000 pickles were eaten in one day—not to break a record but because they taste good. The day begins with a parade and ends with a barn dance. In between are sports competitions, an antique car show, a field full of scarecrows, barbecues, and, of course, pickle judging.

On West Street (it's the street heading west from Central Square, but it was named for a person, not for its direction), ***Ashuelot River Park*** is a pleasant place to stop, sit on a bench, and enjoy the sunshine. The river here was once part of a millpond feeding the factory across the street (now the Colony Mill Marketplace). Today the pond is smaller and bounded by a garden with a footbridge over to an island. On the north side a trail leads through the woods along the banks of the slow-flowing river. The shaded path is a good place to see wildlife, especially waterfowl. Several species of ducks are common visitors. At its north end, the path connects to a paved bike/walking path that, if you go west, will take you to the city's ***Wheelock Park,*** where you will find athletic facilities, including tennis courts and a city-operated camping area. The path allows campers to get to the center of the city without traveling on a public street. For camping information contact the Parks and Recreation Department, 312 Washington St., Keene 03431; (603) 357-9832.

Not long ago, people in Keene used to go across the river to Brattleboro, Vermont, for a fine dinner; now Brattleboro people travel to Keene, especially since Italian-born chef Nicola Bencivenga has opened ***Nicola's Trattoria,*** with a menu of classic and innovative dishes based on impeccably fresh, high-quality ingredients. No shortcuts here: The polenta is real, light in texture, and made the long, slow way instead of the quick-fix, heavy cornmeal mush served as polenta in too many places. The whole menu is enticing, but we usually order the specials just to see what he's created that day. Go on Saturday night for osso bucco or any night for the cioppino. The Risotto alla Milanese is superb—or choose any risotto special. It may be blended with perfectly cooked shrimp and pesto or another equally delicious combination.

Nicola added the Tuscan Room, open later than the restaurant and the perfect place for light meals, dessert, or a late-night chocolate ricotta torte, *tartufo,* or a crisp, freshly filled cannoli after a show at the Colonial. This is the time of night when Nicola can escape the kitchen and meet his guests. Keene's our hometown, and Nicola's is our favorite place for dinner; it's at 39 Central Sq., but you enter from Winter Street, beside the elegant 1858 brick courthouse (you can park behind the courthouse); (603) 355-5242. They're open for dinner Tues through Sun from 5 p.m.

Keene's favorite place for a quick breakfast or lunch is ***Timoleon's,*** on Main Street, just south of Central Square. This is the sort of place where everyone calls the waitresses by their first names, and the menu has all of the old favorites. They are noted for chicken croquettes, meat loaf, and, on Friday, codfish cakes. The breakfast pastries are all baked right there and have earned a "Best of New Hampshire" award. Located at 25-27 Main St., Keene; (603) 357-4230.

The Redfern Arts Center on Brickyard Pond at Keene State College has an active performance schedule (603-358-2168; www.keene.edu/racbp), and Keene supports its own choral group, the **Keene Chorale.** Their professional-quality concerts are held in the spring and before Christmas and may include sacred works, such as masses and oratorios, or operatic choral selections. For a schedule of concerts call (603) 357-1534. During the summer, concerts featuring popular bands are held on Wednesday evenings at the bandstand in the common on Central Square from 7 to 8:30 p.m. (603-357-9829).

Colony House B&B is located a block from Keene's thriving Main Street. It is in a lovingly restored 1819 home that at one time belonged to the owner's great-grandfather. Guest rooms all have private baths and guests have a living room, a butler's pantry with microwave and toaster, and a study as public rooms. Computer access, a fax and copier, and a computer are all available. Entry to the guest rooms is through a private entrance. All of the attractions of the city, including the Colony Mill Marketplace, Colonial Theater, historical society museums, and shopping are within easy walking distance. Located at 104 West St., Keene 03431; (603) 352-0215; www.colonyhouse104.com.

Goose Pond is a recreational nature reserve 4 miles from Central Square on East Surry Road, accessed from Court Street. You will see a sign for the parking area. A trail leads along a stone wall to the undeveloped pond, which once served to power several mills downstream. The trail then circles the pond, close to the shore through woodlands. In one spot it forms a tunnel through overhanging hemlock boughs, but the woods are mostly mixed, with birch, white pine, and maple. Watch for signs of beaver activity here, including their lodge built against the shore, close to the path. The total distance around Goose Pond is about 3 miles, including the short walk from the parking area to the pond.

Just east of Keene, **Granite Gorge** serves as a perfect entry for beginners to the sports of skiing and snowboarding. Granite's specialty is snowboarding, with terrain parks that are noted for their challenges. But they also have alpine and cross-country trails. Granite Gorge, Route 9, Keene; call (603) 358-5000 or visit www.granitegorge.com.

Swanzey, directly south of Keene, has maintained and preserved **three covered bridges** over the Ashuelot River as well as built one new one. The following route will show you all of them. Leave Keene on Route 10 (Winchester Street) and turn left onto Matthews Road just past the veterinary clinic. Go left at the end and through the first of the bridges. When that road ends, go left again and shortly join Route 32 at the **Potash Bowl** (remember where this is—we'll get back to it later). All this sounds complicated, but it's a distance of only 3 to 4 miles. Go south on Route 32 to Carleton Road, where you will find another bridge in a few hundred yards. If it's early spring and the water is high, the bridge may be closed, but you can drive down to watch the river lapping at its floorboards. Return to Route 32 and continue south to Swanzey Lake Road on your right. Follow this winding road until it ends at a T. Go right, and you'll come to West Swanzey. The third bridge is to your left when you reach the crossroads at the top of the hill. Go through it, then turn right, and you will come to Route 10. At Route 10 turn left (south). You will pass auto dealerships, shopping centers, and antiques dealers before coming to a Y intersection. The main road goes to the right, but you should follow the left-hand road to reach the state's newest covered bridge, the **Slate Covered Bridge.** In the late 1990s the historic nineteenth-century covered bridge that stood here was burned by an arsonist. Through the hard work of townspeople a new bridge was built, replicating exactly the one that was lost. In the summer of 2001, it finally opened to traffic. After enjoying this beautiful new/old bridge you can backtrack to Route 10, following it north back toward Keene.

Covered bridges did not originate in New England—they were a common sight in the Alpine regions of Europe for the same reasons early New Englanders built them. The roof protected floorboards and support timbers from the harsh weather and snow buildup that would weaken or break the bridge under its weight. Snow falling on the sloping roof would slide off, as it does on a house roof. The biggest job for road agents was shoveling snow *onto* the bridge so that sleigh runners could slide over them in the time of year when the sleighs replaced carriages and wagons for transport. (In New England the term *road agent* means a person whose job is to maintain roads. It does not refer to a highwayman, as it does in many other places.)

On the east side of Route 10 is the **Swanzey Historical Museum**, which features some interesting exhibits. Here you will find an operational Amoskeag steam fire pumper made in Manchester and a stagecoach. The museum is wheelchair accessible and is open June through Oct, Mon through Fri 1 to 4:30 p.m. and Sat and Sun 10 a.m. to 4:30 p.m. on Route 12 in Swanzey; call (603) 352-4579 for more information.

For more than fifty years, the town of Swanzey has performed Denman Thompson's *The Old Homestead* at an open-air natural arena known as the Potash Bowl (located at Swanzey Center on Route 32). Thompson's down-home plays, filled with moral lessons and country values, delighted New York theater audiences of the Victorian era. This play, performed each July, is a real period piece. Bring lawn chairs or blankets to sit on. Admission is $5.

Close to the Potash Bowl, and to two of the covered bridges, is a newly opened bed-and-breakfast, the **Inn of the Tartan Fox.** In an early 1900s Arts and Crafts–style stone "cottage," smartly renovated to provide private baths (with heated marble floors) for each room and to make one wheelchair accessible, the inn is the essence of comfort. Antiques highlight rooms, which are light and airy, using Scottish tartans in the decoration. Full breakfasts include a main course, as well as freshly baked scones or muffins. Rates are moderate to expensive. The inn is on Route 32, about a mile past the entrance to the airport (follow airport signs from lower Main Street/Route 12) at 350 Old Homestead Highway, Swanzey; (603) 357-9308, (877) 836-4319; www.tartan fox.com.

Stonewall Farm, off Route 9 just west of Keene, is a demonstration farm with an active dairy herd. If you go between 4:30 and 6:30 p.m., you can watch the milking session, especially popular with children. Youngsters also enjoy the other animals that are kept close to the education center—a flock of chickens, a sow with a brood of piglets, goats, sheep, and a calf. The farm's two teams of Belgian draft horses can be seen grazing in the pasture or working on the farm as they plow, hay, or haul sap in the spring for the farm's sugarhouse. Stonewall Farm maple products are sold at the small gift shop in the education center. A 1.2-mile nature walk is self-guided, with the help of a sixteen-page booklet available at the trailhead. Special events include AutumnFest in late September and a traditional Crafts and Fare in mid-November. For a complete schedule of events and programs, contact Stonewall Farm, 242 Chesterfield Rd., Keene 03431; (603) 357-7278, fax (603) 357-6018; www .stonewallfarm.org.

Almost to the Connecticut River (and Vermont), a left turn from Route 9 leads up *Welcome Hill Road,* where residents have created a beautiful place in the spring, which they generously share with total strangers. As you begin to ascend the hill, you see little patches of yellow daffodils beside the road, then a banking of them, then a yard full. And just past the crest of the hill, the road widens enough for a few cars to park, overlooking a beautiful little vale simply yellow with flowers.

A trail winds down through this sea of daffodils, and there is a bench at road level for those who prefer to enjoy the picture from above. As the season progresses, the daffodils are joined by a colorful scattering of tulips; at about the same time the tree above the bench bursts into bloom.

Chesterfield Gorge shows the power of persistence. A relatively small brook has worn a deep gorge through the rocks here as it cascades from pool to pool for a distance of about 0.25 mile. It is an easy hike, just over 0.5 mile, through a forest of beech and hemlock of unusual size. A small pavilion at the head of the trail contains information on the geologic history of the gorge's formation. A shady grove provides a good place for a picnic. The gorge is on Route 9, west of Keene.

Keene's Fireproof House

Fred Sharby was afraid of fire. Two of the theaters he owned burned flat, and he had a terror of dying in a fire. So he tore down his house on the north side of Roxbury Street in Keene and built a new one, all of fireproof materials. Steel girders, stucco, plaster, fireproof floor tiles, doors of solid metal, and a furnace enclosed in cement walls have indeed lasted to this day without a fire. Fred wasn't so lucky. He chose the night of November 28, 1942, to go to the Coconut Grove in Boston and died in that fire.

Farther west, Route 63 crosses Route 9 and leads south to *Chesterfield* and the entrance to *Pisgah* (pronounced "Piz-gee") *State Park.* The road to this wilderness preserve winds along the edge of a hill through mixed hardwood forests. There are no facilities in the 13,000 acres of this park, and camping is not allowed. Twenty miles of hiking and ski trails crisscross the area, which is a favorite with anglers and hunters. Some of the trails connect with *Road's End Farm Horsemanship Camp* on Jackson Hill Road, and you're welcome to hike on these trails as well. For ten weeks in the summer the camp is filled with girls sharing the experience of riding and caring for the camp's horses. In other seasons, experienced riders can call for reservations to enjoy these same trails and the views of Pisgah Park, Mount Monadnock, and even Mount Snow in Vermont. The farm's hilltop setting is unparalleled. The location is Jackson Hill Road, Chesterfield; (603) 363-4900; www.roads endfarm.com.

More trails into Pisgah lead from Route 119 in Ashuelot, at the southern end of the park. This village, part of the town of Winchester, has the elegant and freshly restored 160-foot *Ashuelot Covered Bridge.* Built in the town lattice-truss style, with walking corridors along each side, between 1853 and 1858 (not in 1864 as the sign indicates), the bridge is one of New England's best examples of the American gothic style of architecture translated to bridge design.

Just across the bridge, on the left, is the *Winchester Historical Society Museum* in the Sheriden House. This home of the local gentry has been res-cued from oblivion and is in the slow process of restoration. The two finest rooms, with richly inlaid floors, have been restored and furnished to the late 1800s; others are in various states, which makes it fun to watch the progress. In the barn is a series of very nice horse stalls, and a Sunday "barn sale" helps raise money for the restoration. Admission is free, and the museum is open May through Oct on Sun afternoons from 2 to 4 p.m. and Wed from 9 a.m. to noon. You can see it at other times by appointment; (603) 239-4211.

If you follow it northward, Route 63 winds along the shore of Spofford Lake and into Westmoreland (with the accent on west) and on through the settlement of **Park Hill,** a cluster of noteworthy early buildings, the likes of which are rare outside of Portsmouth or Exeter. *The Meeting House* is one of the state's earliest, built in 1762 with a façade and spire considered among the finest in that period of architectural design. The Paul Revere bell was placed there in 1827. Around the church are several homes dating from as early as 1774.

Follow the signs off Route 63 in Park Hill to the Cheshire County Complex, a county-operated farm, where you can park at the top of the hill to enjoy one of the few walking trails along the banks of the Connecticut River. The *River Trail* overlooks steep banks in places, so you can actually look down onto the canopy of trees, a prime vantage for bird-watching. The trail is being extended, with signage pointing out natural features of the flora along the way.

Back at the farm, stop at the *Master Gardeners Demonstration Garden,* a joint project of the farm and the Cheshire County Extension Service, where you can get ideas for your own garden from their one-acre plot, complete with arbor, pathways, and a small greenhouse.

Cheshire County's Extension Service is a very active one, with innovative programs to promote agriculture in the region and draw the public into farm activities. Check local-events listings (on Friday the *Keene Sentinel* has a calendar for the coming week) for *Open Farm Days* during the summer, when a local farm is featured, and activities are planned for both adults and children. A popular attraction is the appearance of a van from the Granite State Dairy Promotion Board, dispensing unlimited quantities of free ice cream. The highlight of the agricultural year is the *Cheshire Fair* in early August. Although it has a midway with rides, it is still largely an agricultural event, with 4-H members showing their sheep and calves at the southern end of the fairgrounds and the lunch counter in the 4-H building serving up old-fashioned homemade pies.

To learn more about the wide variety of farm-related products in the area, you can get a copy of the free booklet "Monadnock Region Product Directory." Listing dozens of farms where you can buy everything from llama wool to Christmas trees or sign up for classes in soapmaking, the book is available from Stonewall Farm, 242 Chesterfield Rd., Keene 03431; (603) 357-7278; and on their Web site: www.stonewallfarm.org.

Route 63 winds past some of New Hampshire's finest and most fertile farmland, with meadows full of grazing cattle and views across the Connecticut River valley into Vermont. From mid-February until mid-April and from mid-September until the end of November, you can stop for breakfast, lunch, or a snack at *Stuart and John's Sugar House.* It's best in late February and into

March when the sap is running and the back room is filled with steam from the evaporators. The corn fritters and homemade doughnuts are delicious, and syrup comes in a full-size milk pitcher that the waitress plunks on the table when she brings the menu. All you need to decide is what to pour it over. If it's not breakfast or lunch time when you are passing by, try a maple sundae, frappé, or, in the fall, maple apple pie. This place isn't fancy; you sit on folding chairs at church supper–style tables. It's family style, family run, and a favorite low-cost Sunday outing for local families. Open weekends 7 a.m. to 3 p.m. on Route 63 at Route 12 in Westmoreland; (603) 399-4486; www.stuartandjohns sugarhouse.com.

Northern Hills

Walpole looks down onto Route 12, and this picture-perfect village is a good place to stroll around and admire the beautifully preserved and maintained eighteenth- and nineteenth-century homes that encircle the green. On Sunday evenings during July and August, band concerts fill this grassy common with music and people.

The prosperity that built the many homes and public buildings in Walpole resulted from the building of a canal around the Great Falls of the Connecticut River in 1790. The canal allowed river traffic (water was the main means of moving goods in those days) to proceed past here to the north country. The heirlooms of many of these early families have found their way to the **Old Academy Museum.** Silk dresses with the kind of needlework that only prosperous women had the time to pursue have been preserved here along with furniture, tools, utensils and kitchenware, and a completely restored schoolroom from the original academy. Shaker furniture, and the original piano mentioned in *Little Women,* a gift to the Alcott sisters when they were living in Walpole, are just a few of the treasures that have been presented to the museum. Open from 2 to 4 p.m. Wed and Sat, June through Sept. On Main St. in Walpole; call (603) 756-3449 for more information or visit www .walpolehistory.org/.

The chocolates made at **Burdick's Chocolates** by Swiss-trained Larry Burdick are tops. Be sure to try one of their dark, white, or milk chocolate mice. The cafe at the shop serves hot chocolate, tea, espresso, and tempting pastry. Open Tues through Sat 7 a.m. to 9 p.m. and Sun and Mon 7 a.m. to 6 p.m. on Main St., Walpole; (603) 756-3701 or (800) 229-2419 (to order chocolates by mail).

Burdick's also has a restaurant where the freshest, preferably locally produced, ingredients are used to prepare such dishes as grilled beef tenderloin

ALSO WORTH SEEING IN THE MONADNOCK REGION

Colony Mill Marketplace,
West St., Keene;
(603) 357-1240.
Not the usual mall with chain stores, this
carefully renovated historic mill building
is filled with locally owned specialty
shops and eateries.

with bordelaise sauce or seared sea scallops with beluga lentils. Lunch is served Mon through Sat 11:30 a.m. to 2:30 p.m., dinner Tues through Sat 5:30 to 9 p.m., and brunch on Sun 10 a.m. to 3 p.m. Burdick's is located at 47 Main St., Walpole; (603) 756-9058 or (800) 229-2419; www.burdickchocolate.com.

Few dairy farms in New Hampshire produce cheese, but a happy exception is *Boggy Meadow Farm* in Walpole, north of the intersection of Route 63 and Route 12. They sell Swiss and smoked Swiss cheeses under their label Fanny Mason Cheese in a small retail shop right at the farm where they are made on River Road. The shop is open daily 8 a.m. to 5 p.m. You'll find the farm from Route 12 by its discreet farmstead cheese sign; (603) 756-3300, (877) 541-3953; www.boggymeadowfarm.com.

Overlooking the wide Connecticut River valley not far from Boggy Meadow, *Alyson's Orchard* is easy to spot alongside Route 12 because of the beautifully crafted metal apple tree that sprouts green leaves and red apples even in midwinter. This is just a tantalizing hint of the surprises that Alyson's has in store. Bronze cranes and herons fool the eye as they stand in the pond. The orchard grows more varieties of apples than the common Macs and Cortlands—many of the forty-odd varieties are nearly-lost heritage strains—and there are more than a dozen types each of pears and peaches. The hilltop grounds are a popular wedding venue, with sweeping views of the Connecticut River. Alyson's is at 57 Alyson's Lane in Walpole; (800) 856-0549 or (603) 756-9800; www.alysonsorchard.com.

If you have a spare day and a sense of adventure, you could take any road out of Walpole and follow it until it ends in the dooryard of a farmhouse or bumps into Route 12A. The hillsides are covered with well-kept farms and are separated by lovely little hollows. The views over the valley are beautiful when you reach the hillcrests, most of which have been cleared for pastureland.

North of Walpole, Route 123 heads into more hills, following the Cold River (all rivers here are cold; one wonders who decided that this one should be so honestly named). From the village of Drewsville, a road heads north toward Langdon, and in about a mile it passes New Hampshire's shortest covered bridge, only 36 feet long.

More Places to Stay in the Monadnock Region

ANTRIM

Maplehurst Inn
Main St.
(603) 588-8000
www.nh-inn.com
A comfortable country inn. Inexpensive.

CHESTERFIELD

Chesterfield Inn
Route 9
(603) 256-3211 or
(800) 365-5515
www.chesterfieldinn.com
Classy, pricey rooms in a fine, old home overlooking the Connecticut River valley.

KEENE

The Carriage Barn Bed and Breakfast
358 Main St.
(603) 357-3812
www.carriagebarn.com
A block from downtown shops, with three museums and an arts center within a five-minute walk, its location matches the quality of its rooms. Moderate.

Goose Pond Guest House
144 East Surry Rd.
(603) 357-4787
A 1790s home close to the Goose Pond nature reserve and to the golf course at Brentwood, with moderate rates and a continental breakfast.

RINDGE

Cathedral House Bed and Breakfast
63 Cathedral Entrance
(603) 899-6790
Full breakfast; moderate.

WEST SWANZEY

Bridges Inn at Whitcomb House
27 Main St.
(603) 357-6624
www.bridgesinn.com
An attractive B&B within sight of the historic Slate Covered Bridge, with moderate rates.

TO LEARN MORE ABOUT THE MONADNOCK REGION

Greater Peterborough Chamber of Commerce,
Route 101 (P.O. Box 401),
Peterborough 03458;
(603) 924-7234;
www.roninhouse.com/gpcoc.

More Places to Eat in the Monadnock Region

HANCOCK
Fiddleheads Café
Main St.
(603) 525-4432
Opposite the inn, the friendly café serves excellent custom-built sandwiches.

HILLSBOROUGH
High Tide
Route 9
(603) 464-4202
Well-prepared fast-fried seafood,burgers, hot dogs, ice cream. Inexpensive.

KEENE
Ocean Harvest
433 Winchester St.
(603) 357-3553
Skip the chain-brand seafood restaurants to have the area's tastiest (and never greasy) fried clams and shrimp, broiled scallops, and fish sandwiches. Open Tues through Sat, usually from 11 a.m. to 8 p.m. (sometimes later), and until 7 p.m. on Sun.

Papagallos
Route 12 South
(603) 352-9400
Very popular with locals, family dining with an emphasis on Italian but a good mix of other options and interesting wood-fired pizzas. Inexpensive.

PETERBOROUGH
Peterborough Diner
10 Depot St.
(603) 924-6202
It's the real thing, been there half a century. Inexpensive.

RINDGE
Lilly's on the Pond
Route 202
(603) 899-3322
Innovative entrees. Inexpensive.

WALPOLE
Walpole Inn
297 Main St.
(603) 756-3320
www.walpoleinn.com
This beautifully restored 1762 inn has an up-to-the-minute dining room, with a frequently changing menu offering such dishes as smoked pork ribs with sweet potato fries. Moderate.

THE DARTMOUTH-SUNAPEE REGION

The **Connecticut River** flows through a broad, flat valley as it forms the border between New Hampshire and neighboring Vermont. Along its shores and up the hillsides that overlook it are sprawling farmlands: fields of corn, herds of cattle, truck farms, and family farms. Their massive barns and tall, round silos punctuate the landscape. These venerable homes were built by some of the earliest settlers in the valley.

The farms were not always so serene. The river was the major artery of travel for Indians as well as settlers, and the French and Indian Wars were fought along its banks. It was to educate Indians that Eleazer Wheelock founded a school that is now Dartmouth College. Its cultural influence and that of Colby-Sawyer College in nearby New London on the entire upper valley are significant, especially in the performing and fine arts.

To the east of the Connecticut River valley rise the gentle slopes of Mounts Sunapee, Kearsarge, and Cardigan—each about 3,000 feet in altitude—and other smaller mountains. The Appalachian Trail crosses the river on its way south, and nearly every mountain in the region, however small, has a trail to its summit.

THE DARTMOUTH-SUNAPEE REGION

Orford 25A

Baker R.
25

Plymouth

10

UPPER
VALLEY

BAKER RIVER
AND
NEWFOUND LAKE

3A

Newfound
Lake

Hanover
Lebanon

4

Bristol

VT.
N.H.

Danbury

12A

Connecticut R.

Franklin

New
London

Claremont

89

11   11

Newport   Lake
Sunapee

LOWER
VALLEY

12A

SUNAPEE

Warner

Charlestown

10

N

Walpole

0   10 mi
0   10 km

Lakes dot the landscape. This region is a quiet part of the state, and even the interstate that bisects it hasn't changed that. In fact, from the point where I-89 leaves Concord until it arrives in Lebanon, at the Vermont border, there is almost no commercial activity visible along its sides, only miles of forest and farmland backed by mountain vistas.

The Lower Valley

The *Fort at No. 4* was once the northwestern-most English-speaking village in the New World. This museum is an authentic reconstruction of the settlement founded there in 1740. It is New England's only living-history museum of the period of the French and Indian Wars. Within its log stockade are furnished province houses and shops where costumed interpreters carry on the daily work of an isolated colonial village. Dinner is prepared in a huge open fireplace, candles are hand dipped, and wool and flax spun and woven. From the lookout tower, sentries kept watch over the river and valley for signs of attack by the Indians or the French. The skirmishes that took place here in those early years are re-created in full costume each year, and a cloud of smoke from musket fire hangs over the river as it did two and a half centuries ago when, in 1747, the fort was besieged by a force of 400 but withstood the attack. This success resulted in the withdrawal of French forces to Canada and the beginning of English supremacy in northern New England. Of particular interest here is a working blacksmith shop, where a master smith creates the tools and utensils necessary for daily life and work on the frontier. A museum shop carries items of the period at extraordinarily reasonable prices.

theriver'sours 'tilitfloods

New Hampshire's northern border wasn't established until 1842, in the Webster–Ashburton Treaty, which finally set the international boundary with Canada. But the Vermont–New Hampshire line wasn't clear until a 1934 Supreme Court decision set it at the low-water mark on the Connecticut River.

Prior to making a special trip to Fort No. 4 call for the current opening information and hours. Admission is $8 for adults and $5 for children ages six to twelve. The Fort at No. 4 is at 267 Springfield Rd. (Route 11), Charlestown 03603; (603) 826-5700; www.fortat4.com.

Charlestown's *Main Street National Historic District* is lined with distinguished homes, many dating from the early 1800s. It is almost a mile

---

If This Is Africa, Where Are the Lions?

Continental plates are great travelers, but they don't tend to follow the admonition of today's ecotravelers to tread softly and leave no tracks. When these giant pieces of the earth's crust move, they leave lots of tracks; in fact, they leave pieces of themselves hanging about after they've left, which is what the African plate did after it bumped into Vermont. It left New Hampshire behind.

This accounts for the obvious differences in landscape and the wholly different geologies of the two states. The Connecticut River covers the seam, except in one place, where you can actually see where Africa and North America meet. If you go to North Walpole, where the bridge crosses over a deep gorge and into Bellows Falls, Vermont, you can see the two different rocks join in the riverbank below you.

---

long, and fifty-two of its sixty-three buildings are historically important; ten of them date from the 1700s. The Unitarian Church and two of the houses were designed by Stephen Hassam, great-grandfather of the impressionist painter Childe Hassam, who often painted the Isles of Shoals. St. Catherine's Church has four signed Tiffany stained-glass windows. Stop at the office of the town clerk for an inexpensive booklet describing the history of each building.

Known as one of the nation's premier flight centers, ***Morningside Flight Park*** in Charlestown teaches hang gliding and paragliding to all people at all levels of expertise or interest, from the cautiously curious to those with many hours of air time in their logs. For a thrilling sightseeing ride and a new perspective on the Connecticut River valley, you can choose a Tandem Aerotow, a two-person hang glider. With an instructor at the "controls," you can ride as the glider is towed by an ultralight to a 2,500-foot altitude. On release, you'll have a ten- to twenty-minute scenic glide over the river and valley. Morningside Flight Park is on Route 12 in North Charlestown; (603) 542-4416; www .flymorningside.com.

Claremont's early settlers quickly saw the potential of the waterfalls in the Sugar River as it flows from Lake Sunapee to the Connecticut River. The first dam was built in 1767 for a gristmill and sawmill, and other plants soon followed, their machinery powered by the force from the 300-foot drop in the river as it passes through town. Mill buildings still dominate the center of Claremont, and you can learn how they once operated by following a walking tour of ***Claremont Village Industrial District.*** A free brochure available from the chamber of commerce on Tremont Square describes the original uses and evolution of various buildings, including millworkers' housing, owners' residences, shops, the foundry, a weave shed, and other structures, each of which is marked on an accompanying map.

The manufacturing that created the massive mills along the Sugar River also created the wealth to build Claremont's imposing new city hall in 1897, with its tall, prominent clock tower. Its third floor boasted an opera house with one of the largest stages north of Boston. Although the ***Claremont Opera House and Atrium*** now has a separate wheelchair-accessible entry, those who enter through the old building can enjoy the carved archway and oak paneling of the lower lobbies and public areas. The large opera house has a curved balcony and cast-iron-based seats; open one to see its unique reclining back. This outstanding example of public architecture of the past hundred years still hosts varied performances on a regular basis. It is open for performances and from 9 a.m. to 5 p.m. on weekdays. Call (603) 542-4433 for a schedule of events or visit www.claremontoperahouse.com.

About 3 miles west on Route 103 is the settlement of ***West Claremont*** and two historic churches. Union Church, a large, white clapboard building with curved windows, is the oldest Episcopal church building in New Hampshire. It is a surprise to see the oldest one this far inland—and this far from any present-day settlement. Its only neighbor, directly across the street, is St. Mary's Church, the first Roman Catholic church in the state, built between 1823 and 1825 and an outpost mission of St. Bernard's in Keene. The priest who established St. Mary's parish was the son of the Episcopal rector of Union Church across the street. The son had converted to Catholicism. The two men conducted a school for the children of West Claremont millworkers on the second floor of St. Mary's. Today, these vanguard churches stand alone, surrounded only by West Part Burying Ground, the settlement they once served long gone.

The Knights of Columbus have restored the little brick St. Mary's Church, and it is used for small weddings. During the summer it is open on Sunday afternoons and is staffed by volunteers from the Knights. Be sure to go to

EVENTS IN THE DARTMOUTH-SUNAPEE REGION

Dartmouth Winter Carnival,
mid-Feb, Hanover

League of New Hampshire Craftsmen's Fair,
early Aug, Sunapee
(603) 224-3375

Farm Days,
late Aug, Muster Field
Farm Museum, North Sutton
(603) 927-4276

Fall Foliage Festival,
early Oct, Warner

the third floor to see the bright and sunny classroom where the founder, Father Barber, had a school for boys. The white clapboarded Episcopal church across the street is not open at this time but does hold Sunday morning services.

To get there from downtown Claremont, follow Route 12/103 west. About 3 miles out of town look for a historic marker on the left. Take the left over the river and another left turn just after the bridge (this is where the original mills stood). Bear right at the next fork. The churches stand on either side of the road, just ahead. You can also reach the churches from Route 12A, south of the Route 103 intersection. This intersection is also marked with a historic marker.

The Connecticut River flows peacefully between its wooded shores, perfect for traveling by canoe. You can rent a canoe at **North Star Canoe Livery** in Cornish for half-day, full-day, or overnight trips on the Connecticut. The livery provides a shuttle that carries canoes and passengers upstream to put-ins either 4 or 12 miles distant. The 12-mile trip takes four to four and one-half hours; rates are $30 per person. Another option is the covered bridge tour, which is only a 4-mile paddle and costs $18. This can be done as a paddling or a raft trip. Special rates apply for kids. An overnight trip can be arranged so that you can camp on an island in the middle of the river. (You're still in New Hampshire, since New Hampshire owns the normal low-water mark on the Vermont side. When the river floods, Vermont owns the excess.) North Star Canoe Livery is at Balloch's Crossing, Route 12A, Cornish; (603) 542-6929; www.kayak-canoe.com.

The bridge across the Connecticut at Cornish is the longest **covered bridge** in the United States. (The longest in New Hampshire is at Bath; this one doesn't count since its other end is in Vermont.) Built in 1886, it traverses the river in two spans and has an unusual timber lattice-truss construction.

At the turn of the twentieth century, Cornish was the home of a thriving colony of artists, writers, poets, and patrons who built or purchased summer homes around the studio of Augustus Saint-Gaudens. Italian terraced gardens surrounded old farmhouses, and the summer season's social life was one of wealthy bohemia.

The artists are gone, but the genius of the sculptor who attracted them to this retreat lives on in his beautifully situated home. His sculptures are displayed in the studios and galleries and throughout the grounds of the **Saint-Gaudens National Historic Site.** The gardens and grounds, lined with tall pine and hemlock hedges and delicate birch trees, are worth a visit in their own right. The original Stanford White bluestone base for the statue of Admiral David Farragut has recently been moved here from New York City, where it was being damaged by pollution. The house, just as Mrs. Saint-Gaudens left it, is filled with artworks, each piece with some personal significance. A spirited house tour brings the family to life and lifts this site above the usual "home of a famous person" category. Sunday afternoon (2 p.m.) concerts in the summer bring musicians of all styles, along with music lovers carrying picnic baskets to the estate's shaded lawns. The house is open 9 a.m. to 4:30 p.m. daily from Memorial Day through late Oct; the grounds remain open until dusk. Admission is $5; free for children under sixteen. Write to Saint-Gaudens National Historic Site, 139 Saint Gaudens Rd., Cornish 03745; call (603) 675-2175 or visit www.nps.gov/saga.

Beginning with the settlement of Augustus Saint-Gaudens, the other artists, architects, and writers also established summer or even year-round residences. One of these was **Maxfield Parrish,** an illustrator and painter whose work is regaining the popularity it had a century ago. While Parrish's home was destroyed by fire, and his studio is now a private residence, a strong sense of his presence lingers here.

Possibly the most stunning of his work here is in the **Plainfield Town Hall.** In 1916 Parrish and his friends decided to stage a play, *The Woodland Princess,* written by Louise Saunders, the author of *The Knave of Hearts,* which Parrish had illustrated for her. The stage set was designed by Parrish and quite likely was painted by him.

The backdrop curtains show a mountain (said by locals to be Mount Ascutney) rising behind a lake. Along the shore are granite boulders; the side curtains are painted with pine, birch, and maple trees and frame a woodland glen. Above, a gossamer header curtain of colored leaves completes the illusion of autumn. In 1992-1994 the town came together to raise funds to have the sets professionally cleaned and the damages of time repaired. An ingenious lighting system, dating from 1916, allows the set to change from full noon to

Who Actually Painted It?

While most local people believe Parrish did actually paint the set at Plainfield Town Hall, at least one local art collector doubts it. Parrish did not have students or assistants in his Plainfield studio, and it would seem unlikely that local amateurs could have executed such a major work, using the placement, colors, and shading that are so definitively Parrish's. One letter written contemporaneously refers to his creation of the work, but his own records fail to mention it at all. We are satisfied that it is his painting, as well as his design (about which there is no question), but without definitive historical proof, it remains a mystery.

sunset to evening and back through a beautiful dawn. The effect of the slowly changing light on the colors is astounding.

Parrish Blue, a video examining Parrish's life, is shown in the small auditorium. Several original Parrish works are for sale along one wall, and reproductions and publications, including Parrish postcards, are on the other wall. The profits go to maintain the stage set.

The town hall is open Sun afternoons 1 to 5 p.m. from July through Labor Day weekend, or by reservation. Admission is $1. To schedule an appointment, contact Plainfield Public Library at (603) 675-6866 or plfdlib@cyberportal .net. They hold the annual Maxfield Parrish Vintage Print and Collectibles Sale at the town hall on the first weekend of October. Those particularly interested in the artist can inquire at the Town Hall, when it's open, or at the public library across the street for directions to his grave in a nearby cemetery.

Route 11/103 heads east from Claremont to Newport, but a more scenic route follows Sugar River Drive, which you can reach by following Broad Street to Chestnut Street. On the way, **Thyme & Ewe Farm** is worth a stop to meet the animals and learn about this unique farm that has become a home of refuge for abandoned, abused, and neglected farm animals. Tour the organic gardens and shop for herbal and other crafts in the farm store, where you'll also find a splendid array of jams, jellies, pickles, sauces, mustards, and other preserves made on the farm. On the Story Book Trail, kids can meet favorite characters in their homes in the forest. Thyme & Ewe Farm, 688 Chestnut St., Claremont; call (603) 542-1746 or visit www.thymeandewefarm.com.

A busy rail line once connected these two towns, crossing the Sugar River twice on its way. The route is now a walking trail, level and smooth, covering 9.7 miles along the river. En route, it passes through two rare **covered railroad bridges**, the Chandler Station and Wrights. The former is clearly visible, and both are accessible from Sugar River Drive, which parallels the south bank of the river. You can reach the path from Broad Street beyond the Chestnut Street intersection if you want to walk or bike the whole distance, or you can pick up the path at any of several points where it crosses Sugar River Drive.

A cool place to while away a hot summer afternoon is **Pollard's Mills Falls.** Actually a long series of small falls on the South Branch of the Sugar River, the cascades work their way through several hundred feet of a granite chasm lined with boulders. A path through the trees at the top of the embankment brings you to the site of the old mills, their rough stone foundations very evident along the shore of the stream. Be sure to find the large square hole cut into the bedrock to anchor the machinery of the mill. To get to the falls, follow Route 11 west of Newport about 0.5 mile and take a left onto Unity Road. Follow this for about a mile and then take a left onto Pollard's Mills Road.

About 0.4 mile farther, turn right at a Y in the road. Just around that corner is a parking area overlooking the falls. The path is to the left.

We like to find worthy and significant old buildings that have been preserved for other uses when they were no longer needed, so we were happy when **The Old Courthouse Restaurant** opened in Newport's former Superior Court building. The 1826 brick building with its white tower sits behind the **Newport Opera House** (see below), part of a small cityscape that has remained relatively unchanged for the past century. It is listed on the National Register of Historic Places. The restaurant's menu changes weekly, with dishes such as lamb chops stuffed with olives, grilled salmon served over spiced lentils, or seared jumbo scallops paired with braised veal and served with saffron orzo and roasted vegetables. All entrees are reasonably priced; lunch and dinner are served Wed through Sat. The Old Courthouse is at 30 Main St.; (603) 863-8360; www.eatatthecourthouse.com.

The Newport Opera House, reopened in 1896 after a fire, was once one of the largest stages north of Boston and hosted many of the twentieth century's major performers before it dipped into a period of neglect. Restored in the 1970s, it again hosts traveling and local performances; (603) 863-2412; www.newportoperahouse.com.

Sunapee

We have no intention of entering the historical dispute over the original meaning of *sunapee* in the Indian languages. It's a lovely region, in any language, with the mountain and lakes of the same name and the succession of smaller lakes between Mount Sunapee and **Mount Kearsarge.**

To the south lies Warner, with its **Mt. Kearsarge Indian Museum.** The museum's spirit is probably best summed up in the words of Chief Seattle in the late 1800s: "Every part of the earth is sacred to my people . . . every shining pine needle, every sandy shore, every light mist in the dark forest . . . we are part of the earth and it is part of us." The purpose of the museum is not so much to show the incomparable artifacts as to interpret the lifestyle through art and culture and to renew in all of us the positive relationship the Indians experienced between the earth and its people. It succeeds. The exhibits are the lifetime collection of Charles (Bud) and Nancy Thompson, who didn't want to have "a mausoleum of pickled artifacts" but rather a museum with a voice.

The voice is that of Indians. Except for the quotations, there are no written labels or signs in this beautifully displayed collection. Instead, a docent conducts hourly tours, explaining the displays and focusing on those things that catch the visitors' interest. A museum shop sells authentic Indian handwork

Such a Boar

Our high school chum Pat Hanson now lives in Grantham, just north of Newport and quite close to the massive confines of Corbin Park. This huge, private game preserve is surrounded by a high fence, but exotic animals do escape from time to time, and wild boar are not an uncommon quarry for hunters in the adjoining woods. But none of us had ever seen one and had little idea of their size until we were looking at a collection of mounted animals one day in a museum and saw an enormous and unfriendly looking wild boar. "Could you imagine getting one of those out of the woods?" I asked. "Not nearly so hard as getting me down out of the tree!" Pat rejoined.

such as rugs, beadwork, and pottery, as well as books about various Indian tribes. Outdoors, a self-guided walk leads through two acres of native plants and trees used for medicine and food. Open May through Oct, Mon through Sat 10 a.m. to 5 p.m. and Sun noon to 5 p.m.; weekends, Nov to Apr by appointment for groups of three or more. Admission is $8.50 for adults, $7.50 for ages thirteen to eighteen and seniors, and $4.50 for children ages six to twelve; family of two adults and child(ren) under 13 $26.00. Write Mt. Kearsarge Indian Museum, Kearsarge Mountain Rd., P.O. Box 142, Warner 03278; (603) 456-2600; www.indianmuseum.org.

Warner is a town with an air of prosperity, and it has attracted a number of artists and writers. To sample the works of both, stop in at *MainStreet BookEnds,* a combination of art gallery and bookstore, open daily 9 a.m. to 6 p.m. Prominent in the front of the store is an entire cabinet of books by local authors, and the large art gallery in the back not only shows works of Warner artists in all media (including fine woodworking and pottery) but is also the venue of programs every Friday evening. Most are free, many are by authors, and the subjects include everything from the writing life, nature, and the arts to musical performances. The shop/gallery is at 16 East Main St.; (603) 456-2700; www.mainstreetbookends.com.

To see the works of three talented Warner artists, one of whom is also a naturalist and writer, stop at *Carroll Studio,* east of the bookshop in Lower Village. Laurette Carroll paints in the studio, where her work is shown along with that of her son Sean and the nature prints of her husband, the much-acclaimed naturalist/artist David Carroll. His latest book, *Swampwalker's Journal,* is a beautifully illustrated guide to the life and seasons of New England wetlands. Many of the prints from this book and his previous work on turtles are sold in the shop, as are these same images imprinted on T-shirts—an above-average souvenir of New Hampshire. The studio is open all year, Sat and Sun 10 a.m. to 3 p.m., at 237 East Main St. (Route 103), Warner Lower Village; (603) 456-3947; www.carrollstudiogallery.com.

One of the more unusual buildings in Warner is *Clark's Cider Mill,* on Pumpkin Hill Road. This wooden building appears from the road to be a barn, but what you see is actually the upper part of a four-story (or maybe five, depending on what you count) mill, built into the steep banks of a ravine. The mill was built in 1886 and used as a threshing, shingle, and cider mill, as well as an ice house. Its current owners plan to restore it and are using it as an antiques shop (where we found prices amazingly low).

The village of *South Sutton* looks as though it had been dropped there overnight from a previous century. Around its green is an ensemble of notable early buildings crowned by an 1839 meetinghouse with double doors and a curved gallery (you can get a good look inside through the side windows). Behind it is a schoolhouse (note the collection of vintage lunch boxes), and below are several homes, one built in 1756. The *Old Store Museum* was the village store from the early 1800s, and it houses typical store fixtures and goods, as well as collections of farm and household implements. The buildings are open Sundays in the summer, but it is wise to call ahead; you can also arrange an appointment to see them at other times; (603) 927-4117.

In an arrangement somewhat more logical than you often find with New England village names, North Sutton lies north of South Sutton, also along Route 114. Its tidy crossroads is marked by the blue (or frozen) waters of *Kezar Lake* and by the large, white-clapboard *Follansbee Inn.* This is an old-fashioned, warmhearted inn with its own beachfront on the lake and canoes, rowboats, bikes, and snowshoes for guests. Its spacious, bright rooms

If You Find Us in Jail . . .

We travel our home state at all times of year and at all times of day and evening, much of it when the many tiny historical society homes and museums are not open. Sometimes we call for an appointment, but more often we just happen upon a place while we're headed somewhere else. To get an idea of what's inside—and whether we should come back to see more—we walk around and look for windows we can peek through. Sometimes, as in the case of historic meetinghouses, we can see the entire inside, even note the woodworking details or graceful curve of the pulpit. When windows are too high, we sometimes boost one another up to peer inside.

But we do worry that one of these historic buildings will some day be broken into, and it will be our footprints the sheriff will find outside.

have hand-pieced coverlets, and each morning begins with a full breakfast that guests choose for themselves in the kitchen. This moderately priced inn is open year-round and adjoins the ski and snowshoe trails of Wadleigh State Park. Follansbee Inn is in North Sutton; (603) 927-4221 or (800) 626-4221; www.follansbeeinn.com.

Kezar Lake has an island perfect for picnics, and if you are not staying at the inn you can launch your own canoe or kayak from the town beach at the crossroads. Last time we were there, we met a charming gentleman, Dr. Robert Breed from Lynn, Massachusetts, who told us that between him and his father, they had come to Follansbee Inn for 117 summers. The innkeepers have changed over the years, but the hospitality has not, he assured us. He also told us about a rare Native American site across the lake.

Very few tangible sights remain in New Hampshire to show its aboriginal heritage. The Penacook tribe summered in the area and gathered at the lakeshore to roast the abundant mussels they found there, in a spot where they had a view of Mount Kearsarge, which they revered. The *Penacooks' stone-lined cooking pit* is still there. Follow signs to Wadleigh State Park and continue on the road around the lake for 0.5 mile. As the pavement ends, you will see a pull-off and a stone wall. Toward the far end of the stone wall is the pit.

Wadleigh State Park, on Route 114 (603-927-4724 or www.nhstateparks .org) receives few visitors—which is a shame, since its lakefront beach is beautiful and shaded in tall red and white pines interspersed with birch and hemlock. Abundant picnic tables and firepits are well spaced in a shaded grove, and there are changing facilities and a lifeguard. Admission, as to all day-use parks, is $4; children ages six to eleven $2, ages six and New Hampshire residents over sixty-five are admitted free. From the park or from any point along the lake you can walk around the shore, a 3-mile flat walk mostly along unpaved roads with nice views. The park is open weekends mid-May to mid-June, then daily until Labor Day.

If you turn left from the park entrance and then right onto Wadleigh Hill Road, you will climb on a well-surfaced but unpaved road. At just over 1.5 miles is an excellent cellar hole on the right; then you will pass a mill overhanging a ravine. This is one of eighteen that once lined the roaring little brook that drops (along with the road) into *Sutton Mills.* Nearly all these were destroyed in the flood of 1936, but you can see dams and stone foundations along the brook in the village below.

The road past Follansbee Inn leads, after a right turn, into the center of *Muster Field Farm Museum.* This unique collection of historic buildings surrounds the *Matthew Harvey Homestead,* an excellent example of rural architecture of the late 1700s. Basically Georgian, it was updated with a few

Federal-style touches about 200 years ago. In beautiful condition, most of its hand-shaved clapboards are original, and its windows are glazed in original hand-poured glass. The ballroom on the second floor indicates its use as a center for community activities, such as celebrations following musters of the Thirtieth New Hampshire Regiment, which took place in the adjoining fields.

But the house is only the beginning of the museum. The last owner of the 250-acre property, Robert Stannard Bristol, began collecting historic farm buildings and other structures that were threatened with destruction and placing them in the fields along the ridge on which the house stands. He left the property as a museum and working farm to preserve New Hampshire's agricultural heritage. These buildings, which surround cultivated fields of flowers and vegetables that will make any gardener green with envy, include barns, a schoolhouse, corn cribs, two blacksmith shops, the springhouse from Bradford Springs (see the Monadnock Region chapter), and an icehouse, which in midsummer still has firmly frozen blocks of ice cut from Kezar Lake in January.

You can tour these buildings and see the collections of old farm equipment free any day year-round, or go on Sunday in July, August, and September, when the homestead is open from 1 to 4 p.m. and also free. Demonstrations of early crafts and rural skills accompany these summer Sundays. For even more demonstrations and activities, come for one of the several special events, which include late-August Farm Days, an entire weekend that features an encampment and muster, as well as crafts, an engine show, and a chance to try your own hand at several old-time skills. Admission to these special events is $5 for adults and less for seniors and children. For a full schedule of events, visit the farm or call (603) 927-4276 or 526-6643, or visit www.musterfieldfarm .com. The farm stand sells high-quality fresh vegetables, herbs, flowers, and preserves daily from noon to 6 p.m., mid-June through Oct.

Although it's a bastion of *gemutlichkeit* at any time of year, **Alphorn Bistro** at the **Inn at Danbury** really shines during the Christmas season, when the dining room and other parts of the inn are decked with traditional German decorations—European glass ornaments, wooden nutcrackers, and gingerbread houses baked and decorated in their kitchen each year. A kettle of hot *gluhwein* (or warm spiced cider for children) and Christmas cookies on the 1919 stove in the lobby welcome guests. On a Sunday in December the Grafs have a cookie workshop, where guests can join in baking German favorites—lekerli, springerle, drei augen, and linzer cookies from chef Robert's recipes—and each guest takes home a box of cookies. The dinner menu is filled with hearty Alpine dishes: Wiener schnitzel, tangy sauerbraten, beef goulash, chicken paprika, and a wide variety of juicy wursts served with braised red cabbage, spaetzle, and sauerkraut. Most entrees are priced between $15 and $20. The inn is a favorite of skiers at nearby **Ragged Mountain,** with rooms priced at $100 to $160 for two, including a full country breakfast. The Inn at Danbury is at 67 Route 104; (603) 768-3318 or (866) 326-2879; www .innatdanbury.com.

In the Victorian-era railroad station at the village of Potter Place, the **Andover Historical Society Museum** has interesting collections, including an original Western Union Telegraph office. The building itself is intact, a fine example of the ornamented stations that once lined the tracks throughout New England. One of the highlights of the museum is a dugout canoe that is in very good condition; outside on the tracks are a caboose and a plow car used to clear the tracks during snowstorms. Open Sat 10 a.m. to 3 p.m. and Sun 1 to 3 p.m. Memorial through Labor Days; free. There is no phone, but you can visit the museum's Web site, www.andoverhistory.org.

Nearby in Andover is the workshop of young woodworking artist Trip Stiles, who crafts fine, individually made furniture from top-grade hardwoods. His pieces include harvest tables, writing tables, a pencil-post four-poster bed, an early dressing cabinet, blanket chests, and Shaker reproductions. Although he works mostly in cherry, he will make pieces in other woods as requested. All joinery is done with hand-made mortise-and-tenon and dovetail joints, and pieces are finished with four coats of hand-rubbed oil. These are museum pieces of the future, and you can visit the shop to see works in process. **Ragged Mountain Woodworks** is at 7 Pleasant St., Andover; (603) 735-6100, fax (603) 735-6594. Open by chance or appointment.

La Meridiana, on Route 11 in **Wilmot Flat,** is a family-owned restaurant dedicated to the foods of the chef's home in northern Italy. Specialties include a salad of tender calamari, osso buco, gnocchi in a sauce so good that you'll be tempted to mop up the excess with the crusty Italian bread, and tender white veal with lemon served with lightly poached *finocchi.* The choice of desserts is equally varied and tempting: chocolate truffles, tiramisu, raspberry-chocolate cheesecake, *zuppa inglese,* cannoli, or a traditional chocolate sponge cake with ricotta filling. Prices on all courses are inexpensive to moderate, with two-thirds of the entrees under $10. The wine list is quite reasonably priced as well. An especially endearing feature is that they suggest sharing a pasta course, so those without a gargantuan appetite can split a dish of risotto, gnocchi, or agnolotti as a first course and still have room for the entree to follow. They are open for lunch Mon through Fri and for dinner nightly. La Meridiana is on Route 11 and Old Winslow Road in Wilmot Flat; (603) 526-2033.

If you follow Kearsarge Valley Road south from Route 11, turning left onto Kearsarge Mountain Road, you will climb (and climb and climb) until you reach **Winslow State Park** (603-526-6168 or www.nhstateparks.org). Few picnic areas offer better views—180 degrees of valley, lakes, and mountains. Barlow Trail leads into a 1.7-mile loop, and Winslow Trail is 1.1 miles along the upper slopes of Mount Kearsarge. There is a $3 day-use fee for the park; children under eleven and New Hampshire residents over sixty-five are admitted free. Neighboring Elkins borders the shore of Pleasant Lake, where there is a boat put-in. If you stop to enjoy the lake and browse in the antiques shop in the nearby garage in the late afternoon, you may hear the meetinghouse chimes that play at 6 p.m. each day.

New London is the home of **Colby-Sawyer College,** whose stately campus dominates the southern end of the town's main street. Throughout the school year, theater and musical performances keep the local arts scene lively, and then a summer theater takes over the job with Broadway musicals. The town is a good center for hiking and skiing; hikers and walkers can choose from among eight or nine trails leading to or past such varied attractions as a cave, a quarry, cascades, a beaver pond, abandoned farms, and lovely mountain views.

New London Barn Playhouse really is in a barn, converted into a theater that has been performing Broadway musicals since 1934. The barn itself is moving toward its second century, built of sturdy hand-hewn timber frame and sheathed in the original boards that were sawed at the old water-powered up-and-down sawmill at nearby Hominy Pot. The backstage section was added only in 1962; before that actors had to climb ladders for stage-left entrances— pretty awkward in certain costumes. From late June until late August, Broadway actors and interns alike obviously enjoy roles in a repertoire of popular shows, as well as their Monday morning children's shows. The theater is on Main St.; (603) 526-4631 or (800) 633-BARN (2276); www.nlbarn.com.

The **New London Historical Society** maintains a museum that incorporates an entire village of nineteenth-century buildings, plus more than two dozen horse-drawn vehicles. The village is made up of a farmhouse with attached barn, an herb garden, carriage sheds, a blacksmith shop, a schoolhouse, a country store, a violin shop, a firehouse, a hearse house, and a meeting house. From late May until mid-Oct the village is open with docent-led tours Sun from 12:30 to 3:30 p.m., and during July and Aug, it is also open the same hours on Tues. A Holiday Open House in early Dec features hearthside cooking, crafts, and period music. New London Historical Society, Little Sunapee Rd. (Route 114), New London; call (603) 526-6564 or visit www .newlondonhistoricalsociety.org.

By this time, you've probably caught onto the fact that we like bogs, but this is one you must experience—a real quaking bog, where you could fall in and be swallowed up, as several animals have been, if you wander off the boardwalk. So pay attention as you walk through *Philbrick-Cricenti Bog,* or you won't get to see the north country. The bog was formed over a pond of glacial meltwater. About 10,000 years ago, arctic tundra plants began to grow, and their roots created a mat over the surface. Peat formed in the acid waters, made of accumulated plant debris, and the tundra plants continued to thrive in this acidic environment. Part of the old bog has become solid enough to support forests of spruce and eventually red maple within the original shoreline.

You can see all of these environments on a forty-five-minute walk, or just go for the dramatic part, which is on the "quaking loop," where you can feel the unstable mat jiggle under your feet. Believe the trail map when it tells you that those light-green "grassy" patches are only thin layers of moss and sedge. Under them lie cows, deer, and a horse that couldn't read the warnings. To find the bog, bear left onto Newport Road when Main Street forms a Y, following signs to Georges Mills. The trail leaves the left side of the road 0.3 mile from Cricenti's Market. The sign for the bog is not visible from the road, but you will see a small pull-out for parking.

Several restaurants offer dinner in New London, but for a unique dining experience, reserve a table at *The Inn at Pleasant Lake.* Arrive before 7 p.m., when all guests gather for a detailed preview of the evening's menu by the good-humored young chef/owner. (Be sure to order dinner wine before this presentation, or it will not arrive until after your first course.) The menu and price ($52 plus tax, gratuity, and beverages) are fixed, with a choice of a fish or meat entree each evening. Little details of preparation and presentation make up for the lack of choice and the timing problems created by having to serve each course to everyone at once. Entrees for this candlelit dinner might be rack of lamb, pan-seared mahimahi with exotic mushrooms, wood-smoked duck breast with lingonberries, or roasted veal tenderloin in Madeira. Salads get the same careful attention as entrees, with dressings designed to suit the greens; breads are excellent as well. The wine list, beginning at about $25, is well chosen. The restaurant is closed Mon and Tues.

Guest rooms upstairs have woodland or lake views to Mount Kearsarge; some have whirlpool baths. The gabled inn is thought to be where the song "When the Moon Comes Over the Mountain" was composed, and it certainly could be, since the moonrise views are near-perfect, reflected in Pleasant Lake below. The inn keeps a canoe and rowboat for the use of guests. Or you can admire the lake from the porch over afternoon tea with fresh-baked sweets, served to inn guests daily. Rates are $120 to $185; (603) 526-6271 or (800) 626-4907; www.innatpleasantlake.com.

The restaurant at the *New London Inn* is all about fine dining, with creative combinations and elegant presentations. Everything is inspired by the season and the availability of fresh ingredients, and the chef revels in little surprises, pairing ingredients you wouldn't expect to find together or rethinking old favorites. Silky, seared sea scallops are served with a salad of diced watermelon and celeriac, and grilled fresh tuna replaces the usual canned in a salade Nicoise, whose ingredients are not tossed but served more like an antipasto on a bed of baby greens. Entrees keep up the pace, with choices that have included thick-cut and juicy pork chops with chorizo, tiny potatoes, and steamed mahogany clams; striped bass with roasted fresh corn in a creamy sauce; and skillet-roasted loin of venison with sweet potato puree and parsleyed shallots. We don't usually order desserts, but these were irresistible: rich chocolate terrine, creamy cheesecake, fresh strawberry sorbet, or lemon-lavender ice cream. The restaurant is open for dinner only, Tues through Sat. The New London Inn is at 353 Main St.; (603) 526-2791 or (800) 526-2791; www.newlondoninn.us.

In the evening the friendly little cafe, *Jack's of New London,* transforms into a snazzy little bistro, with half a dozen entrees featuring fresh local ingredients. Begin with a sampling of five local artisanal cheeses served with fig jam, raisin toast, and Largueta almonds or beef Carpaccio with shaved red onion, capers, Reggiano cheese, arugula, and white truffle oil before moving on to an entree such as beer-braised lamb shank with soft polenta and fennel fries. In the summer, its sidewalk cafe tables, tree-shaded and surrounded by flowers, overlook the main street. The bistro is open for dinner Tues through Sat; the breakfast and lunch cafe is open daily from 7 a.m. to 5 p.m. Jack's is at 207 Main St., New London; (603) 526-8003; www.jacksofnewlondon.com.

Although New Hampshire's granite bedrock does not form true caves, such as those found in limestone, glacial scouring produced boulder caves and deeply undercut cliffs. One of the best examples of the latter is the *Royal Arch Hill Cave,* overlooking the town of Georges Mills north of New London. The best way to find it is from Georges Mills, from the road that leads from Route 11 in Georges Mills to exit 12A off I-89. Follow this road, under I-89, until it comes to a T. Go right, heading south toward New London, then take your first left, just at the top of a short hill. Just when you see the PRIVATE PROPERTY sign ahead, park and look for the small sign on an old woods road to the left.

The trail is marked to the right, a short way down that woods road. After about half a mile through the woods and a rocky area, the trail begins to climb steeply up Royal Arch Hill, soon arriving at the cave. The trail continues along the ledge in front of the cave and up the ridge behind it, where it angles off to the left and into Giles State Forest, a large tract of wild land that reaches all the way to Route 4A. From above the cave, which is large enough to shelter a small group of people, the view stretches from the town of Georges Mills to Little Sunapee Lake, on the northern boundary of New London.

Although spring-fed *Lake Sunapee* was a very popular resort area in the late 1800s, its shores have never been scoured by bulldozers or scarred by development. The only way to see the fine Victorian cottages nestled among the trees here is from the water. The *MV* **Mount Sunapee II** takes passengers on an hour-and-a-half-long cruise along the 10-mile length of the lake, a tour made even more interesting by the intelligent and good-humored narration about the lake's history and lore. From the boat you can see Sunapee's three lighthouses, said to be the only ones on a New England lake. From mid-May to Columbus Day, the boat sails Sat and Sun at 2 p.m.; in addition, between mid-June and Labor Day, it sails daily at 10 a.m. and 2:30 p.m. from Sunapee Harbor. For reservations call (603) 938-6465 or visit www.sunapeecruises.com.

For a taste of the days of the grand hotels, dine aboard the *MV* **Kearsarge,** a replica of the early lake steamers that brought guests from the train station to their lodgings. The *Kearsarge*'s Victorian interior sets the stage for a buffet supper served during the summer sailings from Sunapee Harbor. For reservations call (603) 938-6465 or check www.mvkearsarge.com.

Until the 1930s, the Woodsum family operated a fleet of steam passenger ships on Lake Sunapee. The *Sunapee Historical Museum* displays the pilothouse of one of these, rescued when the 70-foot SS *Kearsarge,* built in 1897, sank in 1935. Memorabilia of that golden age, including the handmade steam engine of a horseless carriage made in Newport in 1869, a milk delivery wagon, an 1824 fire pumper, an intact eighteenth-century dugout canoe, shop signs, and even a wooden water pipe, fill the museum. Plans are underway to restore the Woodsum Brothers machine shop. The museum is open 1 to 4 p.m. Tues through Sun and 7 to 9 p.m. Wed during July and Aug; open weekends only in the spring and fall. It is at the landing in Sunapee Harbor; (603) 763-9872; www.newlondonhistoricalsociety.org.

Along with its lake, Sunapee is known for its mountain, where Mount Sunapee State Park offers camping and a chairlift that operates in the summer as well as for skiers at the ski area in the winter. Now among the best ski areas in New England, *Mount Sunapee* has come a long way since it was an indifferently funded, state-owned ski area. Some of the best snowmaking and grooming in the northeast have turned this ugly stepsister into a princess. We like the range of challenges here and the fact that those just starting out have an appropriate and separate area where they can gain confidence. Skiers will seldom see such perfectly cared-for trails; even when there is no snow elsewhere, they manage to make and groom it at Mount Sunapee. While it has no on-premises lodging of its own, more than 20 local inns and hotels have packages available. The Sunapee Express Chairlift offers rides on weekends during foliage season and when there are special events at the mountain, as well as for skiers in the winter. The views are spectacular, 360 degrees of lakes, hills, and mountains, clad in orange maples and green pines in the fall. The ride is just over a mile long, climbing 1,402 vertical feet to Mount Sunapee's summit. From there you can see Lake Sunapee and views across New Hampshire to Vermont's Green Mountains. The ski area is located on Route 103, Newbury (close to I-89); (603) 763-3500; www.mountsunapee.com.

New England Handicapped Sports Association at Mount Sunapee offers a unique opportunity for people who may have thought it was impossible for them to enjoy the ski slopes, as well as a chance for active skiers to share their sport with people of all ages and with any number of physical abilities. Mount Sunapee offers lift tickets, and the association provides adaptive equipment and expertise. Volunteers act as instructors, guides, and blockers (e.g., to alert other skiers to the approach of a blind skier) or simply greet newcomers and get them started. NEHSA has its own wheelchair-accessible lodge, and new skiers will enjoy learning on their own private slope. To learn more, to become a volunteer, or to join the program, call NEHSA at (800) 628-4484 or (603) 763-9158; www.nehsa.org.

Not far from the cultural attractions of Sunapee and Hanover is a state park that is possibly the least known of any in New Hampshire. *Pillsbury State Park,* on Route 31, in the tiny town of Washington, is the perfect place for a getaway camping trip, especially if you are a paddler or hiker. The thirty-nine camping sites here are large and well spaced, with several right on the water, each carved out of the woods and providing maximum privacy.

There are four ponds in the park. Butterfield and May Ponds are the largest, and sites on these are mostly accessible by car. Two other smaller ponds (North Pond and Baker Pond) also have remote sites where campers have to paddle in. Because of their remote location, no fires are allowed in these campsites. On the east end, sites 26, 36, 37, and 40 are walk-in sites.

The real draw of Pillsbury for us is the paddling. We like to have a site on Butterfield Pond, a bit marshy but great for exploring in our kayaks. In this part you will find a profusion of reeds, sedges, and water lilies to examine and even a few fish lurking beneath them. On the far side an arm of the pond reaches down to Route 31, where there is a put-in near the dam, which is not on park lands. At the other end a narrow passage leads out into the much larger May Pond. We love being out there at dusk as the autumn sun sets behind the hills across the water. Look for waterfowl in this pond, especially along the east end. Along the shore all that we could see were a few scattered camp lanterns; there is no development at all anywhere around the lake, other than

Yesterday's News

If the little details of local history fascinate you and bring a place to life, as they do for us, you'll enjoy a small, local magazine called *Soo Nipi.* Each issue is filled with old photos of everything from extinct grand hotels to tiny stations on long-gone rail lines that once brought summer visitors to Lake Sunapee towns. Some articles discuss historic items such as the Cornish colony of artists and writers or the old churches of Claremont. Other articles explore walking trails or places to paddle. Look for the magazine locally or call (603) 763-2441 or (800) 339-6094.

the campground. While we haven't fished here, we are told it's pretty good. Canoe rentals are available at the park.

For hikers there are hiking trails on the east end of the park worth exploring. One of the trails starts at a point near campsite 27, crossing over the small stream below the dam of Mill Pond. Another two trails begin close to the bar gate at sites 34 and 35. The one on the left goes to Balancing Rock along a forest trail. The other option, straight ahead, will lead to the Five Summers Trail to the North Pond campsites (numbers 36 and 37). For long-distance hikes, the Monadnock-Sunapee Greenway, a 51-mile trail between the two New Hampshire mountains, passes through the park.

There is a day-use fee of $4; children six to twelve $2, under age six and New Hampshire residents over sixty-five are admitted free. Camping is $21 per site (two adults and dependents under eighteen) per night, $10 additional per person per night above allotted number. Swimming at Sunapee State Beach is included in the camping pass. Reservations can be made up to seven days in advance by calling (603) 271-3628, Mon through Fri, Jan through early Oct, or by visiting the Web site at www.nhparks.org. The park's number is (603) 863-2860.

Late in the nineteenth century, New Hampshire promoted the reuse of abandoned farms as summer homes for the wealthy. John Hay, secretary to Abraham Lincoln, acquired *The Fells* in Newbury, at the southern tip of Lake Sunapee, in 1888. After his death, his son Clarence and his wife created extensive gardens on the property overlooking the lake. The rock garden covers both sides of a gently falling ravine and includes a stone Japanese lantern presented to Hay for his role in the Treaty of Portsmouth in 1905; a small stream flows through the ravine into a rock-lined lily pond before continuing into the forest below. The rose and perennial beds are in more formal terraced gardens, and an easy trail to the lake features placards with nature notes. A 5-mile trail network offers views and wildlife, and the gatehouse has a tiny orientation exhibit. On Route 103A between New London and Newbury, The Fells is open 10 a.m. to 6 p.m. weekends from late May through Labor Day and Wed through Sun mid-June through Labor Day. Call (603) 763-4789 or visit www.thefells.org.

Newbury's *Center Meeting House* was originally built about 1821 but was disassembled and rebuilt on its present site in 1832. It is now located at the intersection of Routes 103 and 103A. A Bulfinch-inspired design, it has a unique interior arrangement; the box pews of the congregation face the entry doors (which would surely discourage late arrivals). The finely executed woodwork of the pulpit is supported by four columns and reached by a double staircase. Sunday services during July and Aug are at 11 a.m.

Railroads were important to the future of small towns when the line to Newbury was built in 1871. To complete it, the engineers had to excavate a massive trench, the *Newbury Cut,* through a solid granite hilltop using nitroglycerin to blast and strong backs to move the rubble, a process that took a year. Although the trains haven't run since 1961, you can get to the still-impressive cut in a leisurely twenty-minute walk along the old rail bed, now a level, birch-lined path alongside a marsh. Park at the town landing, just across the Route 103 intersection from the Center Meeting House, and look for the wide trail behind the small shopping center.

Few people passing through Bradford, just south of Newbury on Route 103, realize how close they are to one of New England's rare stands of virgin pine. Near the intersection with Main Street is *Tall Pines Scenic Area,* accessible by a 0.25-mile trail from the rest area, where you can park. Fourteen trees over 200 years old are among the state's tallest white pines. Such stands of the virgin timber that once covered the state are few and are usually far from roads or on steep and hard-to-reach mountainsides.

Upper Valley

The town of Hanover and *Dartmouth College* are clustered around a large green, decorated in winter by a giant ice sculpture if the weather cooperates. Overlooking this from a slight hill are the white buildings of the original college. Two of the remaining sides are lined with redbrick college buildings, among them Baker Library. The south side is divided between the *Hanover Inn* and the *Hopkins Center for the Performing Arts.* In and around that quadrangle lies an amazing wealth of art.

In the basement of *Baker Memorial Library* is a series of frescoes completed in 1934 by the Mexican artist José Clemente Orozco. A free brochure describing the frescoes is available at the central desk. They are powerful and, since their recent cleaning and restoration, true to their original brilliant colors. They were quite controversial in the 1930s but are now appreciated as a rare art treasure. Even less well known is the **Hickmott Shakespeare Collection,** also housed at Baker Library in the special-collections room, open 8 a.m. to 4:30 p.m. Mon through Fri. The collection includes all four of the folio editions, close to forty quarto editions, all of the pre-1700 editions of *Macbeth,* and many other early editions. In the library's treasure room is Daniel Webster's set of John James Audubon's *Birds of America* in a folio first edition, more than 150 titles of incunabula (works printed before 1501), a 1439 Bible, and a collection of more than 200 volumes illustrating the art of fine bookbinding.

Adjoining the Hopkins Center is the new **Hood Museum of Art,** containing galleries for collections of American, European, African, Indian, and ancient art. The collection of Assyrian reliefs from the ninth century b.c. is rivaled in New England by only one other series. At the other end of history, the Hood is one of the very few American museums to own the entire suite of Picasso's Vollard etchings. There are Roman mosaics; paintings of the Italian Renaissance and baroque periods; landscapes of the Hudson River school; and representative pieces from every major style and period. Traveling exhibits often incorporate pieces from Dartmouth's own collections.

In 1991 the museum acquired the most comprehensive collection of Melanesian art in the country. Nearly 1,000 objects from Papua New Guinea and Vanuatu, ranging in size from miniatures to monumental works more than 8 feet tall, form a collection both comprehensive and rich in detail. Even with its new building, the museum cannot display everything, so inquire if you are interested in a particular subject. Temporary special exhibitions change twice each Dartmouth term. Open all year, Tues through Sat 10 a.m. to 5 p.m. (open to 9 p.m. on Wed) and Sun noon to 5 p.m. Free. You can write for information to the Hood Museum, On the Green, Hanover 03755; call (603) 646-2808 or visit http//hoodmuseum.dartmouth.edu/about for links to a schedule.

The Hopkins Center is as broad in its offerings of performing arts as the Hood is in the fine arts. Call (603) 646-3493 or visit hop.dartmouth.edu for a schedule.

The **Hanover Inn** is an institution almost as revered as Dartmouth College itself. Whenever the inn changes so much as a carpet, some old grad notices and comments. That has not stopped the inn from undertaking renovations to keep it up to date, with modern amenities such as phones with modem ports. As the oldest continuously operated business in New Hampshire, the inn treads a careful balance between maintaining its historical flavor and providing luxurious accommodations and service that anticipates every need. Rooms are elegant, some with real marble baths. The inn is on The Green in Hanover; (800) 443-7024 or (603) 643-4300; www.hanoverinn.com.

If you are a celebrity watcher, you can get the autograph of those performing or speaking at the Hopkins Center by waiting in the corridor that connects it with the inn. They all stay at the inn and use this private lower-level passageway before and after appearances.

In nearby Lebanon, a former bank building is the venue for **Alliance for the Visual Arts** (AVA), where New Hampshire and Vermont artists have their studios and show their work in changing exhibitions. Shown there is a wide variety of styles and media, from very traditional to experimental art. Exhibition gallery hours are Tues through Sat 11 a.m. to 5 p.m. The AVA Gallery and Art Center is at 11 Bank St., Lebanon; (603) 448-3117; www.avagallery.org.

The **Lebanon Opera House,** like so many others, had been locked up and left to decay until the 1960s, when the local music teacher began a campaign to clean it up and attract performers to its stage. A decade later the city took a hand and restored it, so it now brings top performances and Broadway musicals. 51 North Park St., Lebanon, 03766, (603) 448-0400. You can find its current schedule at www.lebanonoperahouse.org.

High on the hill overlooking the airport is the largest cider-apple orchard in America. Yup, right here in little Lebanon. Not only the 100 acres of apple trees, but the cider house where they are transformed from wild-looking little apples with forgotten names like Calville and Brown Snout into world-class ciders that stand proudly beside the finest from Normandy, Britain, and Spain's Basque country. **Poverty Lane Orchards** grows varieties that were once grown on farms across the eastern United States on trees planted by Johnny Appleseed. Choosing the right apples for their nuances of flavor, sweetness, and acidity is the secret of their **Farnum Hill Ciders.** Forget the cloying, grocery store hard ciders and think instead of a fine dry wine for comparison. You can visit the cider house for a tasting anytime by calling ahead, or in Sept and Oct from 8 a.m. until 6 p.m. on weekdays and 10 a.m. to 5 p.m. Sat and Sun. Farnham Hill Ciders is on Poverty Lane, off Route 4 between Lebanon and West Lebanon; (603) 448-1511; www.farnumhillciders.com.

Lower Shaker Village in **Enfield,** while not as extensive as the one at Canterbury, is of special interest for its stone architecture. "The Chosen Vale" (as the Shakers called their lakeside village) is not preserved in its entirety, but many of the stone buildings still stand. Inside the former dairy building is a museum, well stocked with Shaker artifacts interpreted to help visitors understand Shaker beliefs and their way of life. An informative booklet suggests a handy tour of the village and leads to the Shakers' Feast Ground on the hill above. A **small shop in the museum** and another in the adjoining inn feature

Two for Brew

New London and West Lebanon each has a craft brewery with an attached brew-pub. *Seven Barrels Brewery,* whose brewmaster is the author of one of the most popular home-brewing manuals, is in the Colonial Plaza on Route 12A in West Lebanon. In March look for Sugar House Maple Ale and Arctic Lion Bock, and order one of the traditional English pub dishes—cockaleekie pie, toad-in-a-hole, or plough-man's plate—at lunch or dinner; (603) 298-5566.

In New London's *Flying Goose Brew Pub,* the menu is more all-American, with burgers, baby back ribs, and crab cakes to accompany their English-style ales. Golden-colored Split Rock Ale and a hoppy IPA, along with Honey Ale, are among their fifteen brews. Look for the pub, which is open for lunch and dinner, at the Four Corners Grille at the intersection of Routes 114 and 11, just south of town; (603) 526-6899; www.flyinggoose.com.

fine reproductions of Shaker crafts, books on the Shakers and their design philosophy, and even kits to teach the many skills these remarkable people developed. Towering above the vale is the largest Shaker dwelling house built in any of their communities. Four-and-one-half stories tall, it is made of solid granite blocks and the interiors remain much as they were when they were occupied by the Shaker brothers and sisters. Large windows light the rooms and on the walls are examples of the pegs and cabinetry that made Shakers famous. On the lower floor the dining rooms are notable for the stark simplic-ity that marks Shaker art. The museum is open from late May to Oct, Mon through Sat 10 a.m. to 5 p.m. and noon to 5 p.m. on Sun. Winter hours are 10 a.m. to 4 p.m. and Sun noon to 4 p.m. Admission is $7.50, $6.50 for seniors, $5.00 for college students; (603) 632-4346; www.shakermuseum.org.

Northwest from the village of Canaan is the unusual settlement of *Canaan Street.* The main, and only, street is lined on both sides with a mile of distin-guished white homes and churches. These date from as early as 1794. Behind the single row of homes on the east is a lake, and in the other direction is a sweeping view over the valley to the Green Mountains of Vermont. Wide lawns surround the homes, and the broad street is lined with maples and stone walls. The entire scene, so unexpectedly encountered, seems to have been dropped there from the nineteenth century.

One of New Hampshire's first ski lodges, *Cardigan Lodge* is set on the Appalachian Mountain Club's 1,200-acre Cardigan Reservation, on Cardigan Mountain in Alexandria. The AMC property is surrounded by 5,000-acre Mount Cardigan State Forest. Accessible from the lodge are ski trails cut in 1934, still enjoyed by backcountry skiers today. In the summer the lodge is a favorite for hikers, with 360-degree views from the bald summit of nearby Mt. Cardigan only half a mile away. Along with casual lodging, the lodge has a swimming pond, nature trail, and family programs in the summer. The lodge is open year round, serving meals daily from late June through late Oct and on weekends Jan through Mar and during Feb school vacation week. During the full-service season linens are provided for the two private lodge rooms and the bunk-rooms, but in other seasons guests need to bring a sleeping bag and towels. The rate includes dinner, breakfast, and a trail lunch. Rates are inexpensive, even less expensive for AMC members, who pay about $60 a night in mid-summer, meals included. AMC Cardigan Lodge, 774 Shem Valley Rd., Bristol; call (603) 744-8011, reservations (603) 466-2727, or visit www.outdoors.org.

Baker River and Newfound Lake

New Hampshire is filled with stone profiles, and although none rivaled the fame of the Old Man of the Mountain in Franconia Notch, each has its degree of local renown. Some require a great deal of imagination or at least a view from the right spot to distinguish. *Profile Falls,* 2.5 miles south of Bristol on Route 3A, demands both imagination and the right view, but even without spotting the profile, the falls themselves are well worth the short walk. Turn off Route 3A to the east (left if you're traveling south) just before the bridge with the small sign for the falls. A short distance down that road is another small sign and a pull-out area on the right, but it is steep and slippery, so we suggest parking along the road just before the sign. Follow the road to the trail or follow the snowmobile trail, which also leads to the base of the falls. The drop is about 40 feet over a broad ledge, and the profile is supposed to be at the foot of the falls in silhouette against the white water. On hot days local boys can often be found jumping from the high rocks on the right into the pool at the base of the falls. We don't recommend that you try this.

The *Mill Ice Cream Cafe & Fudge Factory,* in the center of Bristol, is like stepping into an old-fashioned ice cream parlor, and the ice cream and fudge are made right there. They also serve organic, fair-trade coffee, hot chocolate, and light meals, as well as vegetarian soups. There is live music on most Saturday nights. The Mill Ice Cream Cafe & Fudge Factory, 2 Central St., Bristol; call (603) 744-0405 or visit www.themillbristol.com.

North of Bristol on Route 3A is a picnic area, maintained by the Rotary Club, in a grove of pines. Shortly past this a road leads to West Shore Road, which hugs the shore of Newfound Lake and offers lovely views of the lake and mountains. Along the road, on a point of land surrounded by the unusually clear waters of the lake, is one of New Hampshire's finest and perhaps least-known beaches. ***Wellington State Park*** has a fine sandy beach under tall pines, so you can choose sun or shade and still be at the water's edge. You can't launch boats from the park, but you can put in canoes or small sailing craft easily. It is a busy, friendly park with plenty of beach and water, so it never seems crowded. It's open June through Columbus Day, 9 a.m. to 7 p.m. daily; $4 adults, $3 for ages six and over, age five and younger and New Hampshire citizens 65 and older free.

At the northern end of the lake, between the attractive village of ***Hebron*** and Route 3A, is the ***Hebron Marsh Wildlife Sanctuary.*** You can park down the dirt road just before the red cottage while you visit the diverse wildlife habitats of freshwater marsh, open fields, and the banks of the Cockermouth River. Follow signs to the southwest corner of the field to find the short trail leading to the observation tower. From here you can look out over the marsh and see wood ducks, buffleheads, pie-billed grebes, great blue herons, ospreys, beavers, and perhaps moose and loons. Songbirds abound, and the trail through the fields gives a closer view of the wildflowers.

Only 1.25 miles down the road is the ***Paradise Point Nature Center*** (look sharp to find its sign on the downhill side of the road next to the driveway). In addition to the trails through an unspoiled lakeshore of coniferous forest, the center includes hands-on exhibits, a library, bird-viewing area, and

Ski Trails

Along with the well-known Mount Sunapee, the region has several smaller ski slopes favored by locals and others who shun long lift lines. Ragged Mountain, in Danbury, has six lifts and thirty-two trails that serve all skill levels. The longest trail is 1.75 miles. Low rates make it attractive to families—$39 for lifts on weekends, or a full package with a lesson, rental, and lift for $60; (603) 768-3475, snow conditions (603) 768-3971, lodging (800) 400-3911.

You would expect a sports- and outdoors-oriented college such as Dartmouth to have its own ski slope, and it does. **Dartmouth Skiway** is where many of the school's racers practice for the Olympics and other events, but it's a popular area for local families as well. Expect some very challenging trails on this surprisingly steep mountain in Lyme, north of Hanover; (603) 795-2143.

Perfect for kids, but challenging enough for the Kimball Union School team's training and meets, **Whaleback** is on Whaleback Mountain Road in Enfield; (603) 448-1489. **Eastman Cross Country Ski Center,** close to exit 13 off I-89 in Grantham, has eight trails covering about 16 miles. It also has a small alpine center for telemark skiing, served by a chairlift; (603) 863-4500.

a fascinating audio-aided exhibit demonstrating the various calls of the loon. A full schedule of naturalist programs is offered, including a sunrise canoe trip. Before walking the trails, be sure to pick up the free visitors guide, with descriptions of the natural history and inhabitants of the area. Try to spot the tupelo tree, rarely found in New England, as you walk alongside the swamp on the Elwell Trail. Its horizontal branches are covered in brilliant red leaves in the fall. The center is open July through Sept 1, daily 10 a.m. to 4 p.m.; trails are open year-round. There is no admission fee, but the Audubon Society, which operates the center, is always grateful for donations to help them continue their work of acquiring and protecting natural habitats. Write Audubon Society of New Hampshire, North Shore Rd., East Hebron 03232; call (603) 744-3516 in July and Aug, (603) 224-9909 Sept through June; or visit the Web site at www .nhaudubon.org/sanctuaries.

Going west from Hebron through *Groton,* a road leads to *Sculptured Rocks.* About a mile from the turnoff, watch for a signpost, although the sign may not be there during the off-season. You'll see a parking area on the left, and the chasm is on the right side of the road. The river here has carved its way under granite boulders, leaving only the crowns of some and forming giant potholes in others that appear to have been the work of a giant ice-cream scoop. Below the bridge a trail leads past falls, pools, and huge moss-covered boulders, culminating in a sheer rock cliff on one side. Notice the full-grown trees on the sidewalls with their roots gripping the walls like fingers.

If you'd like to stay in the area, you should reserve a room at *The Inn on Newfound Lake,* which, as the name suggests, overlooks the lake. This vintage inn has been restored to add modern amenities without losing its charm. Speaking of which, everyone remembers the owners, whose personal attention shows in every detail. Rooms are $135 to $150; suites are $280 to $345 in high season. The dining room is excellent, with creative dishes inspired by a world of cuisines. Dinner may begin with a spicy black bean and tomato soup and move on to veal with proscuitto and aged provolone. Filet of salmon tops baby carrots and green beans in a semiarchitectural presentation, sauced with avocado. Desserts are dramatic: A lemon mascarpone tart is scrolled in raspberry syrup, and crème brûlée will be highlighted with melon liqueur. Vegetables are given serious attention. The chef is dedicated to using locally grown and produced ingredients, so expect to find cheeses from local farms and fresh-picked seasonal vegetables. On Sunday mornings a buffet brunch includes wonderful waffles and enough other choices to keep you fueled all day. The Inn on Newfound Lake is on Route 3A at 1030 Mayhew Turnpike, Bridgewater; (603) 744-9111 or (800) 745-7990; www.newfoundlake.com. It's open year-round.

New Hampshire's Place in Baseball's Hall of Fame

The first baseball glove was designed and made in Plymouth, New Hampshire. In 1882, a local glove maker began producing these for the Red Sox, and by the twentieth century his company had expanded to make baseballs and softballs, as well as the gloves to catch them with.

Quincy Road, which goes off the far end of ***Rumney's*** village green, will take you to the Quincy Bog. Exactly 2 miles from the village green you will see stone pillars on either side of a small road to the left. Down this road 0.1 mile there is another left, which ends shortly at the bog entrance. Nature trails and a viewing deck offer a look at rare bog plants and a wetland ecosystem different from those of shores and marshes. The best months to see the bog plants in bloom are May and June.

On the way to the Quincy Bog you will pass the most unusual ***town pound*** in the state. While pounds were usually made of four sturdy stone walls, forming a square with a gate on one side, the townspeople of old Rumney took advantage of a geological feature as interesting as the pound itself. Huge boulders, which appear to have fallen from the cliffs above, lie in a great tumble. Two of them form protected cavelike areas, and two others form straight walls. By adding only one and a half sides and a gate, the town created a fine enclosure for stray animals, one that even offered shelter from rain and wind. Climb through the space in the center of the back, and you'll find a trail through an arch formed by two huge boulders. You can climb farther and wander amid these granite giants. The pound is a fascinating combination of natural and human history. You'll see one wall of the pound directly across the road from the immense boulder that sits almost in the road.

Along the way to Stinson Lake is the ***Mary Baker Eddy House*** (603-786-9943). The founder of the Christian Science faith lived here in the early 1860s. The house is open Tues through Sat 10 a.m. to 5 p.m. and Sun 2 to 5 p.m., May through Oct. Admission is $3, under twelve admitted free, half off for seniors and students; www.longyear.org.

From here a guide will also take you to another Eddy home in North Groton. The road, which turns to gravel, continues to climb through the woods. Watch for a waterfall to the left just as you cross a bridge. Farther on, as you top the ridge, you will have sweeping views into the White Mountain National Forest, just a teaser for the views you will have as you continue north.

The area around Franklin, just a bit north and west of Concord, lies in the valleys of the Pemigewasset and Winnipesaukee Rivers, beautiful winding valleys where the rivers flow through countryside and past small towns and cities. Route 3 through this region is named the Daniel Webster Highway for its favorite native son. The best and easiest way into the Franklin area is via Route 3. Take exit 17 (Route 4) from I-93 and follow signs for Boscawen and Franklin.

Few New Hampshire residents know of its **State Forest Nursery** on the west side of Route 3 in Boscawen. The forestry nursery was established in 1911 after the state had been largely denuded of its forests by decades of over-harvesting. Since then, more than 72 million seedling trees and shrubs have been distributed from these lands, and today it sells about a half-million trees and shrubs annually. Species that can be seen growing include white and red pine; white, blue, and Norway spruce; balsam, Fraser, and Douglas fir; red oak; black walnut; butternut; and many varieties of shrubs and bushes that provide food for songbirds and other wildlife. There is no visitor center (we wish the state would build one here), but the friendly staff members welcome visitors to look around and are happy to tell anyone about their mission. One of their nursery beds is right along the road, but if that one is empty, follow the dirt road up the hill to see their other acreage. Any resident of the state may purchase trees and shrubs from the nursery, which is open in Apr and May, weekdays 8 a.m. to 4 p.m. Hiking trails and the trout pond are open year-round. A catalogue and price list of available species is available. Contact State Forest Nursery, 405 Daniel Webster Hwy. (Route 3), Boscawen; (603) 796-2323; www .dred.state.nh.us/nhnursery/. For information or their catalogue, write Nursery Mailing List, P.O. Box 1856, Concord 03302.

North of the nursery, cross the Pemigewasset River on Route 3 to get to the main part of Franklin, once a thriving factory town, as the many small, brick mills along the rivers bear testimony. Look to see what is playing at the newly restored Opera House in the city hall. Even though restoration continues, they offer a schedule of events from musical concerts to theater performances (from $5 to $10 for adults), featuring such names as the Shaw Brothers, Randy Avrus, and Susie Burke. Many performances feature local performers, both adults and youth. The **Opera House** is at 316 Central Ave. (P.O. Box 172), Franklin; (603) 934-1901; www.franklinoperahouse.org.

Fine old mercantile buildings line Franklin's main street, part of the Franklin Falls Historic District, one of them housing **Franklin Antiques Market.** The three floors of the restored 1890 department store make a good setting for furniture and decorative glass, china, lighting, and smaller items. There is an especially good selection of primitives and country antiques. Look up to

ALSO WORTH SEEING IN THE DARTMOUTH-SUNAPEE REGION

Polar Caves,
Route 25,
Plymouth;
(603) 536-1888 or (800) 273-1886;
www.polarcaves.com;
Open daily mid-May to mid-Oct.
Chambers and passages formed by

a tumble of giant boulders dislodged by glaciers. Deep inside, natural ice remains into late summer.

The area abounds in **antiques shops,** some of which are open year-round, all of which are open summer and fall.

---

see the original pressed tin ceilings. Franklin Antiques Market, 361 Central St. (Route 3); call (603) 934-2800 or visit www.franklinantiques.com. Starting right in town, opposite the Grevior Furniture store, is the ***Winnipesaukee River Trail,*** a walking and bike trail that follows closely along the banks of the Winnipesaukee River. The trail follows the route of the sewer line from Meriden to the Franklin waste-treatment facility, but the line is buried and doesn't detract from the walk. About a quarter-mile from the beginning, walkers will see the 180-foot-long ***Sulphite Covered Bridge,*** built in 1886. It is the only decked covered bridge remaining in the United States. Farther along, the trail runs along the edge of the river gorge as it drops 80 feet over a distance of 4,000 feet. On New Year's Day, an annual white-water run travels this section of the river. The trail is about 3 miles long and requires a return hike unless another car has been left at the other end.

Back on the west side of the Pemigewasset, take Route 3A north when Route 3 turns and crosses the river. Not far out of town on the west (river) side of the road sits the fine brick Federal-style home known as the ***Maria Atwood Inn.*** Innkeepers Sandi and Fred Hoffmeister have taken this 1830s farmhouse and turned it into a country inn. Guest rooms are very attractive, furnished with a nice mixture of antique and newer furniture; all beds have unique antique quilts, and all rooms have working fireplaces. Many rooms have Internet connections. An unfortunate lightning strike damaged the rear roof a few years ago but led to the happy construction of two large rooms on the third floor with exposed beams, fireplaces, and a double and two single beds, perfect for family stays. Guests have the use of a large living room with television and are served a full breakfast with fresh-baked goodies in the dining room, in the library, or—in good weather—on the patios. Doubles are about $100, singles $65; each additional adult is $25. Children twelve to eighteen are an additional $15, and those under twelve are free and welcomed. The inn is 0.5

mile north of the Route 11 and Route 3A intersection on Route 3A. The Maria Atwood Inn is located at 71 Hill Rd. (Route 3A), Franklin; (603) 934-3666; www .atwoodinn.com.

Another reason for staying at the inn is its proximity to the *Heritage Trail,* which starts a short distance north on Route 3A. The walking trail goes from *Franklin Falls Dam* and follows along the Pemigewasset Valley. Look for the sign for the parking area on the east side of Route 3A north of Franklin. Continue to the end of the road (don't mistake the factory lot for the public lot). There is a nice view here of the dam and the river valley. The dam was built in 1943 to prevent the disastrous periodic flooding that had devastated the valley regularly before its construction. The route of the trail crosses part of the floodplain for the dam, so spring is not a good time to walk here. Along the way, the trail goes through the site of the original town of Hill, destroyed when the dam was built. For more information contact U.S. Army Corps of Engineers at (603) 934-2116. The trail leaves from the northwest corner of the parking lot and requires a return along the same path. In winter it is a snowmobile trail.

For an affordable breakfast or a sandwich at lunch—as well as scoops of locally made Annabelle's ice cream—stop at *Ariana's Cafe.* Sandwiches (the chicken salad is delicious) are all under $5, many under $4, and there is seating indoors or, in the summer, outdoors. Stop here to pick up a picnic lunch to carry on the Heritage Trail. At 428 Main St., Franklin; (603) 934-5577.

West of Franklin, off Route 127, is the little house in which New Hampshire's most famous native son was born. The *Daniel Webster Birthplace* is typical of the first homes built by farmers who settled here when New Hampshire was still a frontier. Webster was born here in 1782, while his father was still serving in George Washington's army. Webster became a lawyer and great orator, was secretary of state under three presidents, congressman from two states, and a leader known for his sense of justice and his ability to find agreement between differing points of view. He was regarded as the greatest statesman of his day. Nearly fifty years after his death, at the turn of the twentieth century, a national poll was taken to determine America's most important historical figures; Webster tied with Lincoln for second place, after George Washington and ahead of all other presidents. His birthplace is brought to life by a Living History Project, with costumed interpreters demonstrating and explaining daily life during Webster's childhood era. You may find them cooking on the open hearth, spinning, tending the herb garden, or playing an early game (which you can join). Admission to the site, which includes the house, museum displays, and a nature trail, is free for New Hampshire residents, Others $7 ages twelve and up, $3 ages three to eleven. Open Sat and Sun, from mid-June to Labor Day. Off Route 127, between Franklin and Salisbury; (603) 934-5057 summer, (603) 485-2034 other times.

Near the turn-off to the Webster Birthplace, about two miles from Route 3, is *Tarbin Gardens,* a little paradise of formal and informal gardens, where afternoon tea is served amid flowering shrubs and plants. A formal garden room is enclosed in tall hedges and a landscape park drops to a scenic pool. Among others are gardens devoted to alpine plants and a bog garden, as well as a sensory garden of plants especially rewarding to sniff and touch. You can wander through on your own or join a guided tour, beginning at 11 a.m. and 2 p.m. daily. The process of turning this forest hillside into expansive English-style gardens is as interesting as the gardens themselves. You are welcome to bring your own picnic to eat in the gardens. Most are accessible to motorized scooters and all can be seen from wheelchair paths. Admission is $8.50 for adults, and the gardens are open Tues through Sun 10 a.m. to 6 p.m. and Monday holidays, from the weekend before Mother's Day through Columbus Day. Tarbin Gardens, 321 Salisbury Rd., Franklin; call (603) 934-3518 or visit www.tarbingardens.com.

More Places to Stay in the Dartmouth-Sunapee Region

BRISTOL

Henry Whipple House
75 Summer St.
(Route 104E)
(603) 744-6157
www.thewhipplehouse.com
Moderate.

CLAREMONT

Goddard Mansion Bed and Breakfast
25 Hillstead Rd.
(603) 543-0603 or
(800) 736-0603
www.goddardmansion.com

Ten beautifully decorated guest rooms in a 1905 summer mansion, with Tiffany chandelier and fine architectural details. Moderate. Breakfast included.

HANOVER

The Trumbull House Bed & Breakfast
40 Etna Rd.
(603) 643-2370 or
(800) 651-5141
www.trumbullhouse.com
Five guest rooms and a cottage with private deck on sixteen acres.

LYME

Loch Lyme Lodge
70 Orford Rd.
(603) 795-2141 or
(800) 423-2141
www.lochlymelodge.com

An old-fashioned family summer camp, with cabins on a pond and canoeing. High moderate.

NEW LONDON

New London Inn
149 Main St.
(603) 526-2791 or
(800) 526-2791
www.newlondoninn.net
Nicely restored rooms overlooking the center of town and the college campus. High moderate.

NEWPORT

Newport Motel
467 Sunapee St.
(Routes 11 and 103)
(603) 863-1440 or
(800) 741-2619
A tidy, well-managed motel with air-conditioning, pool,

TO LEARN MORE ABOUT THE DARTMOUTH-SUNAPEE REGION

Hanover Area Chamber of Commerce,
Main St., Hanover 03755;
(603) 643-3115;
www.hanoverchamber.org.

New London Area Chamber of Commerce,
Main St. (P.O. Box 532),
New London 03257; (603) 526-6575;
www.newlondonareanh.com.

and wireless Internet. Inexpensive.

SUTTON

The Village House at Sutton Mills
14 Grist Mill Rd.
Sutton Mills
(603) 927-4765
Open year-round, this 1857 home offers attractive rooms, as well as a blacksmith shop and the studio of a well-known painter of custom floorcloths.

More Places to Eat in the Dartmouth-Sunapee Region

GRANTHAM

Bistro Nouveau
6 Clubhouse Lane,
Grantham
(603) 863-8000
http://bistronouveau.com
Well-thought-out and well-prepared dining in a club

atmosphere. Large selection of wines is offered by the glass.

HANOVER

Molly's
43 South Main St.
(603) 643-2570
www.mollysrestaurant.com
Put plenty of quarters in the parking meter because service is slow and lunch plates overflow with food. Pizzas are creative in content and cooked on a wood fire.

LEBANON

Three Tomatoes Trattoria
1 Court St.
(603) 448-1711
Possibly the best meal for the money. The wood-fired oven produces pizzas and grilled dishes with panache and they are made using the freshest ingredients. The ambience is very Euro, the food very good. Open for lunch Mon through Fri 11:30 a.m. to 3 p.m. and for dinner nightly from 5 p.m.

NEW LONDON

Peter Christian's Tavern
186 Main St.
(603) 526-4042
www.peterchristianstavern.com
Hearty food and sandwiches, accompanied by a good range of microbrews; open every day.

PLYMOUTH

The Italian Farmhouse
U.S. Route 3, south of Plymouth
(603) 536-4536
www.thecman.com/restaurants/italian-farmhouse/
It's really a New Hampshire farmhouse, its kitchen and parlor transformed into dining rooms, but the restaurant in it is decidedly Italian. Interesting pasta dishes are budget priced.

The Main Street Station
Main St.
(603) 536-7577
Local residents like its traditional menu and moderate prices for breakfast and lunch.

Annie's Overflow Restaurant
Holderness Rd.
(603) 536-4062
Annie's overflows with hospitality—the entire staff greets you as you enter this cheerful spot that's open daily for breakfast and lunch. Eggs are cooked exactly as ordered, and the home-fries are superior. Check the board for daily specials. It's easy to miss the little building near the bridge as you enter town from I-93.

SUNAPEE

The Anchorage
71 Main St.
Sunapee Harbor
(603) 763-3334
www.northendpub.com

An informal place for breakfast or lunch, overlooking the lake. This is the place where the band Aerosmith began—all because the fries were so delicious. Slips available if you arrive by boat.

THE LAKES AND FOOTHILLS

North of the Merrimack Valley and the seacoast region lies an area of rolling farmlands and small mountains. The northernmost of these are the foothills of the White Mountains beyond.

In the center lies Lake Winnipesaukee, an enormous body of water surrounded by several other sizable lakes. The southern shores of Winnipesaukee are covered with popular tourist paths and filled with man-made "attractions" and cheek-by-jowl resorts. While there are some lovely, quiet pockets in this area, it is generally too well known and too heavily trodden to be of interest in this book.

Instead, we shall explore the eastern shore of Lake Winnipesaukee and other lakes east of I-93 and the mountains and forests that border them. Ossipee, Wentworth, Squam, Silver, and Province Lakes are joined by innumerable smaller ones providing reflecting pools for some of the state's prettiest villages. We won't name or take you past all of them, so you should explore the backroads to discover some of them for yourself. Country inns, covered bridges, rock-lined brooks, and old farms lie along backroads here, and at the crossroads are villages that date from the earliest days of the colony.

THE LAKES AND FOOTHILLS

THE
SANDWICHES

Squam
Lake

SQUAM

Holderness

3

Ossipee
Lake

25

OSSIPEE

25

109

Meredith

104

93

Lake
Winnipesaukee

Wolfeboro

Ossipee

16

Lake
Wentworth

Winnisquam
Lake

Laconia

11

Wakefield
Corner

106

WINNIPESAUKEE

Alton

Farmington

28

NEW HAMPSHIRE

MAINE

N

0   10 mi

0   10 km

Winnipesaukee

Memories of New Hampshire's early agriculture are displayed and used at the *New Hampshire Farm Museum* on Plummer's Ridge, just north of *Milton.* Housed in the state's best-preserved series of connected farm buildings (the house and barn are linked by a row of buildings and sheds to facilitate winter access and farm chores), the museum began as a simple collection of early implements. In addition to the house and barn (the latter is filled with fascinating old tools and equipment), there are blacksmith and cobbler shops. Next door is the Plummer homestead, an equally fine set of connected farm buildings, which has recently become part of this museum as an active, working farm. Together they give a rare picture of nineteenth-century farm life. Special weekend events illustrating early farm life include days featuring herbs, dairy farming, fibers, farm animals, and other subjects. The second Saturday in August is Old Time Farm Day, with more than sixty demonstrations of farming skills and crafts. Open May through Oct, Wed through Sun 10 a.m. to 4 p.m. Admission is $6 for adults, $3 for children. Write New Hampshire Farm Museum, Route 125, P.O. Box 644, Milton 03851; call (603) 652-7840 or visit www.farmmuseum.org.

For most of the nineteenth century, *Wakefield Corner* was an important stop on the route north, but then it lost its position to Sanbornville's rail junction. Since then, it has stayed so close to its nineteenth-century appearance that the entire village has been named a historic district. Its white wooden houses sit in gracious, fence-encircled yards, and features such as the hay scales and horse trough are still standing. A Rails-to-Trails project is in progress, converting the former rail bed into a hiking and biking path from Wakefield to Wolfeboro.

The *Wakefield Inn* is a three-and-a-half-story Federal-style inn. The rooms are large, airy, and beautifully decorated, all with private baths. Historical features such as original window glass, a three-sided fireplace, and Indian shutters make the inn as interesting as it is hospitable. John Greenleaf Whittier was a guest in 1891. Full-course dinners are served by reservation Friday and Saturday evenings and room rates are moderate. Write the inn at 2723 Wakefield Rd., Wakefield 03872; (603) 522-8272 or (800) 245-0841; www .wakefieldinn.com.

At the intersection of the village's main street with Route 16 is *Wakefield Marketplace,* a farmers' and crafts market open May through Oct, Sat, 9 a.m. to 3 p.m., and other times when produce is plentiful. For information call Ann Morgan at (603) 473-8762. You'll see the big tent beside the road. If you're heading south, take this turn into the village and continue on the recently designated scenic byway, along country roads shunpiking busy Route 16 from the *farmers' market* all the way to the New Hampshire Farm Museum in Milton.

Route 153 heads toward the Maine border, but just before reaching it at the shores of Province Lake, it passes through the settlement of Woodman, where *Woodman's Forge & Stove Museum* features antique woodstoves. If you're missing the lid-lifter or some other part for your own Glenwood or other antique stove, you're likely to find an original one for sale here, or you can browse among the latest technology in wood-burning in the large stove shop. Woodman's Forge & Stove Museum, Route 153, East Wakefield; call (603) 522-8216 or visit www.woodmanspartsplus.com. Despite all the lakes around, finding a public place to swim can be difficult. *Wentworth Park* on Route 109 between Wakefield and Wolfeboro is a small beach with bathhouses and a picnic area along its sandy shorefront. Nearby is the stone foundation and well of the summer estate of Benning Wentworth, first of New Hampshire's royal governors. This 100-by-40-foot structure, with stories 18 feet high and windows 6 feet tall, is thought to have been the first summer vacation "cottage" in America, built in 1768. Unfortunately, the estate burned not long after the Revolution. The focal point of this 96-acre site, open daily during summer, is Wentworth House's 40-by-101-foot cellar hole.

Across the street from the beach, there is a small granite marker at the beginning of *Ellie's Woodland Walk at Ryefield Marsh,* one of several walking trails and conservation areas of the Wolfeboro Conservation Commission. Five markers identify important environmental sites along the path, including a birch grove, meadow, beaver marsh, and the animals and plants that inhabit them. This is an easy, flat walk through a lowland area. The trail is open every day year-round. Close by the granite marker on Route 109 there is a black mailbox where you can pick up a map of the trail and an explanation of the markers.

The Wentworth Wives

It's easy to confuse the three Wentworths, all of them royal governors and all with a habit of marrying each others' widows, which muddies the waters even more. But Benning, the best known of them, married his housekeeper, much to the shocked surprise of his guests, at a dinner party celebrating his sixtieth birthday. He chose this occasion to announce his intentions, introduce his new love to New England society, and celebrate the wedding itself, catching the rector of St. John's Church, one of the dinner guests, quite by surprise as well.

For a short but beautiful side trip from Route 28 south of South Wolfeboro, take Robert's Cove Road west. The road passes between a handsome set of heavily built, new stone walls and provides a nice view of an arm of the lake. Wolfeboro's Main Street is busy in the summer, but there is a leisurely air here, with no traffic jams. Be sure to walk down Railroad Street and take a look at the restored railroad station where summer visitors once detrained. There's a parking lot here and, just beyond, the **Bridge Falls Walking Trail** follows the former rail bed to the falls section of town. Running 200 yards along the shore of Back Bay, this short and level walk leads to an area that was once used by water-powered mills. After crossing Route 109 (Center Street), the trail continues along the track as far as Sanbornville, but the track and ties have not been removed from a lot of the route, and the going on that side can get difficult.

At the falls, the **Wright Museum** brings memories of World War II to life for those who lived through it and puts flesh on the bones of history for those who don't remember it. The war's effect on the homefront is shown through vehicles, magazines, and even a soda fountain and a dentist's office, while another section exhibits military hardware, including tanks and half-tracks. They even have a Norden bombsight, one of the most secret devices of the war. A special section highlights the role of women in the military, including their little-known role as bomber ferry pilots. Open May through Oct, Mon to Sat 10 a.m. to 4 p.m. and Sun noon to 4 p.m. Admission is $6 for adults; children under eight are free. The museum is at 77 Center St. (Routes 28 and 109), Wolfeboro; (603) 569-1212; www.wrightmuseum.org.

Close to the Wright Museum is the **"Klickety Klack" Model Railroad,** a labor-of-love exhibit of model-train enthusiast Richard Peasley and friends. There are more than 1,000 feet of HO- and N-gauge track, with twenty-two trains coursing over the track, through the tunnels, and over the bridges. The track passes through realistic villages, over mountains, and through quarry and industrial sites both day and night. You can run eleven of the trains yourself, and signs point out special things in the layout. From Memorial Day to July 1 and from Labor Day through Dec, it's open Thurs, Fri, and Sat 10 a.m. to 5 p.m.; from July 1 to Labor Day, it's open Mon through Sat from 10 a.m. to 5:30 p.m. The museum sometimes also opens by appointment, and Richard says it's okay to call him at home. Admission is charged. From Route 109, take Route 109A (Elm Street) a few hundred feet; it's on the left at 8 Elm St., Wolfeboro; (603) 569-5384 or (603) 569-1275 (home).

Farther down Center Street is a spot that preserves the state's long boating heritage, with sleek mahogany Chris Crafts from the fifties and other classic craft such as Garwoods, Penn Yans, and others from earlier and later periods. On display at the **New Hampshire Boat Museum** are examples of small pleasure boats powered by the wind and gas engines, as well as models of watercraft. Many of the craft on display are on loan from their owners so the craft on exhibit provide a changing view of boating history. In addition to displays of recreational craft, a section devoted to boat racing has photographs and trophies from the heyday of lake racing. During the season they host an old boat regatta, a heritage boat auction, an antique car rally, and other activities. The museum shop is a good source of books on boating. Check the Web site for vintage boats for sale on the Trading Dock page. The museum also conducts youth, adult, and family boat building classes, women's kayak building classes, and even model sailboat building. Open Memorial Day through Columbus Day, Mon through Sat 10 a.m. to 4 p.m., Sun noon to 4 p.m. Admission is charged, discounts for seniors and kids. The museum is at 397 Center St. (Route 28), Wolfeboro; (602) 569-4554; www.nhbm.org.

Close to the museum is the entrance to another place for swimming, the **Allen A. Albee Town Beach,** on Lake Wentworth. You'll find the entrance road on the east side of Route 28 (109) just after the **Allen A. Motor Inn.**

Wolfeboro has a lot of opportunities for active recreation. If you like fishing, or think that you want to try it in a serious way, consider **Gadabout Golder,** which provides guided fishing trips around Lake Winnipesaukee and on the Pemigewasset, Little Swift, Bear Camp, and Connecticut Rivers. Their trips follow the season and may concentrate on salmon, pike, bass, trout, or any of the many other native species. They take experienced people and amateurs and offer fly-fishing as well. The half-day (four-and-a-half-hour) guided fishing trip includes all equipment and costs $260 for one person, $300 for two, and $390 for three people. The rates fluctuate with the program, destination, and species. They also do canoe trips, guided snowshoeing, nature walks, guided tracking trips, and ice fishing on the lake. A one-and-a-half-hour dawn lake cruise costs only $90 for up to three people. The company is at 79 Middleton Rd., Wolfeboro; (603) 569-6426 or www.gadaboutgolder.com.

The lakes region also offers lots of bicycling opportunities over terrain that can be hilly or hug the level shorelines. **Nordic Skier Sports** has good, recent-model bikes for rent at reasonable prices. They are at 19 North Main St., Wolfeboro; (603) 569-3151; www.nordicskiersports.com. In winter they offer 20 kilometers of well-groomed and tracked cross-country trails with lake views. This complete center also has lessons and equipment rentals, starting at $25 a day for mountain bikes.

There are a number of choices for hiking and walking in the area. The **Knight's Pond Conservation Area** features a 1.7-mile main trail, with a 0.3-mile option to the end of a peninsula. Along the way it passes around the sides of a beaver marsh and a thirty-one-acre pond that has not had any development. From the trail are views of Caverly Mountain, Rines Hill, and Mount Longstack. A trail map and directions are available at the information center at the intersection of Main Street and Routes 109 and 28. The center also has a sheet of information on more than a dozen hiking trails in the greater Wolfeboro area suitable for family outings.

The town also has an active musical-arts program that runs from the spring through the fall. Past programs have included choral works, ragtime, jazz, Gilbert and Sullivan, the New England Brass, and much more. There is at least one program a month. For information and reservations, write **Wolfeboro Friends of Music,** P.O. Box 2056, Wolfeboro 03894; call (603) 569- 2151 or visit www.wfriendsofmusic.org. Tickets are $18.

For a "lobster shack" feeling without traveling to the coast, seek out **Wolfetrap Grill and Raw Bar,** overlooking Back Bay, the lake, and the Belknap Range on the opposite shore. The long copper bar and the lobster tank provide most of the decor, but it's the fresh seafood you go there for. You can arrive on their vintage boat, which will transport you free from Wolfeboro's town dock. Open June through Labor Day only, Wolfetrap Grill and Raw Bar is at 19 Bay St.; (603) 569-1047; www.wolfetrap.com.

If you follow Main Street north along the shore of the lake, you will come to the **Libby Museum** (Route 109, 603-569-1035). The focus of the museum is natural history, and its exhibits include examples of many of the birds and animals native to the area. There is also a collection of Indian artifacts and items uncovered at excavations at the Wentworth mansion site. In addition to the exhibits, it conducts an Enviro-Arts Summer Program and periodic art exhibits in keeping with the museum's mission. It's open Tues through Sat 10 a.m. to 4 p.m. and Sun noon to 4 p.m. June to mid-Sept. Admission is $2 for adults, $1 for children ages five to twelve; www.wolfeboronh.us/Libby%20 Museum/index.htm.

The Wolfeboro Historical Society operates the **Clark House Museum Complex,** which includes a replica of a mid-nineteenth-century firehouse, an 1805 schoolhouse, and an eighteenth-century farmhouse. Open Wed through Fri 10 a.m. to 4 p.m. and Sat 10 a.m. to 2 p.m. in July and Aug. It's on South Main Street in Wolfeboro; call (603) 569-4997 or visit www.wolfeborohistorical society.org.

An interesting two-hour cruise of the islands on the east side of Lake Winnipesaukee stops at Wolfeboro on Tues, Wed, Fri, and Sat at 11:15 a.m. The captain of the **MV Doris E** points out interesting features on shore and enlivens the cruise with local stories and history. Light refreshments are available. The fare is $16 for adults and $8 for children. For details call (603) 366-2628 or visit www.cruisenh.com.

The **Abenaki Tower,** a little farther along Route 109 in Melvin Village, gives no clue to its origin except the date of its construction. This sturdy wooden structure puts you above the treetops for a 180-degree view over Lake Winnipesaukee and its wooded islands and bays. The Belknap Mountains back it to the south, and the Squam Range to the north. It's a short, easy walk and then a stiff climb, but the view is spectacular, especially at sunset. Notice the unusual raised lines on the boulder near the trail.

Overlooking Lake Winnipesaukee on the west side, **Gunstock Recreation Area** offers activities any time of year. In summer the campground is very popular because campers (as well as day visitors) can hike, ride horses, and enjoy archery, skateboarding, mountain boarding, mountain biking, paddleboats, or tubing. They even have dedicated skateboard and terrain parks.

Gunstock Mountain Resort is at the same time one of the oldest ski areas in the state and one of the newest. Back in the 1930s it came together as a project of the New Deal WPA at the urging of Belknap County officials. Over the years it has continually modernized, adding higher capacity lifts and improved snowmaking and grooming so that it is now one of the best-run ski areas. Its location, only a short ride from the Tilton exit off I-93, makes it a natural for skiers from the Boston and eastern Massachusetts markets and for south-central New Hampshire and southern Maine skiers. Since the beginning, however, there has been a close local connection leading to a strong commitment to ski education and producing one of the best ski schools.

In winter you'll find some of the nicest, friendliest skiing anywhere. The mountain has 1,400 feet of vertical rise, not the tallest but still challenging. It is hardly ever crowded, and its variety of slopes and the great old CCC lodge make it a good family area. Night skiing is offered on sixteen trails, and tubing is also open at night. Gunstock also has 50 kilometers of cross-country and snowshoe trails, and they offer a full rental and instruction facility, located separate from the alpine area. From I-93 use exit 20 and follow Route 3 (also Route 11) east, turning right onto the Route 11 Bypass. Follow the signs to Route 11A and Gunstock. For information call (800) GUNSTOCK or visit www .gunstock.com.

Lyons' Den, overlooking the Glendale marina, offers lake views and a changing menu with continental and New England influences. We like to share the appetizer sampler of grilled shrimp, stuffed mushroom caps, and crab cakes, but the fried calamari is a good option, delicately crisp on the outside, tender and flavorful inside. The chef's signature dish is boneless stuffed duck, slow roasted and juicy tender, but he also treats veal very well. The dessert menu is tempting, especially the tiramisu cake, alternating thin layers of fine white cake with tiramisu, served with whipped cream and rum sauce. Open

Wed through Sun 11:30 a.m. to 8 p.m. (until 9 p.m. on Fri and Sat). Lyons' Den is a little hard to find, but ask for directions to the Glendale Docks to locate 26 Dock Rd., Gilford; (603) 293-8833.

Also on the west side of the lake you will find some of the best ice cream in the state. Call ahead to reserve a table for teatime at *The Topiary at Owl's Rest Farm* in Sanbornton (603-934-3221, www.thetopiary.com). Freshly baked scones include lemon poppy seed, apricot almond, and orange cranberry and are served with Devonshire cream; tea sandwiches are in traditional combinations. Fine china and the floral works of these talented floral artists create the right mood, and tea in season includes a tour of the gardens, where you can wander on your own afterwards. Perennial flowers, herbs, and vegetables decorate the pastoral landscape, changing with the seasons from tulips, daffodils, and other spring bulbs to the asters and colorful foliage that highlight the gardens in September and October. Every Friday and Saturday from Thanksgiving until Christmas you can tour the twelve rooms of the nineteenth-century farmhouse, each decorated for the holidays. Refreshments are served and the shop is filled with floral and herbal gifts and holiday decorations. From exit 22 on I-93 follow Route 127 south, turning right on Prescott Road. When it ends, go left onto Brook Road, where Owl's Rest Farm is the second driveway on the left; (603) 934-3221; www.thetopiary.com.

Ossipee

Unlike New Hampshire's western border, where the Connecticut River makes a clean separation with Vermont, the border with Maine, north of Wakefield, is merely a surveyor's line. Roads and villages that grew up prior to this line sprawl and meander from one side to the other. Route 153 is one of these, not only a lovely road to travel but a good alternative for shunpikers seeking to avoid the traffic of Route 16. On its way to Conway, this road weaves through valleys and around the shores of little lakes. Province Lake nudges it over the line into Maine for a few miles until it reenters New Hampshire at South Effingham.

The Effinghams, and there are four of them, were once a very prosperous community based on a group of mills built along the Ossipee River in the 1820s. Center Effingham overlooks the road from a hill, with an imposing town hall that doubled as a Masonic lodge. That accounts for the emblem on the clock face. A Grange hall, a Baptist church at the foot of the hill, and several eighteenth- and nineteenth-century farmstead homes complete the historic village. Learn more about this surprising town's architecture at the *Effingham Historical Society,* whose free museum is open Tues and Thurs afternoons,

June through Oct. Effingham Historical Society, Route 153; call (603) 539-6715.

To the north is Effingham, also known as Lord's Hill. This cluster of early-nineteenth-century buildings includes a church, a 1780s hip-roofed house, and several impressive homes of 1820s origin. Just down from the crest of the hill is a road with a historic marker describing the Effingham Union Academy. A short distance up that road, set among manicured lawns and huge shade trees, is *Squire Lord's Mansion.* For its size and the quality of its architecture, this would be an impressive building in Portsmouth or Exeter. Here, come upon suddenly in such a rural setting, it is astonishing. Its three stories rise in clean lines, the eye drawn upward to the tall, octagonal, domed cupola. A Palladian window in the second floor surmounts the wide Federal doorway. No longer open for public tours, the mansion is now a private home. Please respect this and continue down the road a few yards to the Effingham Union Academy, on the right, to turn around. This stark building was erected in 1819 as a school but was reorganized in 1829 as New Hampshire's first "normal school," a teachers college, under the leadership of James W. Bradbury, a first in education.

For an unbeatable fall-foliage tour and a once-a-year chance to visit more than twenty such historic buildings, homes, and gardens that are not open to the public, reserve early for *Tour of the Towns,* usually held the first Saturday in October. A limited number of tickets are sold for $20 in advance or $25 the day of the tour, if any are left. The ticket includes admission to a Friday evening preview party, where a presentation about the sites helps you choose which to see. The tour sites vary from year to year but include the towns of Freedom, Effingham, Ossipee, Chocorua, Tamworth, and Wolfeboro. Past tours have included the Squire Lord's Mansion, an Italianate Masonic temple with trompe l'oeil murals, and several early homes with antique interiors. For information on obtaining tickets, write to Tour of the Towns, P.O. Box 2559, Conway 03818.

The town of *Freedom* lies along a small river, its two streets lined by fine homes, many with interesting decorative trim. On Maple Street is the *Freedom Historical Society,* which operates the Allard House and Works Museum on Old Portland Road. The Allard house collections include furnished rooms and the attached barn has collections of farming tools, and pre-motor vehicles and equipment. The house's Victorian parlor is particularly illustrative of life in these prosperous mill towns during their heyday, with its ornate fainting couch and stereoscope viewer. Open Memorial Day to Labor Day, Sat 10 a.m. to noon or by appointment; call David Buswell at (603) 539-6520 or visit www.freedomhistoricalsociety.com.

If you're staying at ***Purity Spring Resort*** (www.purityspring.com), you don't have to look for activities to keep your family busy, since each day at this casual family resort brings new activities, from a Monday-morning breakfast cooked over a campfire and a Thursday lobster-and-steak cookout on a private island to a Friday-night steamship smorgasbord. The dining room in the old-fashioned, American-plan resort offers a choice of five entrees each evening, always including a meatless alternative. Nonguests are welcome at meals—some families come every week for the lobster cookout, and reservations are highly recommended.

Everything here is included: day care, tennis, canoes, rowboats, and all outdoor activities, except an all-day canoe trip on the nearby Saco River. Grandparents who first came here as children are still returning to this comfortable, homey resort. It is also wheelchair accessible. Write them at 1251 Eaton Rd., Route 153, East Madison 03849; (603) 367-8896 or (800) 373-3754; www.purityspring.com.

Purity Spring Resort is on ***Purity Lake,*** and you don't have to be a guest there in order to explore this beautiful spot. It's surprising to discover that, although the lake stretches along a road, there is very little settlement around its shores. The pond is long (about a mile and a half), narrow, and fairly shallow at the edges, making it a great place for flat-water paddling.

Start at the south end at the intersection of Toll Hill Road. There you will see a grassy area with a path to the Audubon sanctuary. You will usually be able to drive up the path about 75 feet to the south end of the pond, next to the dam. Put in and paddle past Purity Spring Resort's beach. This is in a small pond, and at the end you will find a narrow, river-like, stretch of water that leads to the next pond. Watch for the kingfishers that guard this narrows. Along here on the right is an esker, a long ridge of sand and gravel deposited during the last ice age.

At the end of the esker, you will see an opening to the east, leading to a totally wild place with lots of wildlife. Even this close to a resort, there is not a sign of mankind. In places you will see bog plants, where a base of thick peat and sphagnum moss grows over the water and supports a number of plants on its surface. Look for pitcher plants, cotton grass, bog laurels, and other species of grasses and sedges. Along one shore is a big beaver lodge. You will also find a number of different bird species in this deep cove; the Audubon Society has placed duck houses here to encourage black ducks.

Back on the lake, follow along the undeveloped east shore to a secluded cove at the far end. There are some nice marshy areas to explore here, too.

To reach Purity Lake from the south on Route 16, take Route 25 east in Ossipee, just south of Ossipee Lake. When you reach Effingham Falls, take Route 153 north to Purity Lake. From Conway take Route 153 south.

King Pine Ski Area, just up the road, is small, but it has trails for those of all skill levels. Six trails and slopes are lighted for night skiing. Facilities are up to date, but prices are old-fashioned and made even better with joint ski-lodging packages with Purity Spring. A complete ski school and the relaxed atmosphere of King Pine make it a particular favorite of families. It's located on Route 153 in East Madison; call (603) 367-8896 or (800) 373-3754, or visit www.kingpine.com.

The *Madison Boulder,* off Route 113 between Conway and *Madison,* is the largest known example of a glacial erratic in New England and one of the largest in the world. Enormous freestanding boulders are not uncommon in New Hampshire, but none even approaches the size of this 83-foot, 5,000-ton giant. This is not just another big rock. Such erratics were broken from large outcrops of granite by glaciers, then carried away and dropped in spots sometimes several miles distant. This one is thought to have come from cliffs about 4 miles away, but some geologists believe it came from Mount Willard, 25 miles north in Crawford Notch.

One beautiful way to see the White Mountains is from the saddle of a bike. Whether it is in spring, summer, or foliage season, this is one way to connect to the land. *Bike the Whites* has tours of the region throughout the season at prices starting at $299 in May and rising to $499 in the fall. Beginning on Sunday, these three-day tours include lodging, breakfasts and dinners, maps with points of interest noted, luggage transfers, transportation to the starting point, and emergency assistance if needed en route. Other itineraries can be arranged. For information call (877) 854-6535 or visit www.bikethewhites.com.

Overlooking the postcard-perfect Crystal Lake in "downtown" Eaton, the *Inn at Crystal Lake* looks exactly like what it is—a hostelry that has welcomed travelers to this tiny village since the 1880s. Its three layers of porches, rows of rockers, and columned façade mark it even before you see the sign. Inside this period piece, simply furnished rooms are comfortable and breakfasts delicious. The pub serves hearty dishes such as shepherd's pie. Unique in New Hampshire is the live opera that accompanies the inn's monthly opera nights, held on the fourth Thursday of the month from September through May. These are so popular that advance reservations are essential to get a table. Discussions, illustrated by recordings and live singing by innkeeper Tim Ostendorf, cover operas that are announced in advance, so you can choose a favorite. The program is included with a four-course dinner and a glass of wine. Ostendorf trained as an opera singer and has sung professionally. The chef creates each dinner menu to fit the featured opera. The dining room and pub are open Tues through Sun, 5 to 8:30 p.m. The inn is on Route 153, Eaton Center; (603) 447-2120 or (800) 343-7336; www.innatcrystallake.com.

Around the corner from the inn, the ***Eaton Village Store*** faces the lake. Along with being the general store and community gathering spot, it also serves a good lunch. Eaton Village Store, Route 153, Eaton; call (603) 447-2403 or visit www.evps.org.

White Lake State Park packs three attractions into one compact park that surrounds a crystal-clear lake. The lake's swimming beach stretches along one end, with the rest of the shore bordered by trees. A walking trail encircles its perimeter, a campground offers well-spaced sites under tall pine trees, and the forest floor is padded by a soft carpet of pine needles. Across the lake is a stand of pitch pines that have been declared a national natural landmark. Close to the northern tip of their range, the pitch pines here are especially large, which indicates age, but they are hard to date because they don't grow even rings for each year's growth. Pitch pine trees have difficulty reproducing except after a forest fire, since their cones need the heat to spring them open and release the seeds. Open from the end of May to Columbus Day, White Lake is in Tamworth; call (603) 323-7350 or visit www.nhstateparks.org. A day-use fee of $4 is charged, ages six to twelve $3, under age six and New Hampshire residents over sixty-five admitted free.

Another interesting pine-forest environment is located a short distance away along the road between Silver Lake and ***West Ossipee.*** The ***West Branch Pine Barrens,*** part of which is owned by The Nature Conservancy, is considered one of the world's finest examples of pine barrens. Its layer of birch and scrub oak grows under a canopy of pitch pine, with blueberry bushes closer to the ground. The barrens is home to several rare moth varieties that feed on its trees.

Tamworth doctor Edwin C. Remick joined his father's practice, which had begun in 1894, and continued it until his own death in 1993, missing a round century by less than a year. When he died he left the family farm, dating from the late 1700s, to the town as the ***Remick Country Doctor Museum and Farm.*** Much of the interest of the museum, which includes two homes, barns, and outbuildings, is its emphasis on how the traditional country doctor grew vegetables and kept livestock just like his neighbors. The interplay between the two themes—medicine and farming—keeps the Remick property lively.

Two doctors' offices show the two generations at work, and a fascinating set of photographs and artifacts discusses topics from World War II to how the doctors reached patients' homes in the winter. During special events, the farm is abuzz with activity: butter churning, cheese and sauerkraut making, sledge rides behind a team of draft horses, barn tours, a chance to use a corn sheller, and blacksmithing demonstrations.

Tamworth is west of Route 16. The Remick Country Doctor Museum and Farm (58 Cleveland Hill Rd.) is open Mon through Fri 10 a.m. to 4 p.m. year-round. July through Oct it is also open on Sat and occasionally on Sun of special-event weekends. Admission is $3. For information call (603) 323-7591 or (800) 686-6117, or visit www.remickmuseum.org.

Across the street from the museum stretches the friendly clapboard façade of the *Inn at Tamworth.* The inn has been welcoming guests to its comfortable rooms and dining room for many years, and its dining room has quickly made its way to the upper ranks of area restaurants. Interesting and innovative dishes depend on locally grown and raised products whenever possible. But those who long for their old favorite country-inn dishes will also find them on this menu, sharing space with the more updated and stylish treatments. The wine list is of extraordinary quality, but with surprisingly reasonable prices. On evenings when the Barnstormers are performing at the summer theater just down the street, it's wise to time your reservations after their 8 p.m. curtain time. Before that the kitchen is scrambling to get everyone served and to the show on time; after 8 p.m. it may have run out of one of the evening's specials, but the pace will be more relaxed, and the ambience quieter. The dining room is open Tues through Sat for dinner. If you arrive early for dinner or are staying at the inn, stop for a glass of wine in the friendly little pub, where the walls are decorated with vintage wooden skis, snowshoes, and sleds—it's a fine collection. Guest rooms upstairs are freshly redecorated but remain moderately priced at $115 to $300 on highest peak weekends. You can't miss the inn on Main Street, Tamworth; (603) 323-7721 or (800) 642-7352; www.innat tamworth.com.

Something Was Missing

On an October morning in 1915, as she was hanging out her daily laundry, a woman glanced up at the mountain that she had looked at every morning since she could remember. But something was different about the familiar view of Mount Chocorua. The white two-story house that stood just below the summit seemed to have disappeared overnight.

Peak House, built in 1884, was an inn for climbers, anchored firmly (or so its owner thought) by chains to the surrounding rock of Chocorua's barren summit. But an October gale ripped the chains loose and literally blew the house away, scattering it board by board all over the craggy slope. Only bits and pieces of either the house or its contents were found. It was never rebuilt, but the Jim Liberty shelter for hikers was later built near the site.

Dreamworks Antiques and Collectibles shares a pretty little cottage near the crossroads with ***Grammy Gordon's Bakery,*** and the combination encourages enjoying a cup of tea or coffee while browsing. The bakery case is always full of fresh-made scones, cookies, bars, and whoopee-pies, and the bakery has a menu of meals to take home ready-to-eat, a nice option for cottage vacationers or those considering a picnic dinner. Grammy Gordon's caters especially to those with gluten intolerance, vegetarians, and other food preferences. Grammy Gordon's Bakery, 29 Tamworth Rd., Tamworth; (603) 323-2005. Climb out of town on Cleveland Road, past the Remick Museum, to find a most unusual monument beside the stone enclosure of the 1801 ***Town Pound.*** There, atop a large glacial erratic boulder, is a memorial to Tamworth's first minister, who was ordained on top of the boulder. You'll have to climb the 17 steps to the top to read about it.

Just north of the village of Choc-orua, you'll see a sign for the ***River-bend Inn*** on the west side of Route 16. Although only a short distance from the traffic, it seems to be deep in the woods. The inn overlooks a deep curve in the Chocorua River, and in good weather guests have breakfast outside on a ter-race that extends out over the riverbank. The inn is as lovely as its setting, with richly decorated guest rooms in deep jewel colors. Gregarious owners Jerry Weiss and Craig Cox have furnished the public rooms with wood carvings and other art from their extensive travels. A library of well-chosen books on a variety of subjects tempts guests to curl

they're smaller now

The snowmobile was invented by Virgil White, longtime owner of White's Garage, a familiar land-mark in West Ossipee, where more than 20,000 of these were made between 1913 and 1929. They worked on two axles of rear wheels joined by caterpillar trac-tion, fitted onto a Ford chassis with two runners on the front; he patented the name, along with the machine.

up and read in front of the fireplace or on the terrace overlooking the river. Several special package weekends are available, such as one that includes kayak or canoe rental and transport. Write to the inn at P.O. Box 288, Route 16, Chocorua 03817; call (603) 323-7440 or (800) 628-6944. You can see pictures of the rooms at www.riverbendinn.com.

The distinctive silhouette of ***Mount Chocorua*** is probably the state's most photographed view. Not only is it a perfectly shaped mountain, but it rises alone, and at its feet is a lake placed like a looking-glass to reflect it. Behind the lake rises a hill, and as Route 16 drops over the crest, travelers are treated to a view, across an open field, of the mountain and lake. Below, just at the foot of the hill, a left turn takes you to the shore of the lake, where there are parking spaces and benches under a stand of giant red pines.

Chocorua offers more to travelers than its pretty face. Several trails ascend to its rocky peak, one of the most satisfying to reach, since it really is pointed on top. (So many mountains are really quite flat at the summit, even though they appear to form a point.) The easiest climb is via the Piper Trail, which begins on the left side of Route 16, not far north of Chocorua Lake. A tougher climb, but also very scenic, is the Champney Falls Trail, which begins from Route 112, the Kancamagus Highway, not far west of Rocky Gorge. A short distance up (straight up, it often seems) is Champney Falls, at their best in the spring or after a heavy rain.

Don't be put off by the fear of looking like the two fat pink pigs on the sign of The *Yankee Smokehouse* at the intersection of Routes 16 and 25 in West Ossipee. This is an authentic open-pit barbecue, one of the few in New England. The service is so unremittingly cheerful and eager here that it reminds us of Disney World. Servers describe each specialty and suggest the best deal. "You'll get more of the same thing for less money by ordering the sampler for one and splitting it," our waiter once advised us after mentally totting up our order. Beef or pork ribs or slices, chicken, and delicious baby back pork ribs are their specialties, but you can have the sliced smoked beef or pork in a sandwich or the chicken made into a wonderful smoked salad. Don't miss the corn chowder (it's unlikely that your waiter will allow you to order a meal without it), which is solid with chunks of potato, bacon, and corn, seasoned with herbs and plenty of pepper. You can roll up your sleeves and eat until you can't hold another bite and still have trouble making the bill come out to $12 each. If you have a group of at least eight, order the Smokehouse Feast for $56.99. It says on the menu that it feeds four to six, but it's enough for a regiment on the march. Open 11:30 a.m. to 9 p.m. daily all year, except Apr and from mid-Nov to mid-Dec; (603) 539-RIBS; www.yankeesmokehouse.com.

South of the Yankee Smokehouse on Route 16, a former state fish hatchery has been converted to *Sumner Brook Fish Farm.* Fly-fishing enthusiasts can practice their skills in the pond on a catch-and-release basis, or those who prefer can catch their supper at 30 cents an inch. The farm also sells trout or will stock your own pond. Open weekends spring and fall, daily Memorial Day through Labor Day; (603) 539-7232.

The Sandwiches

Some of New Hampshire's quirky private museums—collections gathered over the years by people with a particular hobby or interest—have signs by the roadside inviting people in, and some don't. Even when you're in the **Old Country Store** (603-476-5750; www.nhcountrystore.com), at the crossroads of Routes 25 and 109 in Moultonborough, you might not notice the sign by the stairs pointing to the museum. The whole upper floor is filled with local history—saws, axes, and other tools; a wooden snow shovel; blacksmithing tools; maple-sugaring equipment; advertising cards; cigar-store Indians; yarn winders—neatly labeled, often in some detail. Much of what is up there was probably sold downstairs when it was new. The building and the store are believed to date from the late eighteenth century. There is no curator and no charge; you just wander around at your leisure. You might want to show your appreciation by taking home some common crackers or some cheddar cheese from the wheel in the glass case downstairs or stopping for a Moxie or a cream soda from the big old ice chest, but everybody's very pleasant even if you don't buy anything. Outside in the barn, and visible from outside through a large window, is an original Concord coach that is thought to be the oldest Concord-built stagecoach in existence.

DDT and other pesticides of the last century, as well as increased pressure from the growing popularity of lakes as recreational assets, almost led to the extinction of the American loon. These beautiful birds with their black heads, red eyes, and gray-and-white-striped breasts are perhaps best known for their plaintive cry in the evening. The **Loon Center** and **Markus Wildlife Sanctuary** have the dual mission of creating a habitat for the protection and propagation of the species and teaching the public about the birds and the impact of human activity on their welfare. Displays and materials in the center teach about the birds. Outside is the sanctuary, covering 200 acres of rare wilderness land on the shores of Lake Winnipesaukee. The Loon Nest Trail travels through the forest to the shore of the lake. It then follows along the shore, passing among huge glacial erratics left here in the last ice age, and continuing into a marsh where the loons nest. The Forest Walk Trail is another pleasant option for a walk in the woods. A gift shop features loon material, of course, including framed photos, carved decoys, and books and pottery with a loon motif. From Route 25 in Moultonborough, take Blake Road at the Central School, following signs for The Loon Center. At the end of the road, turn right onto Lee's Mill Road and look for the center on the left. It is an Audubon sanctuary and is free to the public. Open Mon through Sat 9 a.m. to 5 p.m. year-round and the same hours on Sun in July and Aug. Visit the center at www.loon.org/facilities.html.

The village of Center Sandwich is largely made up of houses built in the first half of the nineteenth century. The houses are clustered into a handful of tree-lined streets, an open invitation to stroll through town. Along with the

Get Your Big Foot Out of My Sandwich

Hollis is not alone as a sighting spot for Sasquatch. In the area around Sandwich—Mount Israel and Sandwich Dome—there have been reports since the early 1940s, and they have even been backed up by 3-foot-long footprints, four-toed and claw-less like other Big Foot tracks recorded, in the mud beside the road. Recent reports on file with the state police all describe a fur-covered creature about 8 feet tall. Everyone agrees that however startled and alarmed they were, Big Foot seemed just as frightened and ran into the woods immediately.

antiques and craft shops, be sure to stop at the *Sandwich Historical Society Museum.* Its furnishings include a kitchen, household implements, and a wide variety of artifacts from the town's eighteenth-century beginnings through the early twentieth century. Open late June to early Oct, Tues through Sat 10 a.m. to 4 p.m. There is a $3 suggested donation. The museum, at 4 Maple St., has events throughout the summer and fall. Call (603) 284-6269 or visit www .sandwichhistorical.org.

Follow Grove Street and then bear left at road signs for *Sandwich Notch.* It is reached by a gravel road that is not maintained for winter use. The stone walls beside it once outlined the fields of farms now overgrown into forests. A cart track, the road was put through the notch in 1801 as a route for north country farmers to get their produce to the markets of Portsmouth and Portland and return with supplies and goods not made on their own farms. Later bypassed by other routes, the road through this notch has not changed very much for the past century and a half.

A parking area on the right marks the short trail to *Beede's Falls.* Where the trail meets the river, an island cuts the river into two small channels. To the right, the water slides over ledges and drops in a series of cascades into a moss-lined pool below. The wooded area at the bottom is surrounded by a tumble of boulders, some of which form caves and crevices. If you go upstream along the island, you will see the brook rushing through a foot-wide shoot. A short distance above that, the river flows down a ledge and then drops 40 feet into a sandy pool. More rocks lie in giant tumbles here, too. Some of these overhang enough to form a cave that, legend has it, sheltered a stray cow for an entire winter. Above the main falls there are two more cascades. Because there are no signs here, it would be easy to miss the main falls to the left and to assume the cascades downstream to be Beede's Falls.

Not far up the road, between two bridges over the Bearcamp River, is a cliff shaped like the prow of a ship. Called *Pulpit Rock,* it was used as a pulpit by a long-ago Quaker pastor. The head of the notch, 7 miles from the center of Center Sandwich Village, is marked by a small sign high up on a tree and not easy to see. For a well-written history of the notch, read *The Road Through Sandwich Notch* by Elizabeth Yates.

There are more entrees on the daily special blackboard at the **Corner House** (603-284-6219) in Center Sandwich than most restaurants have on their printed menus. These dishes allow the chef to take advantage of ingredients with short seasons and the chance to serve his latest original dish. This might be a double lamb chop stuffed with a blend of ricotta, parmesan, and spinach. The printed menu is not ho-hum either, with such offerings as medallions of chicken breast stuffed with ham and artichoke hearts or veal smothered in chunks of lobster with broccoli and béarnaise sauce. A grinding of nutmeg on the cappuccino tops off a fine dinner here. Prices are moderate; lunch (try the crab cakes) and dinner daily and Sunday brunch are served year-round. Visit the restaurant's Web site at www.cornerhouseinn.com.

At the edge of the village on the road to North Sandwich, the Quimby Barn is the home of town's Concord Coach. **Sandwich Creamery,** in North Sandwich, isn't a place you will stumble upon, unless you are a really dedicated backroad follower. But it's worth looking for this dairy farm of placid cows that produce the milk and cream for a cave-full of farmstead cheeses: aged or smoked cheddar, Caerphilly, Coulommier, Jersey jack, brie, and several fresh soft cheese spreads. It's the ice cream they're best known for, creamy and rich, made with fresh local peaches, berries, maple syrup, and even pumpkin in season. We like the black raspberry with chocolate chips and the black currant sorbet. The door is always open, so if you crave a pint of ginger ice cream at 7 a.m., you can get it from this honor-system dairy. Picnic tables in the yard invite you to sit right there and eat it from the box as you watch the butterflies play in the flower garden. To get there from Route 113A, turn onto Wing Road, going right onto Hannah Road. As you go down the hill you will see the creamery on the left. Sandwich Creamery is on Hannah Road in North Sandwich; (603) 284-6675; www.sandwichcreamery.com.

Squam

The quiet of **Squam Lake** is almost legendary. Its irregular shape, with bays, inlets, and islands, makes it virtually impossible for power boats to get up any speed, so there is very little to disturb the loons that nest here. Cottages along the shore are tucked behind the trees, giving it the feel of a wilderness lake.

Squam, along with Winnipesaukee, is one of the best landlocked salmon lakes in the state. Squam is a gem of a lake with nesting loons, and **Science**

Center Lake Cruises has ninety-minute boat tours that showcase the high points. Explorer Cruises depart daily late May to mid-June at 1 p.m., and from mid-June to mid-Oct daily at 11 a.m., 1 p.m., and 3 p.m. from the docks on Route 3 in downtown Holderness. From July through mid-Oct there is also a Nature of the Lakes Tour led by a naturalist at 4 p.m. on Tues, Wed, and Thurs. A Loon Cruise is added on Fri from mid-June through mid-Sept at 3 p.m., led by a naturalist from the Loon Preservation Society. The fare is $12 for all passengers. For more information contact the science center at (603) 968-7194; www.nhnature.org/.

A group of businesses in Holderness has prepared maps of summer and winter recreational routes showing mountain bike and hiking trails, and snowmobile and cross-country trails, respectively. You can get a copy from most businesses in town or from Squam Lakes Association (Box 204, Route 3, Holderness 03245; 603-968-7336; www.squamlakes.org), or Riverside Cycles (Route 3, Ashland 03217; 603-968-9676). The association also has boat rentals at it headquarters on Route 3 and manages twelve remote unserviced campsites on islands in the lake and in a forest preserve. Camping is also available at the Mead Conservation Center in Sandwich Notch. Check the Web site for details on the camp sites.

The *Manor on Golden Pond* is a romantic lodging choice with its broad lake and mountain views. It started life as the country retreat of Florida real-estate magnate Isaac Van Horn in 1907 but has spent much of its existence as a manor-house inn. The rooms are beautifully decorated in a style that matches the elegance of the home, but with easy comfort in mind. The inn has its own dining room, and six times a year the inn's chef has specially themed cooking lessons. Packages are available. The manor is on Route 3, Holderness; (603) 968-3348 or (800) 545-2141; www.manorongoldenpond.com.

In 1897 two summer encampments were started on the shores of Squam Lake, one Rockywold and the other Deephaven. Over the years, the tent platforms became cabins and the two camps one, now *Rockywold-Deephaven Camps,* but the magic remains. They don't advertise and families have returned here for generations. Rustic wooden cabins, many with fireplaces, sit spaced among tall pines and granite outcrops on trails over a peninsula jutting into the lake. Meals are family style in one of two large, open wooden dining halls. Ice cut on the pond over the winter and stored in an old-fashioned ice house is delivered to each cabin daily, along with firewood. Check their Web site to watch a video of the ice harvest from Squam Lake. Two libraries and lodges also serve the campers. This is an authentic, old-fashioned family camping experience, a treasure that we thought had left with the fifties. If you want modern conveniences, creature comforts, and speedboats, don't even think about this place. If you want peace, camaraderie, connection with nature, and space for thought, you'll find it here. Call or write them for rates and family packages; it's all by reservation. Cottages average $2,500 per week for two persons. The address is Rockywold-Deephaven Camps, P.O. Box B, Holderness 03245; (603) 968-3313; www.rdcsquam.com.

One of the nicest views in the lakes region is reached by a gentle climb up *West Rattlesnake Mountain,* just east of Rockywold-Deephaven. All you snake lovers out there will want to know that it overlooks Rattlesnake Cove on Squam Lake, but there's no recorded history of rattlesnakes at either of them. A bit over 5 miles east of Holderness on Route 113, look for a parking area on the north (left) side of the road. You have to park here, even though the trailhead is a five-minute walk back along Route 113. The Old Bridle Path leaves from the opposite (south) side of the road, easy to follow as it climbs at a gentle grade. The only fork is well marked to the left. Although this is an easy climb for children, be aware that the view is from the top of steep ledges, not a place for untethered small-fry.

The *Squam Lakes Natural Science Center* on Route 113 in Holderness encourages visitors to explore six different natural communities along its exhibit trail. Signs and staff members explain the ecosystems of the marsh, field, pond, stream, forest, and lake, showing how plants and animals live together in each setting. Signboards explore such questions as "If the marsh were drained, who would suffer?" The marsh community is reached by a boardwalk, often covered with little bodies lying on their stomachs watching painted turtles, leopard frogs, and trout below. Birds are everywhere, perched on fences or signposts or darting among trees. The setting is attractive and well maintained, a good way to understand the woods, fields, and waters as you travel around the state. Young travelers will enjoy the Children's Activity Center, where they can descend into a groundhog hole, climb a giant spiderweb, or invent an insect of their own design. The Science Center is open May through Oct 9:30 a.m. to 4:30 p.m.; last admission at 3:30 p.m. Adults $13 (ages sixteen to sixty-four), seniors (sixty-five and older) $11, ages three to fifteen $9. For a calendar of the science center's many special events, write P.O. Box 173, Holderness 03245; call (603) 968-7194 or visit www.nhnature.org.

Kirkwood Gardens is a one-acre garden at the western side of the historic Holderness Inn, a building listed on the National Register of Historic Places, but currently in use as Squam Lake Artisans Gallery, filled with high-quality local crafts. A bluestone terrace overlooks a garden of ferns, one to attract butterflies and another with a fountain and native shrubs chosen to attract birds. You can also reach the gardens on trails from the Squam Lakes

Natural Science Center. Admission to the garden is free, and it is located on Route 3 in Holderness; (603) 968-7194.

Anyone interested in art will want to stop in Meredith to see *The Old Print Barn*, one of the largest galleries in New England dedicated primarily to prints. Their collection includes more than 2,000 graphics from the United States and Europe, covering the period from the eighteenth century to the present. Media include all techniques: lithograph, metal plate, woodblock, linoleum, and photography.

The gallery started life as a nineteenth-century barn but has been artfully remade into a series of mini-galleries to better showcase the prints. Their New Hampshire pieces include works of the nineteenth-century artists W. H. Bartlett and William Oakes. The Old Print Barn has put together an illustrated paperback book entitled *New Hampshire's First Tourists in the Lakes and Mountains*, which uses reprints of antique materials to tell the story of the birth of the tourism industry in the state. More contemporary works of New Hampshire artists include those of wood engraver Herbert Waters, considered to be one of the top ten in the country. Their European collection includes older works of Manet, Piranesi, Delacroix, Lalanne, Legros, and Daumier, as well as works by newer artists such as Joop Vegter, Pino Finocciaro, Fulvio Ara, and contemporary Egyptian and Chinese prints.

In addition to their prints, the print barn has a collection of nineteenth- and twentieth-century oil paintings that can be seen upon request. These works include some by Benjamin Champney, one of the earliest New Hampshire painters of the White Mountains.

Riding Rails in the Lakes Region

Wide-open lake vistas mark the route of the *Winnipesaukee Scenic Railroad*. On its regular one- and two-hour trips between Meredith and Weirs Beach the train is rarely out of sight of the lake as it travels along the tree-lined shore, making it especially appealing in the autumn foliage. Along with these daily runs, longer trips during foliage season cover sections of rail that are rarely seen. On weekends in October a train makes the four-hour round trip from Meredith to Livermore Falls in Campton, north of Plymouth. This route climbs over a hill to Ashland, where the old rail station has been restored. It then follows the Pemmigewasset Valley northward, crossing the river on a three-span bridge and providing views of waterfalls and rapids, as well as long vistas of the valley framed by red maple hillsides. At Livermore, the river flows through a deep canyon, where an old bridge framed in foliage begs for photos. A buffet lunch is served in the historic Plymouth railway station and is included in the ticket price. Contact the Winnipesaukee Scenic Railroad at (603) 279-5253 or www.foliagetrains.com.

ALSO WORTH SEEING IN THE LAKES REGION

MS *Mount Washington,*
(603) 366-5531.
Cruises depart Weirs Beach two or three times daily, May through Oct, calling at Wolfeboro, Center Harbor, and Alton Bay. Evening cruises offer dinner and dancing to live music.

Winnipesaukee Scenic Railroad,
(603) 279-5253.
Carries passengers along the scenic shore between the stations in Meredith and Weirs Beach for two-hour rides, leaving at 10:30 a.m., 12:30 p.m., and 2:30 p.m., with a one-hour tour leaving at 4:30 p.m., May through Oct.

The gallery is also engaged in the sale of estate art and as such often has private collections on view and for sale. As one would expect, these change frequently. The Old Print Barn also provides authentication, evaluation, restoration, and framing services. From Route 104 in Meredith, take Winona Road north at the traffic light (look for White Mountain Orthopedic) about 2 miles, following signs. It is open daily 10 a.m. to 5 p.m. all year, closing only on Thanksgiving and Christmas; (603) 279-6479; www.lakesregion.org/oldprint barn/. You will need to make an appointment for appraisal or other services.

Ashland has a trio of small museums—quite an accomplishment for a town of its size. The ***Whipple House Museum*** is a home built in 1837 and occupied by the same family until the 1970s, at 14 Pleasant St., just off Main Street (Route 3). It is open July through Labor Day, Wed through Sat 1 to 4 p.m. The ***Pauline Glidden Toy Museum*** is an 1810 cape displaying a collection of more than 2,000 antique toys, including dolls, miniatures, games, trains, and books. It is entered from the Whipple House and open the same hours (and sometimes more frequently). The third is the ***Ashland Railroad Station Museum,*** an 1869 station, one of the state's best preserved. In it are collections relating to rail history, and it is open July and Aug, Sat 1 to 4 p.m.; www .oldashlandnh.org/Ash01.htm. The Glidden Museum charges a $1 admission, but the other two are free. All are run by the Ashland Historical Society, P.O. Box 175, Ashland 03217; www.oldashlandnh.org.

More Places to Stay in the Lakes and Foothills

ALTON BAY

Lakehurst Cottages
9 McKone Lane
(603) 875-2492
www.lakehurstcottages
.com
Available May and June by
the night; July, Aug, and
Sept by the week only.
Nice, well-kept cottages
on the water. Reservations
suggested, heavily booked.
One bedroom $864/week
(sleeps four); two bed-
rooms $918/week (sleeps
six).

FREEDOM

**Freedom House Bed and
Breakfast**
17 Old Portland Rd.
(603) 539-4815
www.freedombb.com
A beautifully restored Victorian home in the center

of the village, open year-
round.

HOLDERNESS

The Inn on Golden Pond
Route 3, P.O. Box 680
(603) 968-7269
www.innongoldenpond
.com
Beautiful inn/B&B accom-
modations overlooking the
lake in an 1879 farmhouse.
Expensive, lower off-sea-
son; including full breakfast.

Squam Lake Inn
Shepard Hill Rd.
(603) 968-4417, outside
New
Hampshire (800) 839-6205
www.squamlakeinn.com
Elegant country inn in the
Victorian style. Expensive,
includes full breakfast and
afternoon tea.

LACONIA

Lake Opechee Inn
62 Doris Ray Court
(603) 524-0111
(877) 300-5253
www.opecheeinn.com
The newly renovated mill

building overlooks Lake
Opechee, and along with
the spa the inn has thirty-
four individually decorated
guest rooms with fire-
places. Many rooms have
balconies with lake views
and double whirlpool tubs.
Expensive, packages and
spa packages available,

MOULTONBOROUGH

Olde Orchard Inn
Lee Rd.
(603) 476-5004 or
(800) 598-5845
www.oldeorchardinn.com
A 1700s Federal home with
attractive rooms. Moderate
to expensive.

WOLFEBORO

**Tuc-Me-Inn Bed and
Breakfast**
118 North Main St.
(603) 569-5702
www.tucmeinn.com
Comfortable, seven rooms,
in town location with free
WiFi. Expensive, less
off-season; including full
breakfast.

TO LEARN MORE ABOUT THE LAKES REGION

**Greater Ossipee Chamber of
Commerce,**
Routes 16 and 25W,
West Ossipee 03890;
(603) 539-6201 or (866) 683-6295;
www.ossipeevalley.org.

Squam Lakes Association,
Route 3, Holderness 03245;
(603) 968-7336; www.squamlakes.org.

Wolfeboro Chamber of Commerce,
32 Central Ave.,
Wolfeboro 03894;
(603) 569-2200 or (800) 516-5324;
www.wolfeboroonline.com/chamber.

More Places to Eat in the Lakes and Foothills

ASHLAND

The Common Man
Route 3
(603) 968-7030
Right in the center of town, with a dependable and varied lunch and dinner menu; moderate prices.
For other dining options, see Plymouth, in The Dartmouth-Sunapee Region chapter.

MOULTONBOROUGH

The Woodshed
Lee Rd.
(603) 476-2311
www.thewoodshed restaurant.com
Best known for its prime rib and lamb and for its breads; moderate to expensive prices.

WEST OSSIPEE

Purity Spring Resort has a dining room open to the public.

Whittier House Restaurant
Route 16
(603) 539-4513
A bright and airy dining room serving lunch and dinner daily at moderate prices.

WOLFEBORO

El Centenario
14 Union St.
(603) 569-3445
Serves authentic Mexican dishes (not Tex-Mex).

Dockside Grille
11 Dockside St.
(603) 569-1910
Seafood platters, burgers, and more, open all year.

The Morrissey's Front Porch
286 South Main St.
(603) 569-3662
A family restaurant and ice cream bar, serving three meals daily Apr through Dec.

THE EASTERN WHITE MOUNTAINS

The **White Mountains** are the stuff of native legend and settlers' folktales, of larger-than-life explorers and pioneers. Until the discovery of Crawford Notch, these mountains presented a barrier that kept the lands to the north in isolation.

In the nineteenth century they were "discovered" again, this time by wealthy families from the cities escaping the heat and dust. With maids, nannies, and enormous trunks, entire families boarded trains in New York, New Haven, Boston, Hartford, and other cities bound for Jackson, Glen, Twin Mountain, and Bretton Woods. Hotels sent elegant Concord coaches, resplendent in canary yellow or cherry red with gold-leaf scrollwork, to welcome guests. They stayed all summer, hiking, riding, swimming (called bathing), playing lawn sports, and dancing to a full orchestra every evening. This annual social season lasted until World War II and the invention of air-conditioning. Now most of the grand hotels are gone, but the few that remain have retained the fine traditions that made them famous in their golden age.

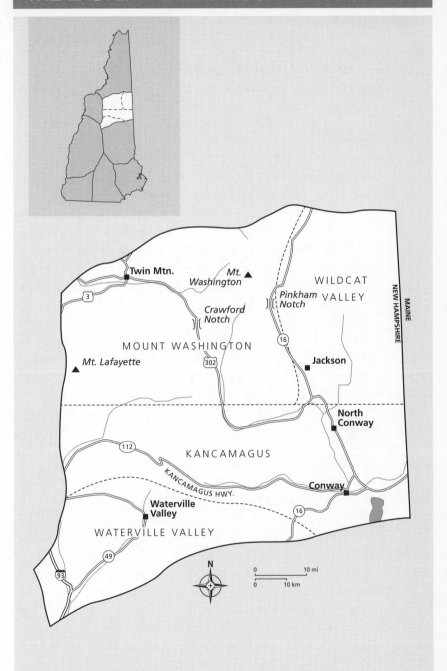

Waterville Valley

Waterville Valley is a cul-de-sac cut deep into the White Mountain National Forest. Route 49 follows the Mad River, which is really quite benign except in the spring, when it carries the runoff from a vast watershed and pours it into the Pemigewasset River. After 12 miles of narrow wooded passage, the valley opens suddenly into a broad floor of fields and a resort village reminiscent of an Alpine ski town.

During the 1960s the little town of Waterville Valley became known as a purpose-built resort with all-season facilities and as the occasional playground of the Kennedy family and other well-known celebrities. Since then the resort has continued to grow into a mature and well-designed operation, offering year-round sports, from skiing and skating to mountain biking and hiking.

The **Waterville Valley Resort** ski area covers one of the largest areas in New Hampshire, with more than 255 skiable acres on fifty-two trails. The vertical on this big hill is more than 2,000 feet, making it one of the highest in the state, and one of the trails is almost 3 miles long, perfect for cruising. As with most of the true resorts, lodging is available close to the slopes and a regular free shuttle service takes skiers to and from the slopes all day, as long as the trails are open. Waterville is especially popular for its attention to families. Ski lessons are given in a separate area to free learners from interference. Lift capacity is good and long lines are rare, meaning increased time on the full range of slopes. While many of the skiers here are staying at the resort, it is a very popular area for day skiers as well. In addition to alpine skiing, Waterville also has about 75 kilometers of Nordic skiing trails and a full Nordic center with lessons available. The resort also offers indoor skating and sleigh rides. Waterville is off I-93 at exit 28; follow Route 49 northeast. Contact Waterville Valley Resort, 1 Ski Area Rd., P.O. Box 540, Waterville 03215; call (800) GO–VALLEY or (603) 468-2553, or visit www.visitwatervillevalley.com/lodging/.

Waterville also includes 22 miles of hiking trails and several mountain summits whose trails begin in the valley. One of the shorter trails for more casual hiking begins at the bottom of the Snow's Mountain ski lift and leads to **The Cascades.** Follow the signs, climbing up the ski slope and then to the left. Be sure that you are following the sign for the Cascades trail and not the Snow's Mountain cross-country ski trail. Once you are in the woods, look for yellow trail blazes. There are very few steep places on this easy trail. Once you get to the cascades, cross the brook and continue up the other side for the best views of the continuous series of waterfalls and pools.

A pleasant, if moderately difficult hike, the **Welch-Dickey Mountain Trail** combines views and natural history with a touch of mystery. To reach the trailhead parking area, take Upper Mad River Road, near the Thornton town line, then follow signs at the third junction to the right. Two trails begin here, joined into a loop that connects the two small mountains; the easier route begins with the right-hand trail toward Welch Mountain. Much of the trail is in the open, across ledges that give good views to the south and east. Before reaching the summit of Welch Mountain, the trail passes several stands of jack pine, exceedingly rare in New Hampshire. On Dickey Mountain, look for a cairn marking a stone circle carved into the bedrock. The origin of the circle is unknown, but if you stand inside it and look back toward the large triangular rock, you are looking at the exact point of the sunrise at the summer solstice. The 4.5-mile climb takes about three and a half hours.

Okay, we admit it: We like the trappings of luxury, and our favorite place to stay in the valley is the ***Snowy Owl Inn.*** Summer or winter, its three-story-tall fieldstone fireplace identifies it as a ski lodge. In the big downstairs lounge

Walking Lightly

Many casual—or even serious—hikers don't think about the effect their shoes or boots can have on the landscape and flora along the way. Each trail disrupts the landscape to some degree, packing the surface so water flows over rather than into the soil. During the spring melt, trails often create miniature streams that wash out steep places, form mud holes, or make going rough. To avoid these, hikers take detours, trampling plants to create a new trail, which only increases the damage in following years.

Hikers also take shortcuts, bypassing a curve in the trail by making a beeline through the woods. Not only does this practice kill a new set of plants and damage more tree roots, but these straight lines make more direct paths for water runoff, increasing the danger of erosion.

Staying on the trail and avoiding trails altogether in the early spring or after prolonged heavy rains, when they are muddy, protects the trails and the plants around them that would be damaged by detours and when wet.

Staying on the trail and boardwalk while hiking through a bog is even more important, since bog plants are especially vulnerable to crushing. Also, in a floating bog you always run the risk of stepping right through the delicate mat.

When hiking above timber line, stay on the trail—if there is one—or step from rock to rock, carefully avoiding tiny plants and trees that grow between them. These alpine plants are fragile and often rare, and they have enough trouble surviving the extreme weather and winds without being kicked or stepped on by hiking boots. The little stunted tree beside the trail may have been clinging to that crack between the rocks for one hundred years.

EVENTS IN THE EASTERN WHITE MOUNTAINS

July Fourth Family Day,
North Conway
(800) 367-3364

Highland Games,
mid-Sept,
Loon Mountain Resort, Lincoln
(603) 229-1975,
Tickets: (800) 358-7268

Fall Railfan's Day,
mid-Sept,
North Conway
(603) 356-5251, (800) 232-5251;
www.conwayscenic.com

Polar Express,
Dec,
Conway Scenic Railroad,
North Conway
(Tickets available by lottery only; visit
www.polarexpress.org. for information.)
(603) 447-3100

area, a sunken pit provides guests a place to gather by the fire in the evening. In the afternoon, wine and cheese await returning hikers and skiers. Rooms are spacious; especially nice are the upper-level rooms with loft bunks for the kids. In-suite whirlpool baths, an indoor swimming pool, and a kids-stay-free policy make this contemporary inn an old-fashioned value. Winter rates begin at $120; rates drop in spring, fall, and summer. Call (800) 766-9969 or visit www.snowyowlinn.com.

Several lodging options cluster around Corcoran Pond, including Town Square Condominiums. These are geared to families, with multiple bedrooms and big kitchens. In the same complex are a coffee shop, restaurant, and convenience store, and the condos all have WiFi. Kids love the third-floor bedroom space all to themselves in the three-bedroom condos, with bunk beds and their own TV. Reserve Town Square Condominiums at (603) 236-8175 or visit www.townsquarecondos.com. Except in winter, when the road is closed, a nice alternative route out of the valley is over *Thornton Gap,* a small notch reached from a road to the left at the village library. Follow signs to Tripoli (pronounced "triple-eye") Road, following a mountain brook through the forest.

After you crest the gap, you drop down into the Pemigewasset Valley near *Russell Pond Campground.* For those who enjoy camping as a sport, not simply as a way to reduce lodging costs, this national forest campground offers well-separated sites, deep in a hardwood forest that drops into a lovely small pond. No buildings mar its shore; there are a canoe launch, a fisherman or two, and the deep quiet that only lakes that ban motorboats can offer. There are no electric outlets at the campground and no RV hookups. It's hard to believe that such quiet wilderness can be so close to an interstate highway. On Saturday afternoons, rangers present nature programs. Call the Pemigewasset Ranger Station at (603) 536-1310 or (888) CAMPSNH, or visit www.campsnh .com for open dates.

Leaving or entering Waterville Valley on Route 43, it's a 4-mile side trip north on Route 175 to have breakfast at **Benton's Sugar Shack.** From mid-February through mid-April, they are likely to be boiling maple sap into syrup in the back room, but they serve weekend breakfasts year round. They are best known for stacks of pancakes swimming in their own maple syrup, but they serve a full menu that includes French toast, omelets, even biscuits and gravy. Buy their syrup, maple candy, and jams at the shop. Serving from 8 a.m. until 2 p.m. on weekends and during holiday weeks. Benton's Sugar Shack, 2010 Route 175, Thornton; call (603) 726-3867 or visit www.nhmapleoutlet.com.

The Kancamagus

Only one road cuts directly east and west through the center section of the White Mountain National Forest—the Kancamagus Highway. Not really a highway but a paved two-lane road, it climbs from Lincoln to Conway over the 2,860-foot **Kancamagus Pass** via a long switchback. Be sure to stop at the pull-out areas to enjoy the view back across the mountains. No commercial development mars this route; you'll just find the woods, the views, small trailhead parking areas, and a handful of national forest campgrounds.

At its beginning on the west end is **Loon Mountain,** well known for its ski area. Less known is the geological site at its summit, reached by a trail from the top of its chairlift (which runs in the summer). A well-built stairway allows you to climb down among a tumble of giant boulders tossed there by a glacier to form caves and passageways that will fascinate kids (and adults). On Sunday mornings there is a nondenominational service in an outdoor chapel at the summit, and a pancake breakfast is served at the summit restaurant.

At valley level, the **Wildlife Theater** presents lively shows with native animals, birds, and reptiles during the summer. The shows are very informative and very popular with kids, who jump at the chance to actually pet a snake and love watching the ferret "weasel its way" through a PVC pipe. The emphasis is on learning about the environment. The park also has an Equestrian Center. It is located on the Kancamagus Highway; (603) 745-8111.

Loon Mountain ski resort expanded in 2008 with the addition of South Peak and Loon's first double-black diamond trail, Rip Saw. Ski it if you dare, but don't say you weren't warned. The resort's Adventure center, located opposite the main parking areas, has a cross-country center and skating rink, with rentals of skates, skis, and snowshoes.

Loon Mountain and the town of Lincoln combine to make this a major center for outdoor activities year round. Near the ski area, rent snowmobiles and join guided tours of the snow-covered mountains with SledVentures (603-238-2571; www.sledventures.net), and in Lincoln, Art's Outdoor Outfitters offers canoe and kayak rentals, complete with pick up and drop off for paddles down the Pemigewasset River. Bicycle rentals are also available (603-745-4806).

At the eastern end of the Kancamagus, watch the south side of the road for the sign for **Sabbaday Falls.** From the picnic area, the path is broad, smooth, and quite well marked to the foot of a flume, where the river flows through a 10-foot gap between straight rock walls more than 40 feet high. At the base there is a water-worn pothole about 4 feet in diameter, and nearby a 2-foot-wide stripe of dark basalt runs through the granite shelf that forms the viewing platform.

The trail along the rim is secured by a log railing, so you can safely look straight down into the flume. Full-grown trees cling to the opposite wall, their roots like giant fingers gripping the rock. You can see here very clearly the dramatic upstream march of the vertical wall of a waterfall. As potholes are formed by whirlpools, their walls are washed or worn away, and the ledges are undercut.

About 3 miles east of the Sabbaday Falls trailhead is the **Russell-Colbath House.** This 1805 farmhouse has been restored to the mid-nineteenth century, providing an interesting look at the isolated lives of the families who settled the Passaconaway Valley. Ruth and Thomas Colbath lived here in the late nineteenth century in the house built by her father. One day in 1891 Thomas told Ruth that he was going out for a spell, but didn't return. For the next 39 years Ruth kept a lighted candle in the window every night waiting for his return. She died without ever seeing him again, but he finally did show up three years later. The house is in Passaconaway, on the Kancamagus Highway, and is open daily 9 a.m. to 4:30 p.m. between mid-June and Labor Day and on weekends after Memorial Day and until Columbus Day. Call (603) 466-2727 for information.

Behind the house, **Rail 'n River Forest Trail** is a 0.5-mile level loop that offers a unique view of the logging that once took place here and of the regrowth of the forest. Signs and a free leaflet explain different kinds of forest environments, how timber was carried out of the valley by rail, and methods used to fight forest fires. The tale of the timbering that once stripped this entire area of its forests is now told only by ghosts, such as the pilings of a railroad bridge in the bed of the Swift River, visible from this trail. For a closer look at these rough-and-tumble days read *Tall Trees, Tough Men* by Robert E. Pike. The trail is wheelchair accessible.

On Route 16, after it becomes the main street of **Conway,** you'll see the **Eastman Lord House,** a museum run by the local historical society at 100 Main St. It's no ordinary period house but an 1818 home with each of its twelve rooms restored to a different period, from the year of its building to 1945. The last is the kitchen. Instead of showcases of artifacts with placards, each item is displayed in its place of use, so it's like walking from era to era through someone's home. Their enlightened view of history as a continuing story has created a museum well worth seeing. It's open Memorial Day through Labor Day, Wed 2 to 4 p.m., Thurs 6 to 8 p.m., and by appointment other days in the summer and in May, Sept, and Oct; (603) 447-5551; www.conwayhistory.org.

Route 16 from the northern end of Conway to above North Conway is so beaten a path that on summer and fall weekends the traffic may be backed up for hours. But there is a way around it, and it takes you past two delightful corners that people honking their horns on Route 16 never hear about. But first you have to find West Side Road. Just opposite the intersection where Route

Forest Service Parking Fees

Be aware that the White Mountain National Forest charges a use fee. A $20 charge ($5 for a one-week pass) is levied not on the person but on the car, whether you take a five-minute walk to a waterfall or spend the whole summer hiking. You can use the trails all you want as long as somebody drops you off or you park outside the national forest. It is hard to find a place to get a pass. You can buy a site-specific pass for $3 per day at some national forest parking lots (look for a box on a post near the trailhead), but don't count on it. There is a fine for not having a pass. For locations of sales points visit www.fs.fed.us/r9/white, ask at information booths, or call (603) 528-8721 for the current list of places to buy passes. Canada has done this with its national parks for years, and it's happening in other states as well. Don't blame New Hampshire, as many people have done quite loudly: It was a decision made in Washington, NOT, we can assure you, something the state volunteered for.

On the plus side, the Forest Service and the White Mountain Interpretive Association provide free nature programs all summer long at the campgrounds throughout the national forest. You may learn about medicinal plants, weather, lumbering, raptors, canoeing, animals, llama trekking, salmon, geology, or any other facet of the White Mountains. Programs begin at 7:30 p.m. on Friday and Saturday evenings at Dolly Copp Campground, Saturday nights in others. For a schedule, stop at any ranger station or call (603) 466-2713.

153 heads south to Eaton Center is a street going north. Take it and then the left at the fork (straight ahead is one of Conway's **covered bridges,** and to the left you will pass another one just a few yards up the road). Follow this road through lovely farmlands that open out to some of the valley's finest views of the Presidential Range. When the road comes to a T, you should go left to bypass North Conway or right to reach the ski area or the northern edge, above the outlets.

Taking full advantage of those views with a beautiful 70-acre setting along the Saco River, **Stables at Farm By the River** is a year-round center for horseback riding, as well as sleigh, wagon, and carriage rides. Pony rides for children and riding lessons for all ages are also available. Stables at Farm By the River, 2555 West Side Rd.; call (603) 356-2694 or (603) 356-6640 for reservations.

Less than a mile north of the North Conway intersection, on West Side Road, is the trailhead to **Diana's Baths.** Look for a sign on the west side of the road after two fenced fields. A parking lot is cut into the woods. The falls, only a short distance along a fairly level trail, were once the site of a gristmill. You can still see the foundations and the chute that fed it water. Above, falls and pools are interspersed with cascades over sloping granite. Each of these succeeding shelves is marked by potholes cut into its surface, like a series of children's marble holes on a playground. As you continue to climb, you will find the ledges flatten and the falls shorten. But the swirls and scoops in the granite become even more dramatic.

Another way of getting to North Conway without encountering the outlet traffic is to ride the Conway Scenic Railway from the quieter town of Conway. The tracks cut through the peaceful, historic heart of the valley, passing fields, meadows, woodlands, the Saco River, and an abandoned lumber mill. The Presidential Range fills the north end of the valley, and dramatic ledges line the west. Or, if you begin the trip in North Conway, you can enjoy a good lunch en route in the dining car, a period piece in honey-colored wood and etched glass. Trains run daily from mid-May through foliage season and on weekends as early as April and as late as November, but to ride from Conway and have any time in North Conway, you have to ride between May and October, when there are multiple trains each day. The train also travels north to Bartlett and, once a day, beyond and all the way through Crawford Notch to the tiny Victorian railway station that once served Crawford House. It's five hours of mountain scenery and a don't-look-down crossing of the Frankenstein Trestle. The trains begin at the depot in downtown North Conway; call (603) 356-5251 or (800) 232-5251, or visit www.conwayscenic.com.

Green B&Bs

Bed & Breakfasts Inn Mount Washington Valley is a group of ten B&Bs between North Conway and Shelburne that have joined not only to promote their inns, but to promote green initiatives for themselves and their guests. Throughout the year the inns find ways to make getaway weekends more fun for their guests with programs such as March Maple Madness, Ghost and Goblin Trail in October, and a June weekend celebrating green living. At March Maple Madness, guests receive a booklet mapping out the locations of local sugar houses and the participating inns. Part of the fun is the "Sap-enger Hunt" and a puzzle to assemble of pieces gathered from each inn. Questions involve the inn or the local attractions. Clues and hints are liberally provided by the innkeepers, as are the items needed for the scavenger hunt. The prizes are well worth competing for, but the other reward is sampling each inn's favorite maple recipe, along with sweets from the maple sugar houses on the trail. To learn of upcoming events, visit www.BBInsMWV.com.

You don't have to ride the train to enjoy the museum at the *North Conway Depot,* a beautifully restored Victorian railway station in the center of town at the northern terminus of the trip. Displayed in the old waiting room are brochures, lanterns, uniforms, photos, and other historical items. Be sure to ask for the flyer identifying the buildings, railway cars, and engines in the rail yard. Many of the cabooses are private homes; other cars and engines are in the process of restoration. For information call (603) 356-5251.

Before the return ride to Conway, walk across the wide town green to *Zebs General Store,* which carries only products made in New England. Look for fine foods from small farms and bakeries, unique handmade items, books, soaps, and an array of other items you won't find elsewhere. Call (603) 356-9294 or visit www.zebs.com.

Under the towering rock cliffs of Cathedral Ledge, in the White Mountain Hotel, *The Ledges* dining room is defined by a large semicircular glass wall with views over forest to Mount Cranmore. Inside, a split-level floor affords patrons in the back of the room the same views. But the food beats even the views. Specials may include smoked duck, mako shark, or ribs of Angus beef, but the menu's fifteen entrees give a wide range of choices, such as orange-scented scallops in Grand Marnier and crème fraiche. Dinner is served nightly all year, and lunch is served from late spring until mid-fall. The Ledges is at the *White Mountain Hotel* resort, West Side Road, North Conway; (603) 356-7100; www.whitemountainhotel.com.

Dog-owners will be happy to hear that North Conway has a B&B where the dogs are welcomed with the same warm hospitality as their owners. In fact, Whitman and Lilly will be right at the door of *Spruce Moose Lodge and Cottages* to join the innkeepers in the first hello. Cheery sunlit rooms are decorated in a comfortable cottage style in the lodge, and the cottages and bungalows sleep as many as twelve, making them ideal for family groups. Visiting dogs get a discount on anything they (or their traveling companions) buy at Four Your Paws Only, North Conway's center for all things canine. Spruce Moose Lodge and Cottages, 207 Seavey St.; call (800) 600-6239 or (603) 356-6329, or visit www.SpruceMooseLodge.com.

Very few people know about the *Pudding Pond Trail* in North Conway, which we found while looking for something else. It's a nice walk in the woods, good for a family, and not too strenuous, but don't expect to swim there. Pudding Pond is actually a string of small ponds connected by marshlands and a stream. The trail is a joint effort of The Nature Conservancy and the town of Conway.

You will notice signs of beaver activity as soon as you reach the water. Several beaver lodges are visible, as well as the telltale gnawed stumps of small trees that were used as building material. Especially in the morning and evening, keep a sharp lookout for the typical V-shaped wave that beavers make in the water as they swim. You will also notice, especially in the spring, the large variety of wildflowers that abound here, which seem to be guarded by their own air force of voracious mosquitoes—the price you must pay to see spring wildflowers in such moist places.

The trail starts along a wide old road and parallels a powerline easement and then forms a T intersection with other trails. At the intersection take the trail to the right. A wide and easy dirt trail leads uphill before descending a gentle slope. Ignore the first trail that goes off to the right. At the base of the hill look for a sign that shows the Pudding Pond Loop Trail to the left. This is the other end of the loop trail, and we suggest that you follow the path to the right. It leads to a small stream that is the exit of the pond. Take the path left as it changes direction and follows along the marsh. The trail can become rough in this area, with lots of roots protruding to catch your feet, so be careful. Another part of the trail is over planks that span the low spots.

To find Pudding Pond, take Artists Falls Road, which leaves the north side of Main Street (Route 16) in North Conway, beside the Eastman Inn. Go right onto Thompson Road and look for the PUDDING POND sign on the right, with parking at the trailhead.

Green Hills Preserve is a 4,222-plus-acre tract of Nature Conservancy land in North Conway, with 1- and 2-mile trails. One leads up 1,734-foot Peaked Mountain, where rare plants grow. Also on the property is a red pine forest, an unusual phenomenon for its altitude. Take Artist Falls Road to the east (left as you head south) off Route 16/302, at the southern end of North Conway. Just short of its end is a public parking space, with a trail board at one side. Pick up maps here before hiking the trails. For information call (603) 356-8833 or visit www.nature.org.

Just south of North Conway, U.S. 302 diverges east from Route 16 through a dot on the map marked Redstone. This was once a very active village because of the Redstone Ledge, where a richly colored red granite was quarried, and because of a spring known for its restorative properties. During the Victorian era, "taking the cure" became high fashion, and grand hotels were built around springs whose water tasted even faintly odd. These mineral springs were fairly common in Vermont and the Hudson Valley but quite uncommon in New Hampshire, where we've been able to track only three. All that's left of the fashionable **White Mountain Mineral Springs** are some foundation stones and one of the most surprising sights you'll come upon in a walk through the New Hampshire woods.

Only a short distance from the Route 16 intersection, look for a pull-out area in a pine forest, where you'll see a gate barring an old road. You'll also see a sign and a trail map, but you won't need a map. Park and follow the old road on foot through woods and across a powerline cut to a large, round field. As you enter the field, look to the woods on your right. You'll see what at first appears to be the fanciful cupola of some long-collapsed grand hotel, but if you walk to it, you'll find a pavilion under a spreading curved dome, sort of an offshoot of the Karelian/Victorian architectural style of the North Conway railway station. The spring still fills the pool in its center, and the place stands dilapidated and overgrown; near where the road enters the field, you'll find

The Case of the Missing Tourist Attraction

In the heyday of the grand hotels—from the Civil War to the end of the century—guests arrived by train and stayed for weeks, so it was up to the hotels to amuse them. Each day they offered excursions, and one of the favorites near Conway was a circuit that stopped first at Echo Lake, then at the gigantic Washington Boulder, and then at White Mountain Mineral Springs in Redstone. The wooden springhouse, as you know, is still there, but not a trace remains of the presumably more durable Washington Boulder. Despite its having been named for the "Father of his Country," it was quarried in 1900, and you can see it now in neat blocks as the foundation to the public library in Conway, at the intersection of Routes 113 and 16.

some foundations of a guest house, really a large farmhouse, and a building where the water was bottled.

It's the terrible weather—world-record winds, driving rain, dense fog, sleet, snow—that makes conditions at the top of **Mount Washington** so formidable, and so interesting. And you can learn all about it, without going to the top, at the **Weather Discovery Center** in North Conway. Small, but very well done, it's filled with hands-on exhibits that demonstrate the forces of wind and show how (and why) we study weather patterns. The center is in direct contact, by photo and weather instruments, with the Mount Washington Observatory, so you can see the wind, barometric pressure, and other readings as they happen. Exhibits are designed for all ages, with plenty of interactive displays for kids and the scientifically challenged. The Weather Discovery Center is at 2779 North Main St. (Route 16) in North Conway; (603) 356-2137; www.mountwashington.org. Admission is $5 for adults and $2 for ages six to twelve.

Mount Washington Valley Children's Museum is a low-tech museum designed for children eight years and younger, offering a puppet theater, costumes for impromptu plays and make believe, a construction area with a kid-size log skidder, a carpeted wall where children can arrange their own village of movable buildings, and an area designed just for toddlers. The museum is open Wed 10 a.m. to 1 p.m., Thurs through Sat 10:30 a.m. to 5 p.m., Sun 9 a.m. to 1 p.m. The cost is $5 per person for a day's multiple admission (good for short toddler attention spans or a lunch break). The museum is located at 2936 White Mountain Hwy. (Route 16), north of the village center; (603) 356-2992; www.mwvchildrensmuseum.org/.

In the same little shopping center is the (literally) world-famous **Stan and Dan's Sports,** where you can get custom-fitted ski boots at prices real people can afford. *Snow Country* called Stan and Dan's the top ski shop in the country and *Ski Magazine* has twice awarded them gold medals for their custom boot fitting. Not surprisingly, the owners are named Stan (Millen) and Dan (Lewis), both of whom acquired their expertise at Carroll Reed's, a gone-but-not-forgotten North Conway landmark. Their shop fits about 1,100 pairs of ski boots in an average season. At two to three hours a pair, that's a lot of hours spent heating boots and snapping buckles. The best time of year to shop is September through Thanksgiving, when they have the largest stock. If you go in ski season, the best time of day is between 10:30 a.m. and 3 p.m., although they are open 8 a.m. to 6 p.m. Stan and Dan's is in North Village Common on Route 16, just north of the village; (603) 356-6997; www.stananddansports.com.

Running parallel to often-busy Route 16 through Intervale is Route 16A, which was bypassed by the new road. Now a quiet residential byway, the road

For Cookie Lovers

In mid-December, the **Annual Inn-to-Inn Christmas Cookie Tour** takes place throughout the Mount Washington Valley. At least eighteen inns and B&Bs dress up in their holiday finest and bake up their favorite cookies. Tickets are $20 for two days of self-guided inn touring, and it's a good idea to get tickets in advance. Call (603) 356-9460 or visit www.countryinnsinthewhitemountains.com.

was once lined with inns and hotels. A few remain, among them **Glen Oaks Inn,** which has hosted travelers continuously since it opened in 1890. Rooms on the top floor have recessed windows set inside the slope of the mansard roof. Groomed cross-country ski trails begin at the door, and downhill skiing is minutes away. Glen Oaks is part of *"Bike the Whites"* and a similar cross-country ski package with two other inns (see The Lakes and Foothills chapter). Glen Oaks Inn is on Route 16A; call (603) 356-9772 or (877) 854-6535, or visit www.glenoaksinn.com.

Bernerhof Inn is surrounded by beautifully kept gardens, and its rooms are just as well maintained. We like the quirky arrangement and shapes of rooms tucked into the turrets and gables of this Victorian mansion. Prices are moderate and include a full breakfast. You can't miss it beside Route 302 in Glen; (603) 383-9132 or (800) 548-8007; www.bernerhofinn.com.

Wildcat Valley

Tucked into a corner, away from the bustle to the south, is the village of **Jackson,** with its red covered bridge and white church. Artists discovered its scenic beauty in the mid-1800s, and by the turn of the twentieth century, Jackson had twenty-four lodging places, including several grand hotels. By the late 1970s, only **Eagle Mountain House** and a few smaller guest houses were still operating.

But this story has a happier ending than most. Today a number of these have reopened, including the Victorian treasure Wentworth Hall. Not all of its original thirty-nine buildings could be saved from years of neglect and abandonment, but the three central ones and several other cottages, with their curved porches, round towers, wide gables, and quirky architectural detail, are once again the showpiece of the village center.

The **Wentworth Resort** is just as nice inside as it is outside, with real feather pillows, giant bathtubs, and an air of grandeur that is comfortable, not intimidating. Rooms in the Arden, Wildwood, and Amster cottages are unique, taking advantage of the architecture of each. In the main building, the Thornycroft suite is our favorite, with its carefully restored antiques, custom-built bed, window seat, sleigh settee, marble fireplace, and even a fireplace in the ample Jacuzzi room.

The dining room is just as memorable; the menu is innovative, and each season brings new dishes as the chef takes advantage of the freshest ingredients. A meal could begin with smoked trout or a monkfish medallion with a coriander crust and shiitake mushrooms. Entrees may include lemon-thyme chicken breast with stone-ground polenta or lamb shanks in a white bean cassoulet. The public is invited to dine here but should call to make reservations. The hotel is open year-round. Expensive. Write the Wentworth Resort Hotel, Box M, Jackson 03846; call (603) 383-9700 or (800) 637-0013, or visit www.thewentworth.com.

A short walk up the road is *Jackson Falls,* a series of cascades with potholes that invite jumping into, if the weather is only halfway nice. The hotel has a pool, of course, but these falls must have been the original inspiration for water slides. There is a circular route of 6 miles (called, for some reason, the Five Mile Drive) that begins at the Wentworth and goes up the Carter Notch Road past the falls. Instead of continuing to the top of the notch (where the road turns into a trail), turn right and cross the river for views across highland meadows to the mountains.

On the way to **Carter Notch,** tucked under the wing of the Eagle Mountain House, is the bright and appealing **Carter Notch Inn.** Engaging hosts have created a haven filled with character, including a room with a loft that kids love. Rooms range widely in price, higher in summer and fall, including breakfast—but all are nicely furnished and very pleasant. Moderate. Eagle Mountain's golf course, with fine views, is in sight. Carter Notch Road, Jackson; (603) 383-9630 or (800) 794-9434; www.carternotchinn.com.

Golf Clubs

At least a dozen golf clubs in New Hampshire are over a century old, built in the 1890s when golfing was the latest rage. By the 1920s dozens of golf clubs, most attached to grand hotels, flourished in the White Mountains alone. Several of these have outlived the hotels—the Maplewood in Bethlehem and the Waumbec in Jefferson among them—and others are long gone. But at the **Wentworth Resort Golf Club** you can still play the two oldest holes in the state. Holes Twelve and Thirteen were in use when Grover Cleveland was president. Of the original six holes, two have been altered and two taken out of play entirely.

Eagle Mountain House itself was one of the smaller of the grand old White Mountain hotels, with a mere ninety-three guest rooms, and one of very few to survive. Lodging is expensive. The menu is classic New England with nice seafood options and they have kept some old favorites from the hotel's previous life, including the roast turkey dinner—slow-roasted turkey breast with stuffing, gravy, and cranberry sauce. Moderate. Eagle Mountain House is in Jackson; (603) 383-9111; www.eaglemt.com.

Black Mountain Ski Area (800-475-4669 or www.blackmt.com) is usually forgotten in the razzmatazz of its bigger neighbors, but this end-of-the-road place is a favorite of anyone who has ever skied there. This is a real gem of a mountain, with over 1,100 feet of vertical drop and more than 98 percent of the trails covered by snowmaking. Black Mountain is popular with families for more than one reason. First is cost, since it has some of the least expensive rates in the state: Weekend tickets are $39 for adults and only $29 weekdays, with correspondingly less expensive rates for kids and seniors. Special packages, including room and lift tickets (some with meals), are available from Whitney's and other local inns and B&Bs. Another reason is its genuine north-country hospitality and friendliness. Kids are safe here and they are treated like family. Black Mountain has an exceptional ski school for all ages, with an atmosphere that provides just the right setting to make novices into confident skiers. And the mountain itself, served by four lifts, is another reason for Black's popularity. Beginners can ski with confidence and advanced skiers will find some nice challenges.

Skiing on Black Mountain has been synonymous with Whitney's since "Ma" Whitney bought the old Moody Farm in 1936 and welcomed skiers to the first overhead ski lift in the East on Black Mountain, literally out her back door. The lift was made from Sears Roebuck shovel handles. Generations of skiers later, **Whitney's Inn, Jackson,** still welcomes skiers, Black Mountain has grown into a full-service ski area whose lift rates are one of the best ski values in the White Mountains, and "Ma" Whitney has retired to a house on the edge of the slopes above the inn. There has been a complete renovation of the old inn recently bringing the inn to the next level. Comfortable rooms, a hearty breakfast, and special facilities and programs for children make Whitney's popular with families. It's a year-round resort as well, with special summer packages that include a Wednesday night lobster cookout. Starting rooms rates are on the low end of moderate. Whitney's address is P.O. Box 822, 357 Black Mountain Rd. (Route 16B), Jackson 03846; (603) 383-8916 or (800) 677-5737; www.whitneysinn.com.

In summer, Black Mountain Stables, located at the Ski Area, offers horse back riding. The hour-long guided ride is $45. Trail rides start at 10 and 11:30

Christmas in the Mountains

In early December the Jackson area is abuzz with its annual *Traditionally Yours* holiday celebrations. Santa arrives and the Christmas tree is lighted the weekend after Thanksgiving, but the following weekend brings the Jingle Bell Chocolate Tour, when horse-drawn sleds stop at inns and restaurants for chocolate goodies. The Women's Sewing Club Silver Tea and Christmas sale is at the Community Parish House. On Sunday, Eagle Mountain House hosts a gingerbread workshop for children, and in the afternoon Nestlenook Farm hosts a Winter Wonderland, with free ice-skating on their big pond. Contact the Jackson Area Chamber of Commerce at (603) 383-9356 or www.jacksonnh.com.

a.m. and 1, 2:30, and 4 p.m. For kids there are pony rides on gentle Tinkerbell at 10:30 a.m. and 3:30 p.m. They also have two five-day riding camps (9 a.m to 4 p.m.) in July and Stay and Ride packages are available using local inns and B&Bs. Reservations are suggested. Black Mountain Stables, 373 Black Mountain Rd., Jackson; call (603) 383-4490.

Cross-country skiing is an art form in Jackson. This is the home of the *Jackson Ski Touring Foundation,* which maintains 150 kilometers of exceptionally well-groomed trails throughout the village and all over the surrounding hillsides. In winter, with no leaves to obscure the view, the neighboring mountains, including the southern slopes of Mount Washington, are visible from every hillside. It's so beautiful on a crisp winter day that it's hard to concentrate on skiing. Grooming here is state of the art, and they offer quality rental equipment and lessons. Jackson XC, as they call themselves, hosts an amazing array of programs from the beautiful new lodge, often several a week. These range from wax demos to snowshoe nature tours, "ski with a ranger," group skiing, and ski demo days, when you can try out the new stuff. If you have never tried Nordic (cross-country) skiing we urge you to start here. Look at the page for beginners on the Web site, then sign up for lessons. The scenery around Jackson is one of the world's best stress relievers. For the latest conditions and the calendar of events, contact them at 153 Main St., Jackson 03846; (603) 383-9355 or (800) 927-6697; www.jacksonxc.org.

High above Jackson, with a full view of Mount Washington, *The Inn at Thorn Hill* sets a standard for relaxed but luxurious country lodging. The original inn, designed in 1895 by Stanford White, burned in 2002. The new inn follows White's style and perhaps trumps it. The rooms are decorated in Victorian style, with elegant, comfortable furnishings and stunning views from the windows. Each room has a gas fireplace and a two-person Jacuzzi tub.

Accommodations are available in the Main Inn, the Carriage House, or cottages, and rates vary. Rates in the Carriage House are lower. Expensive. Frequent specials are offered. There are several outstanding restaurants in Jackson, and the dining room at the inn is among them. Guests can dress casually, but the settings and surroundings are undeniably elegant and the service far from casual. The menu adds a Mediterranean accent to New England traditions and is based on fresh local ingredients when possible. Pignoli nuts add sparkle to a crisp-skinned salmon served with braised baby beets, and roasted halibut is served with a roasted red pepper coulis and truffle vinaigrette. And the Thorn Hill wine cellar, with more than 3,000 bottles of the world's finest wines, remains as outstanding as before. Along with direct access to the network of cross-country trails and proximity to four ski areas, the inn offers tobogganing on the property, even at night. Art and photography workshops with artists from Cape Ann are a long-standing tradition at the inn, which is on Thorn Hill Road (P.O. Box A), Jackson Village; (603) 383-4242 or (800) 289-8990; www.innatthornhill.com.

If you ever long to slip into an idealized, Currier and Ives world that never was, spend some time at **Nestlenook Farm** in Jackson. No one at Nestlenook pretends that this is what life was really like in the good old days, although the gingerbread trim, patterned shingles, splendid woodwork, stained glass, and furnishings are all quite authentic.

The inn faces a pond that meanders into coves and past islands and under arched wooden bridges. Bonfires at its shore on winter evenings welcome skaters to warm their hands. On special winter weekends, people dress up in Victorian costumes to skate, a visual treat that adds to the fairyland ambience. At the inn's front porch, a team of Belgians and a large Austrian sleigh stop for passengers, then set off past the pavilion and into the snow-covered woods to circle the lake, sleighbells jingling.

The inn has a fully equipped kitchen for guests' use. Fresh-baked muffins and cookies are always available. Multicourse breakfasts are sumptuous, and in guest rooms hang original oil paintings by Benjamin Champney and other White Mountain artists whose works are usually seen only in museums. Visit www.nestlenookfarm.com for more information.

If all this is too much and you long for a more modern take on easy living, head up the hill to **Luxury Mountain Getaways'** smart new condos, under the same management. Spacious rooms sport all the modern amenities and are within easy reach of swimming pools and a new state-of-the-art fitness center with views across the valley. Both properties are on Route 16A, Jackson; (603) 383-9443 or (800) 659-9443; www.luxurymountaingetaways.com.

Near the top of Pinkham Notch on Route 16 is a trio of short, rewarding hikes. Look for the parking area for **Glen Ellis Falls** on the west side of the road. This short walk, beginning at the tunnel under the highway, leads to the cliff-lined Ellis River, which plunges over cascades and then through a narrow cleft in the granite, falling 65 feet into a basin before continuing through its boulder-strewn bed.

The Appalachian Mountain Club Visitor Center, just up the road, is the starting point for the 0.5-mile walk to *Lost Pond.* Cross Route 16 to the east side. The trail crosses a bridge, then runs south for 0.5 mile to the pond. While the falls show the wild side of nature, this shallow pond shows a gentler, more tranquil wilderness. At the southern end is a beaver dam and a jumble of boulders dropped here from the slopes above. In dry weather the path continues on to Glen Ellis Falls. You can get your national forest permit here, but note that if you park here for Glen Ellis Falls, you don't need a pass. If you park in the area at the falls, you do.

Crystal Cascade is an easy fifteen-minute walk up the trail behind the visitor center, following the Cutler River upstream. Although called a cascade, this is really a waterfall, the water dropping almost vertically 60 feet into a deep chasm and then falling another 20 feet. We have always felt that the best place to view a waterfall is facing its midpoint, a vantage usually reserved for winged creatures. But the unique bend in the river provides an overlook at exactly the right point for viewing this one.

A wide variety of programs and classes are held by the *Appalachian Mountain Club* (AMC) at their Pinkham Notch Visitor Center. These go on year-round and include nature, mountaineering, hiking, botany, photography, igloo and snow-shelter building, animal tracking, and other subjects of interest to those who revel in nature and the outdoors. Some are day or half-day programs, others are weekend classes that include lodging and require advance reservations. Free evening programs with illustrated travelogues are often combined with inexpensive dinners featuring dishes from the destination. The AMC operates a hikers' hostel inn here, with comfortable rooms and nightly dinners that are among the best values in the White Mountains. Served family-style at long tables and priced under $20, the multicourse dinners may feature hearty entrees such as pork loin roasted with rosemary and garlic. There is always a vegetarian option, which might include risotto primavera or couscous with sautéed cannelini beans and a vegetable medley. It's a good idea to have reservations on weekends. For a complete schedule, contact them at P.O. Box 298, Gorham 03581; (603) 466-2727; www.outdoors.org/lodging/pnvc.

The 4,000-foot summit of Wildcat Mountain brings visitors face to face with Mt. Washington's eastern slopes, carved and shaped by the deep glacial scours of *Tuckerman's Ravine* and *Huntington's Ravine.* The upper slopes of the mountain are so close across the narrow valley that without even using the telescopes at the summit, you can follow the progress of climbers making their way up the trails. Ascend to this view via New Hampshire's highest gondola ride, the four-passenger *Wildcat Express,* in a vertiginous twelve minutes; on a really clear day, from the top you can also see to the Atlantic Ocean and into Canada. Wildcat Express Gondola serves skiers in the winter, but it operates daily through the summer and until mid-Oct, 10 a.m. to 5 p.m.; (603) 466-3326; www.skiwildcat.com.

A bit farther up Route 16, at the head of Pinkham Notch, you'll find the entrance to the *Mount Washington Auto Road,* opposite the site of the long-gone Glen House, one of the grand hotels. Its carriage houses remain, and in them you can see some of the vehicles that have carried passengers up the scenic road since its building: the first coach, two wagons, a Pierce Arrow, and a wood-paneled Beach Wagon. In the wagon days, they had to replace all the brakes entirely after each trip down the mountain. You can drive along the road in your own car or ride up in one of the fleet of new vans with a guide who'll point out everything from historic sites to the unusual geologic formations beside the road. Fee for car and driver is $23, $8 each additional adult passenger (ages thirteen and older), $6 ages five to twelve, ages four and younger free. Van prices are: $29 per adult, $25 seniors and military, $12 children five to twelve. Located on Route 16, Pinkham Notch, Gorham; (206) 466-3988; www.mountwashingtonautoroad.com.

For a shorter climb on Mount Washington, rather than tackling the entire mountain, you can take the auto road to reach the *Alpine Garden.* Begin at the Huntington Ravine Trail crossing, where there is parking space. Follow that trail down (trying not to think about the reverse of the old axiom: "What goes down must go up") until it meets the Alpine Garden Trail in less than half a mile. The trail through the gardens is fairly flat and continues for more than a mile to the spectacular view down into Tuckerman's Ravine. Along the way are other fine views of the mountains to the east. Because the plants here are unique to the alpine environment, you should bring a guide to alpine wildflowers, available at the Pinkham Notch Visitor Center. The plants are interesting all summer, but bloom is the best in June. Please be careful to stay on the trail; these plants are not only rare but fragile, despite their ability to survive their harsh environment.

The Mount Washington Auto Road and *Great Glen Trails* share the same headquarters building. Great Glen has more than 40 kilometers of trails on Mount Washington that are available free to hikers. Mountain bikers are also welcomed, with a fee of $8 for a full day ($25 rental for a bike, including helmet and a trail fee). Great Glen also has nature walks, archery, a concert series, barbecues, kite flying, and a climbing wall that's available all year. They

Road Records

In 1853 a man made the descent on the auto road on a tricycle in fifty-five minutes.

In 1887 a record ascent by a horse-drawn vehicle clocked in at one hour and nine minutes.

In 1899 Mr. and Mrs. Freeland Stanley made the first engine-powered vehicle ascent on the auto road in a Stanley Locomobile, taking two hours and ten minutes.

In 1907 two men made the first road ascent on skis, as far as Halfway House, and skied back to the base in twenty minutes. The first round-trip to the summit on skis was made by members of the Dartmouth Outing Club in 1913.

In 1926 Arthur Walden (musher for several Arctic expeditions) and several friends drove the first team to the summit and back, which took fifteen hours. In 1932 Florence Clark was the first woman to make the trip with a dog team.

also have full- and half-day paddling excursions on the Androscoggin River and rafting trips. In winter the trails become cross-country trails, covered in natural snow. Several trails have snowmaking, so there is almost always skiing available. The lodge has skis for rent as well as skates and kick sleds, popular in Finland but relatively unknown here.

Great Glen also offers a *snowcoach* service, operating between December and March, which takes passengers 4.5 miles up the auto road to a point above the tree line where they can get out and experience the mountain in winter. Cross-country and telemark skiers and snowshoers then have the option of going back on foot. It's first-come, first-served and no reservations. Open daily 8:30 a.m. to 4:30 p.m. The price is $40 for the 1.5-hour trip, $25 for ages six to twelve. Located on Route 16, Pinkham Notch, Gorham; (603) 466-2333; www.greatglentrails.com.

Mount Washington

At just over a mile high, Mount Washington is the highest mountain in the northeast, but its weather conditions are among the most severe in the world. Arctic equipment is tested at its summit. Only slightly below it stand other mountains named for presidents—thus the name Presidential Range.

Crawford Notch, a break in the almost solid chain of the White Mountains, lies due south of Mount Washington. Geologically, the notch is a classic glacial scour. During the last ice age, boulders frozen into the ice caught onto chunks of loose bedrock as the glacier moved down mountain slopes. In valleys, where the action of the glacier became more concentrated, the scouring was at its greatest, carrying off boulders and pieces of broken cliffs, which in turn scraped even deeper as they moved, giving a characteristic U-shaped curve to the valley walls.

In the early days of settlement, vast forests of very tall trees covered all but the tops of the mountains, so the settlers couldn't tell where the notches and the passes were. About all they could do was follow the riverbeds, hoping to find the easiest and lowest route.

Usually, these routes were discovered more or less by accident. So it was with Timothy Nash the day he climbed a tree on Cherry Mountain while moose hunting and saw the gap in the line of mountains. He went to Portsmouth to ask the royal governor (the same Benning Wentworth we met earlier) for a piece of land and a road through the notch. The governor told him to bring a horse through the notch, which Timothy and a friend did by lowering it over the cliff on a rope. Nash got his land, and eventually the road was built, opening a much shorter route to the north country.

The trees that filled the notch, like those of the Passaconaway Valley, fell to the lumber market. Entire towns sprang up around the lumber camps, and some of them died with the industry. ***Livermore,*** a ghost town today, lies along Sawyer River Road, which meets Route 302 just north of the bridge over the Sawyer River about 5 miles north of Bartlett. A 1.5-mile walk up Sawyer

Author's Note

As a child, tucked into my sleeping bag on summer nights beside the Ammonoosuc River, my sleep was sometimes interrupted by the long, mournful whistle of the train as it passed almost over my head on its way between Fabyan Station and Twin Mountain. But I never rode it farther north than Conway. Later, after the train line was abandoned—forever, everyone thought—we walked the tracks, but only as far as the trestle, where the land dropped straight down into the notch. The track was deteriorating, and it was too late to ride the train through the notch as I had dreamed of doing on those long-ago nights.

Finally, I rode that train I thought was gone forever, through the notch and past the scenes of childhood summers—past Notchland, with its strange stone house where there used to be a thank-you-marm in the road; over trails I'd climbed to waterfalls; and over the trestle where I still didn't dare to look down. When the train came through the rocks at the Gateway to the Notch, I half expected to see Crawford House, a phoenix arisen from its ashes like the railroad. Even if it had been there, I wouldn't have been able to see it through the tears. You CAN go home again.

—Barbara Radcliffe Rogers

River Road, you'll see a barred gate and some foundations, which are all that is left of Livermore. It was once a thriving community of 200, built in the late 1800s and reached by both road and railroad. Of its homes, stores, boarding-houses, offices, and two sawmills, you'll find only ruins. Walk to the river and into the woods upstream to find cellar holes and the ruins of a beautifully con-structed concrete-and-brick sawmill. All of these have full-size trees growing out of them now. It's easier to find the cellar holes in the fall when the leaves are missing. Look for the one with the company safe clearly visible.

Just north of the Sawyer River Road is the **Notchland Inn,** a granite man-sion that has been a Crawford Notch landmark since its construction in 1862.

bitofablow, itwas

On April 12, 1934, the highest velocity wind gust ever recorded rocked the observatory on top of Mount Washington with a force of 231 miles per hour. On the same day, the one-hour average velocity was as high as 173 miles per hour, also a record.

The front parlor of this Victorian home was designed by Gustav Stickley; an adjoining country schoolhouse has been transformed into two suites. Guests can join a guided walk to a dramatic gorge and swimming hole located on the property. Nonguests are welcome to dine here but must reserve for the fixed-price dinner, which costs $38 for inn guests and $40 for nonguests ($45 nonguests Fri, Sat and holidays). The Notchland Inn is on Route 302, Harts Location; (603) 374-6131 or (800) 866-6131; www.notchland.com.

The head of the notch was once home to the historic Crawford House Hotel, unfortunately a victim of fire in the late twentieth century. Today the hotel site is home to the new **Appalachian Mountain Club Highland Center,** offering lodging, dining, outdoor activities, and learning. Simple but attractive rooms allow families to stay together and a separate bunkhouse in the historic Shapleigh studio accommodates hikers. The center hosts a con-stant series of seasonal education programs throughout the entire year and serves as a center for hiking, bicycling, and other outdoor activities in the vast woodlands around it. While there, be sure to look into the environmentally friendly techniques used to build and operate it. Free environmental tours are offered daily, and all the evening nature programs are free and open to the public, not just to overnight guests. An added plus to all their programs, which include year-round hikes, climbs, and other sports, is free use of the abundant clothing and equipment provided by L.L. Bean. These range from winter boots, insulated gloves, and snowshoes to hiking boots, sleeping bags, and backpacks. Sophisticated, healthy, family-style dinners, which are worlds away from the pass-the-meatballs style of most hiker meals, are served nightly and priced under $20. A vegetarian option is always offered, such as a hearty lentil and vegetable stew. The AMC Highland Center is on Route 302, Crawford Notch; call (603) 466-2727, or contact the Appalachian Mountain Club, 5 Joy St., Boston, MA 02108 (617-523-0655 or www.outdoors.org/lodging/lodges/highland/highland-lodge.cfm).

The happy news is that with the reopening of the railroad through the notch, trains arrive once more, and if you check the schedule of the Conway Scenic Railway, you can be there to see one come through the "Gateway to the Notch" and pull up to the station. Better yet, you can be on one (see the Kancamagus section in this chapter).

Less than half a mile behind the railway station is a waterfall where the abolitionist Henry Ward Beecher liked to swim, so it was named **Beecher's Falls** after him. Follow the Avalon Trail across the tracks and over Crawford Brook. Shortly beyond, a side trail to the left climbs a very short way to the falls. The brook channels through a narrow chute and drops about 25 feet into a pool below. Follow the brook upstream to a second falls and then to a third.

The best view of Crawford Notch is down into it from **Mount Willard,** an easy climb (more accurately, an uphill walk) along an old bridle path to the summit. From there you can see the great scoop of the notch below you, as well as the shimmering cascades that fall off the mountains through rocky ravines. Watch overhead for peregrine falcons, which have nesting sites near the summit of Mount Willard.

Past Saco Lake, which is the source of the Saco River, is Mount Clinton Road, which leads to **Jefferson Notch.** Possibly the least known of the White Mountain notches, its 3,009-foot elevation is the highest point in the state reached by a public road. Gravel all the way, the road passes through deep woods along Monroe Brook, which cascades over rocks between moss-covered banks. At the top, the forest is still too tall to allow any panoramic

The First Trail

The Crawford Path, which begins at the top of Crawford Notch, is the oldest continuously used mountain trail in America, a fact confirmed by a sign erected on the path by the National Forest Service. Cleared in 1819 by Abel Crawford and his son Ethan Allen Crawford, the trail reached the tree line near the summit of Mount Clinton. In 1840 it was widened to bridle-path width. Ethan Allen Crawford, by this time seventy-five years old, used it to make the first ascent of Mount Washington on horseback.

views, but drive into the parking lot for a good, close view of Mount Washington's summit, 3,000 feet above you. The road descends into the town of Jefferson; the entire trip is 9 miles.

While the Cog Railway to the summit of Mount Washington is one of the state's best-known attractions, the **Cog Railway Museum** at the base station enjoys less celebrity. Located opposite the ticket window on the ground floor, its displays include cutaway versions of an early coach and boiler, showing how these were originally built and how they worked. There are also exhibits on the mountain's unusual weather, the history of the railway, and other related subjects such as the fall of the Old Man of the Mountain. There is no admission charge. The museum is open daily May through Oct. Call (603) 846-5404 or (800) 922-8825, or visit www.cog-railway.com.

Our favorite trail up the mountain leaves from just below Base Station. The scenic **Ammonoosuc Ravine Trail** passes a waterfall before it begins any serious climbing, a pleasant short walk for those who do not wish to tackle the peak—or for days when climbing is unadvisable. High up on the mountainside, the trail breaks through the tree line and skirts **Lake of the Clouds,** passing **Lake of the Clouds AMC Hut** before the final climb to the summit via the Crawford Path. The round-trip will take about nine hours for someone in reasonably good shape, assuming the weather is good.

It's a beautiful climb on one of the easiest trails, but for many the summit is a great disappointment. Tourists arriving by train, van, and private car crowd the summit, which on a nice summer day seems more like Hampton Beach than a mountaintop. But the views are spectacular, and you can have lunch at the top and visit the observatory at which the world's highest wind velocity was recorded. A little museum in the lower level tells about the arctic flora and fauna. An older summit house is also a museum, restored to its original interior and furnishings. The museum is open whenever the road is open; $2 for adults.

Although the busy tourist bustle at the top may diminish the sense of conquest afforded by lesser peaks with foot trail access only, the fact remains that climbing Mount Washington is an accomplishment in itself. We've been doing it since we were kids, and it's still a thrill to stand at the top and look out at 360 degrees of mountaintops below. Sometimes there are no mountaintops except the one you stand on, with only a sea of clouds bathed in sunlight.

With the world's worst winter weather, the top of the Presidential Range is not where you'd want to spend much time outdoors at that time of year, but it's cozy inside the **Mount Washington Observatory.** From December through March, a limited number of guests can spend the night, arriving after a two-hour ride up the mountain by snow tractor. It's an adventure suited

If You Climb Mount Washington

Because of its infamous weather, this is not a trip to be undertaken on the spur of the moment. Wait for a day that promises good weather, begin early, and take layers of warm clothing. Even if you plan to lunch at the summit, take plenty of high-protein food and at least two quarts of water. Wear hiking boots (the top is rocky and, if wet, quite treacherous) and be sure you have a sturdy, waterproof windbreaker, even if it's hot and still, without a cloud in sight, when you leave the bottom. The weather above timber line can change from crystal-blue sky to a pea-soup fog in less than fifteen minutes. Never begin a climb here without being prepared to spend the night unsheltered on the mountain. The chances of that are very slight but always there.

only for those in good physical condition, because should the tractor break down halfway through the four-mile trip, it means hiking back to the base or to the top of the mountain. Guests join the staff for dinner and a tour to learn about their work, and most trips include special programs and workshops with experts in related subjects, from winter photography and mountain safety to meteorology, global warming, and geology; www.mountwashington.org.

While the *Mount Washington Hotel* is a White Mountain landmark, few know the *Bretton Arms,* a former chauffeur's quarters that served as home to the secretariat during the Bretton Woods Monetary Conference in 1944. Now an inn and a National Historic Landmark, the Bretton Arms offers newly renovated guest rooms and a more intimate atmosphere than the grand hotel up the hill. Be sure to see the magnificent Victorian stable building just past the inn, where horses, sleighs, and carriages are still housed. The Bretton Arms is located on Route 302, next to the cross-country ski center at *Bretton Woods;* (603) 278-1000 or (800) 314-1752.

The dining room at the Bretton Arms is small and intimate. The menu, too, is different, making the most of opportunities the grand hotel's large dining room doesn't have. Try as we might to sample different starters, we can't resist the smoked duck with cheddar-walnut ravioli. If wild boar in mountain berry plum sauce is on the menu, don't miss it.

The Mount Washington Hotel exudes the opulence of its era, as it should, and it's been restored by owners who really care about the details. (They studied old photos and sent to England for replicas of the original Axminster lobby carpets.) It also exudes history. Nearly every nook and cranny has its story, many of which involve the princess. The hotel's first owner died only a few years after its opening, and his widow remarried a European prince. They continued to return to the hotel for summers, living in Paris in the winter, and she had her magnificent bed crated and shipped with her twice each year. The princess's bed, now retrofitted to queen (Why does this strike us funny?), is in an executive room at the hotel, with a Jacuzzi the princess would have had crated up and shipped to France each winter, too, had it been here then. Speaking of Jacuzzis, Room 114 has one in its bay window nook overlooking the mountains.

For the first time in its history, and just short of its one hundredth anniversary in 2003, the Mount Washington Hotel remained open in the winter of 1999-2000, launching it into the spotlight as a winter resort. Renovations with complete insulation and winterizing have prepared it to do so for at least the next century. Along with the skiing and other winter sports, winter hotel guests enjoy a gala round of special theme events centering around food, holiday celebrations, and music. The Mount Washington Hotel is in Bretton Woods; (603) 278-1000 or (800) 314-1752; www.mtwashington.com.

While you can argue that the hotel is not off the beaten path, the three free tours they give certainly are. You don't have to be a hotel guest to join; just ask at the activities desk. Each of the staff members who leads them has different stories to tell—perhaps of the princess sitting behind a curtain in a little balcony watching the ladies descend to the dining room each evening before choosing which gown to wear to dinner—but you'll certainly see the

The Kind of Ghost You Like to Have Around

I was staying at the Mount Washington Hotel with our daughter, who was at the time about eight years old; it was a warm evening, and we left our big windows open to sleep in the fresh mountain air. In the morning the windows were firmly closed. Odd, I thought, but I said nothing. The next night, the same thing happened, and in the morning I mentioned it to Julie, who not only sleeps like a granite boulder but also was too short to have reached the windows. She suggested that the window might simply have slipped down, but when I checked, the balance and suspension were perfect, and the windows stayed exactly where I put them. "Must be the ghost of the princess," Julie laughed.

When the housekeeping staff came to do up the room, I mentioned the windows. Without so much as a twinkle in her eye, the woman said quite matter-of-factly, "She was probably afraid the little girl would get up in the night and fall through the screen, so she shut them." After that, we left the windows down and saved the princess that stop on her nightly rounds of her hotel.

—Barbara Radcliffe Rogers

ALSO WORTH SEEING IN THE EASTERN WHITE MOUNTAINS

Mount Washington Cog Railway,
Off Route 302, Bretton Woods;
(603) 846-5404 or (800) 922-8825.
Operates Sat and Sun in May, daily
June through late Oct. Departures hourly
from 8 a.m. to 5 p.m. Reservations
suggested for this memorable train that
has been chugging to the summit of
Mount Washington since the 1860s.

Attitash Bear Peak,
Route 302, Bartlett; (603) 374-2368.
Open daily mid-June to mid-Sept,
weekends through mid-Oct with alpine
and water slides, horseback riding, and
a chairlift to the top for 360-degree
views. In winter it is a ski resort.

Tiffany windows and the table where the Bretton Woods Monetary Agreement was signed, and you'll find out why the dining room is round.

The other tours take you to the print shop, where the menus are still hand set in type each day and printed on a press the Smithsonian wants, and to the Stickney Chapel, where one of the windows is signed by Louis Comfort Tiffany and the others are made by his students. If you can, go on a sunny afternoon when the sun is backlighting the chapel's front window. Bretton Woods Mountain Resort combines top-quality family skiing with eye-boggling views across the valley to the Mount Washington Hotel, with its distinctive red roof, and behind it in their full majesty Mount Washington, Mount Clay (now Mount Reagan by federal fiat), and Mount Jefferson. Once known as a small ski area, this is now the largest ski resort in New Hampshire, with more than 101 trails and glades spread over 434 acres of mountainside. Encompassing two (and soon to be three) peaks, the area has a vertical drop of 1,500 feet, access to which is provided by nine lifts. More than 92 percent of the trail area is covered by snowmaking. That, plus its north country location and attention to grooming, assures good skiing all season. The trails here are well balanced in their challenge, with 29 percent beginner slopes, 39 percent intermediate slopes, and 32 percent advanced slopes. On a clear day it's very hard to concentrate on skiing with those views in front of you. Alpine and Nordic skiing are both available, as are equipment rentals and instruction in both styles of skiing. Skiers over age sixty-five take note: You get the astounding daily rate of $16. Located on Route 302, Bretton Woods; (603) 278-3320, snow phone (603) 278-3333, (800) 258-0330; www.brettonwoods.com.

Instead of leaving the area via Jefferson Notch, you can continue along Route 302 to the *Zealand Campground,* where there is a nice picnic area along the Ammonoosuc River. If you continue up the Zealand Road, about 3.5 miles to its end, you can take the Zealand Trail to *Zealand Falls,* a 2.5-mile easy hike. Getting to the top of the falls is the only climbing involved—there is only about a 350-foot difference in altitude from the parking lot to the top of the falls. The falls is really a cascade, and at its top, from the AMC hut, is a view of New Hampshire's hidden notch. Only hikers can see the dramatic shape of Zealand Notch, for no road penetrates it at any point. Take a lunch to eat by the falls as you enjoy the view. Along the trail you will follow the bed of a nineteenth-century logging railroad and pass through hardwood forests. It's hard to picture this entire valley laid waste by uncontrolled lumbering and the resulting fire and erosion damage, so great was the ability of the forest to rejuvenate itself here.

About halfway up the Zealand Road is the *Sugarloaf Campground,* one of the loveliest and most secluded in the mountains. Roomy sites are carved out of young forest, some with direct paths to the rocky Zealand River below. For information, write to the district ranger, White Mountain National Forest, Bethlehem 03574. Call (877) 444-6777 for reservations or (603) 536-1315 for information; www.campsnh.com.

The *Twin Mountain Fish and Wildlife Center,* on Route 3 north of Twin Mountain, has a museum featuring local wildlife and an excellent exhibit on Water on the Move. It shows water in all its habitats, in a flowing stream, riffle area, cold-water pool, beaver pond, and wetland, each with its fish life. Although we think it was intended for kids, we found it fascinating, and we learned a lot about our finny neighbors. You can also tour the hatchery and hike a nature trail. It's free and open May through Oct daily 8 a.m. to 4 p.m.; the center is open 9 a.m. to 4:30 p.m. For information call (603) 846-5429 or visit http://www.twinmountain.com/hatchery.php.

More Places to Stay in the Eastern White Mountains

CAMPTON

Mountain-Fare Inn
Mad River Rd.
(603) 726-4283
www.mountainfareinn.com

An 1840s village house with antiques and flower gardens; rates low end of moderate.

CONWAY AND NORTH CONWAY

The Buttonwood Inn
Mt. Surprise Rd.
(603) 356-2625 or
(800) 258-2625
www.buttonwoodinn.com

Spacious rooms with sitting areas, some with fireplaces and whirlpool tubs, are in a secluded setting with walking trails right out the back door. Families are welcome, and one of the owners is a chef, so breakfasts are a treat. Rates begin in the lower moderate range.

The Cabernet Inn
Route 16
(603) 356-4704 or
(800) 866-4704
www.cabernetinn.com
Elegantly furnished
throughout, Cabernet is
a pampering refuge for
adults, with large, bright
guest rooms and a com-
mon area that opens onto
a garden terrace.

The Farm By the River
2555 West Side Rd.
(603) 356-2694 or
(888) 414-8353
www.farmbytheriver.com
An original land-grant farm,
still in the same family since
King George III. Horses,
cross-country skiing, and
fishing on the property.

Fox Ridge
off Route 16
(603) 356-3151 or
(800) 343-1804;
www.redjacketresorts.com
Motel-style rooms are
large, with nice decora-
tive touches and balconies
or terraces with views.

Swimming, tennis, and a
location close to the outlet
shops.

Green Granite Resort
Route 16
(603) 356-6901 or
(800) 468-3666
www.greengranite.com
Family owned and one of
the most attractive, hospitable lodgings in town, with
indoor heated and outdoor
pools, an exercise room,
and a sauna.

GORHAM
**Appalachian Mountain
Club**
Route 16
(603) 466-2727
www.outdoors.org
The Pinkham Notch Visitor
Center offers rustic lodging
and three meals a day at
reasonable prices.

JACKSON
Christmas Farm Inn
Route 16B
(603) 383-4313 or
(800) HI–ELVES
www.christmasinn.com
A charming country inn and
resort with a full service
spa on 15 acres.

**Lincoln Mountain Club at
Loon**
Loon Mountain Resort
(603) 745-2244 or
(800) 229-STAY
www.mtnclub.com
A modern hotel that keeps
the atmosphere of a ski
lodge; indoor parking, balconies, pools.

WATERVILLE VALLEY
Black Bear Lodge
(603) 236-4501
(800) 349-BEAR (2327)
www.blackbearlodgenh
.com
Two-room suites with
kitchenettes. Ideal for families, with pool in building
and moderate rates.

TO LEARN MORE ABOUT THE EASTERN WHITE MOUNTAINS

**White Mountain Attractions
Association,**
Route 112 at exit 32 off I–93,
200 Kancamagus Highway,
North Woodstock 03262;
(603) 745-8720 or (800) 346-3687
outside New Hampshire;
www.visitwhitemountains.com.

**Mount Washington Valley Chamber of
Commerce,**
Route 16, P.O. Box 2300,
North Conway 03860;
(800) 367-3364;
www.mtwashingtonvalley.com.

The Valley Inn
(603) 236-8425 or
(800) 343-0969
www.valleyinn.com
A full-service hotel with the warmth of an inn, moderate prices, and some real bargain specials. The restaurant offers hearty standards—steak, fried chicken, burgers—in a pub-like setting, at moderate prices.

More Places to Eat in the Eastern White Mountains

CONWAY

Chinook Café
Route 16
(603) 447-6300
Serving healthy, innovative breakfasts and lunches with plenty of vegetarian options, Chinook Café also offers cooking classes on subjects ranging from bread baking to cooking winter vegetables.

LINCOLN

Gypsy Cafe
Route 112
(603) 745-4395
Just down the road from Loon Mountain, in the center of Lincoln, the cafe serves a worldly, eclectic menu with especially interesting Latin dishes, such

as Cuban pork—a grilled tenderloin with habanero-orange mojo. Moderate.

NORTH CONWAY

Maestro's
6 Reporter Court
(603) 356-8790
Hidden in an alley off Main Street, this tiny restaurant is known by locals for its good Northern Italian food, served in a far from fancy but very friendly cafe. They carry a small selection of imported Italian specialty ingredients, too, in case you want to cook in your condo. Moderate.

Stonehurst Manor
Route 16
(603) 356-3113
www.StonehurstManor.com
A New Hampshire Farm to Restaurant member, Stonehurst serves a changing menu to take advantage of as much locally grown produce as possible. Breads are baked at the inn, which is well-known for its innovative pizzas.

NORTH WOODSTOCK

Cafe Lafayette Dinner Train
Hobo Railroad Station
(603) 745-3500 or
(800) 699-3501
www.nhdinnertrain.com
A restored, 1952 Pullman dome car travels at a stately speed along the

Pemigewasset Valley while passengers enjoy dinner and a changing panorama. Between Memorial Day and Columbus Day, it runs four days a week, with a few runs late in the fall.

WATERVILLE

Wild Coyote Grill
White Mountain Athletic Club
(603) 236-4919
http://wildcoyotegrill.com
Serving dinner every day and weekend lunches, featuring such specialties as pork chops encrusted with walnuts and flavored with a hint of apple, or chicken marinated before slow roasting.

WATERVILLE VALLEY

The Campton/Waterville/Loon Mountain area is right on the border of our division between the Eastern and Western White Mountains, with North Woodstock and Thornton right on the line. Be sure to look in the "More Places to Eat" pages of the next chapter for dining and lodging options in these two towns close to Lincoln and Waterville Valley.

THE WESTERN WHITE MOUNTAINS

The summer social season on this side of the *White Mountains* involved not only guests at the grand hotels—Profile House, Forest Hills, Sunset Hill, and the resorts of Bethlehem—but an increasing number of wealthy people who built their own summer estates, especially in Sugar Hill and Bethlehem. When the era of hotel summers ended, these families continued to return. Some retired here, giving the area a permanent cultural tradition that shows today in regular art and music events.

This land is beautiful, and the mountains a little less craggy than the Presidential Range to the east. Towns here have less of a seasonal air about them, being year-round communities with their own economic base. Downtown stores cater more to local needs than to tour-bus shopping expeditions. Hospitality is warm, and visitors return to the same inn year after year.

Country stores, covered bridges, farms, and mountain streams punctuate the miles of forests bordering the winding country roads. Only the stone walls that wind through the woodlands remind us that much of this land was once cleared for farming. This is a place for relaxing, exploring, and savoring.

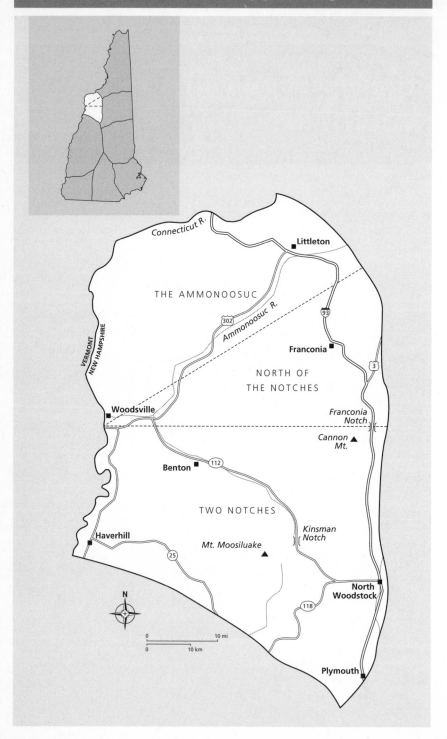

Connecticut R.

Littleton

THE AMMONOOSUC

302   Ammonoosuc R.

93

VERMONT
NEW HAMPSHIRE

Franconia

NORTH OF
THE NOTCHES

3

Woodsville

Franconia
Notch

Cannon ▲
Mt.

112

Benton

TWO NOTCHES

Kinsman
Notch

Haverhill

Mt. Moosiluake ▲

25

North
Woodstock

N

118

0   10 mi
0   10 km

Plymouth

Two Notches

The ***White Mountain National Forest's*** westernmost segment begins just south of Sugar Hill and Franconia. Route 116 continues past the Frost Place to the town of Easton, high in the hills and completely surrounded by the national forest. South of Easton on Route 112 is a wild and beautiful notch almost completely overshadowed by the fame of neighboring Franconia Notch.

The road through Kinsman Notch winds and curves and climbs until it reaches tiny Beaver Lake, a high mountain tarn, rockbound and icy cold. In its center rises a rocky, pine-clad island. The landscape here is wild and almost desolate under the slope of Mount Blue—but nowhere near as forbidding as it must have looked to Asa Kinsman and his wife. With their household goods on a two-wheeled cart pulled by oxen, they discovered that they had taken the wrong track to their new home in Landaff. Instead of turning back to go around the mountains that lay in their way, they hacked a path through the notch. If you take a turn you didn't plan on or miss the road you wanted, just remember the Kinsmans and take heart.

At its top the notch opens out, giving excellent views down the valley to the east. The narrowness and curves of the road at the top give a real sense of this being a pass, more so than some of the better-known notches. For some reason we can't understand, ***Agaziz Basin*** is never listed among the natural attractions of the White Mountains, whereas less interesting gorges and water-falls are. It's also easier than most to get to, right beside Route 112, just west of North Woodstock. In the summer, there's a sign; off-season, look for a parking lot on the south side of the road. One of the safer of New England's gorges to visit, the site includes a bridge over the falls.

Lost River really isn't lost, it just plays hide-and-seek for a while among glacially jumbled boulders, falling into huge rock chambers and through caves. Boardwalks and stairs make the trip easier, and you can simply walk through, or you can wriggle through the "lemon squeezer" or other tight passages that the claustrophobic should probably avoid. It's a beautiful area, and at the top is a garden with examples of woodland wildflowers, some of them quite rare. You can see the garden without paying the $12 admission to go through Lost River. Also at the entrance is a re-created "mining sluice" where kids can pan for real semi-precious stones that they can keep. Open mid-May to late Oct 9 a.m. to 5 p.m. and until 6 p.m. in July and Aug. It's on Route 112 West in Kinsman Notch; (603) 745-8031; www.findlostriver.com.

Farther along Route 112, the entire family can experience the real thing, panning for gold in the Wild Ammonoosuc River. Stop at Twin River

Campground (603-747-3640) to buy an inexpensive pan and join other "prospectors" in the shallow river to find a few flakes to take home.

Dinner on the *Cafe Lafayette Dinner Train* is not the usual pretty-views-with-mediocre-food tourist train ride. In fact, the scenery is not spectacular—no broad mountain vistas but a lovely woodland trip along a rocky river. And the meal served on this leisurely ride is excellent, prepared on the train and artistically presented. Each of the antique rail cars has been restored, bringing to life the aura of railroading's glory days. As dusk falls, outside lighting casts a spell on the passing woods. The dinner train runs May through June and late Oct, Tues, Thurs, and Sat; July through mid-Oct, Tues, Thurs, Sat, and Sun. Boarding time is 5:15 p.m. (4:30 p.m. Sun), and the trip takes about two hours. The dinner and ride cost $65; $45 for children three to eleven. Located on Route 112, 0.25 mile west of exit 32 on I-93, North Woodstock; outside New Hampshire call (800) 699-3501, in New Hampshire call (603) 745-3500; www.nhdinnertrain.com.

Using the same tracks along the Pemigewasset River is the child-pleasing *Hobo Railroad*, which leaves from a station just off I-93 exit 32 in Lincoln, at the beginning of the Kancamagus Highway. The onboard hobo clown doubles as crossing flagman to stop traffic on Route 112 before taking up the role of onboard entertainer with magic tricks and spoofs. The conductor tells about the train line's history in the logging days as you roll past views of the river framed in the maple and birch trees. In the 1850s, when the whole of northern New Hampshire was filled with lumber camps, the Boston and Maine Railroad built its line from Boston to Montreal through Plymouth. Loggers in the woods along the Kancamagus Pass floated the logs they had cut all winter down the Pemi to Plymouth, where they were loaded onto southbound trains. In 1880 the railroad was extended to Lincoln, and paper mills were built there to process pulpwood as it was cut. But chemicals from those mills killed everything in the river, until the Clean Water Act gave the mills a choice in 1975: clean up or shut down. The Lincoln mills closed and when the B&M abandoned the track, locals turned it into a tourist railroad. The Hobo Railroad operates daily through foliage season, weekends only in the spring, with departures at 11 a.m., 1 p.m., and 3 p.m. Before traveling a long distance, it's always a good idea to confirm times; call (603) 745-2135 or visit www.hoborr.com.

In the village of North Woodstock may be the most complete breakfast menu in the White Mountains, at the *Clement Room Restaurant,* in the Woodstock Inn. Munch on their famous sticky buns as you browse several pages of entrees that include a dozen tempting varieties of Eggs Benedict alone. The toast is made from their own bread, which also arrives fresh from the oven at dinner in the Clement Room. The more intimate atmosphere in the evening is the setting for an innovative menu of choices such as veal medallions with lobster chunks, asparagus, and hollandaise, or venison served with cranberries, walnuts, and venison sausage in a port-wine demi-glace laced with maple syrup. Woodstock Inn's Brewery, entirely visible through a glass wall in the brew pub, takes the usual tastings and tours a step further with Brewers Weekends. Owner Scott Rice says, "The guests take over the brewery; the brewers just stand by to advise and teach."

There's a lot more than dining and drinking at the **Woodstock Inn.** Several fine old buildings in North Woodstock's little downtown cluster around the main inn, each with its own style of accommodations. Two are Arts and Crafts–style cottages with nicely preserved interiors, and one, Cascade lodge, is a classic old Adirondack-style lodge, furnished entirely in beautiful hand-crafted rustic furniture. In the common room big cushy sofas face a huge river-stone fireplace with a birch mantel. In the guest rooms, king-size beds are made of peeled birch logs and accessories are museum-quality Arts and Crafts reproductions. Don't think rustic in terms of comfort, through—these rooms have heated bathroom floors and whirlpool tubs. The Woodstock Inn, Main St. (Route 3), North Woodstock, call (603) 745-3951 or (800) 321-3985), or visit www.woodstockinnnh.com.

Franconia Notch, until May 2003, was the home of the state's symbol, the **Old Man of the Mountain.** It was to protect the fragile ledges of this famous stone profile from the dangers of blasting that I-93 was stopped just below the

An Old Friend Slips Away

In May 2003 New Hampshire was stunned by the loss of its symbol, the **Old Man of the Mountain,** which fell into Franconia Notch. For almost everyone it was a loss that was personal and deeply felt.

For ten to twelve thousand years, he looked out from his cliffside, but it wasn't until 1805 that he was discovered, by workmen Nathaniel Hall and Luke Brooks, who were repairing the road through the notch. Over the past two centuries, a few dedicated people, especially E. H. Geddes from 1916 to 1937 and Niels Nielsen and his family from 1954 to 2003, made a tremendous effort to shore up the cluster of huge loose ledges that made up the face. But nature and the immutable laws of physics have won out, to the great loss of New Hampshire and the people who loved the profile.

But the Old Man will not be forgotten. A special state commission is considering ways to commemorate him, and an expanded museum is likely to open in Franconia Notch.

Modest, but True

Native son Daniel Webster is credited with the following observation about the Old Man of the Mountain:

"Men hang out their signs indicative of their respective trades. Shoemakers hang out a giant shoe, jewelers a monster watch, and a dentist hangs out a gold tooth; but up in the White Mountains of New Hampshire, God Almighty has hung out a sign to show that there he makes men."

notch and resumed just above it. The Old Man may have slid into the notch, but he is far from forgotten. You can learn more about the Old Man's geology at the small, free ***Old Man of the Mountain Museum,*** at the beginning of the path that leads to Profile Lake. Along with pictures of volunteers dangling on ropes in front of the Old Man's nose, you'll see a varied collection of memorabilia picturing the profile and Profile House, the grand hotel that once looked out across Echo Lake, at the head of Franconia Notch.

Most of the souvenir plates, cups and saucers, engravings, stereopticon views, and silver spoons are at least a hundred years old, many dating from the late nineteenth century, the golden age of the White Mountains grand hotels. Connected to the museum is a tiny shop where you'll find the new generation of Old Man of the Mountain souvenirs. You can also buy huge, top-heavy cones of the White Mountains' local homemade ice cream from Bishop's in Littleton.

The Face That Shouldn't Have Been There

The Old Man of the Mountain (no "s" at the end, please) shouldn't have been there as long as he was. The top two of the five granite ledges that formed the great stone face were cantilevered out well beyond the carrying capacity of the distance for which they penetrated the mountainside. "There's nothing holding them up; they should have fallen into the notch centuries ago," explained the man who knew these famous ledges better than anyone else. Niels Nielsen climbed down over the Old Man's face, suspended on ropes, every year from 1960 to the 1980s, when his son David took over the job, to measure slippage and seal any cracks that might allow water to freeze inside and split the ledge. Equipment for this annual face-lift was brought up by helicopter; the Nielsens were volunteers, and the first time David went down the face, he was eleven years old.

The Old Man of the Mountain Museum is located at the head of Franconia Notch, near the base of the aerial tramway, and is open daily from mid-May through mid-Oct; www.oldmanofthemountainmuseum.org/. For more information about the museum (or anything else in the White Mountains), contact White Mountain Attractions at (603) 745-8720; www.visitwhite mountains.com.

Also at the head of the notch, by the base of the aerial tramway, is the **New England Ski Museum.** Permanent and changing exhibits tell the story of this sport with historical equipment, photographs, art, and even changing fashions in skiwear. Open daily Memorial Day through the end of March, 10a.m. to 5 p.m.; admission is free. The New England Ski Museum is in Franconia Notch; call (603) 823-7177 or visit www.skimuseum.org.

The **Rim Trail** can be reached from the top of the aerial tramway (look for one of its original 1930s cars at the Ski Museum) or via the Kinsman Ridge Trail from the head of Franconia Notch. It offers hikers panoramic views into the notch and across the Franconia and Presidential Ranges along the exposed rim and from the observation tower at the end. Notice the scar on the steep facing slope of Mount Lafayette, caused by a 1959 landslide that covered the road through the notch with 27 feet of debris. Even today, the physical forces of weathering and erosion continue the work of the glaciers in changing the landscape of the notches. Be sure to watch for peregrine falcons that nest on Eagle Cliff below, where golden eagles once laid their eggs.

A trail from the glacial formation known as **The Basin** leads to **Cascade Brook** and **Kinsman Falls.** Although these cascades are less than a ten-minute level walk from The Basin, they are never crowded and provide a fine place to picnic or just explore. The ledges over which the brook slides and drops have been worn into graceful curves, potholes, tiny flumes, and gorges by the brook. In places the water spreads over the granite in a smooth sheet; elsewhere it falls in ribbons from pool to pool. You can climb through the woods along the trail or up the sloping face of the ledges. When water is high or the weather rainy, it's better to stay on the trail and avoid the slippery rocks.

Below The Basin (turn left when the trail forks right to Kinsman Falls) is a pretty trail along the river, past a narrow little flume. The brook is the upper part of the Pemigewasset, well named by the Abenaki, who described it with their word for "swift." It is the prime watershed (river into which smaller streams empty) for Franconia Notch and for much of the hill country it flows through as it moves south, draining over 5,000 square miles. The river begins at Profile Lake, at an altitude of 1,900 feet. About 60 miles downstream it becomes the Merrimack River, which finally empties into the Atlantic Ocean, after a 185-mile trip, at Newburyport, Massachusetts.

Frostbite Follies,
early Feb, Franconia
(603) 823-5661,
(800) 237-9007

Lilac Time Festival,
late May, Lisbon
(603) 838-6673

Fields of Lupine Festival,
June, Sugar Hill and Franconia
(603) 823-5661, (800) 237-9007;
www.franconianotch.org/special-events/
lupine-festival.aspx

**Music in the White Mountains
Summer Festival,**
July–Aug,
Lincoln and Sugar Hill
(603) 869-3154

Quilt Festival,
mid-Oct, Sugar Hill and Franconia
(603) 823-5661, (800) 237-9007

North of the Notches

Over the hills, on Route 117, lies Sugar Hill, stretched along the top of a ridge overlooking some of the White Mountains' most beautiful scenery. It's the kind of genteel town where people wave to you from their front porches as you go for an evening walk. **Harman's Store** should be your first stop, for fine aged cheddar that bears no resemblance to the grocery store stuff. Harman's sends cheese and first-run New Hampshire maple syrup to people all over the country who don't really believe there is a town named **Sugar Hill.** The secret of their cheese is that they buy fine cheddar and then age it themselves. You'll find New Hampshire jams and jellies, soldier beans, common crackers, and whole-wheat pancake flour here, too, and all grades of the New Hampshire maple syrup that gave Sugar Hill its name. They also sell Vermont syrup for those people who won't believe that maple trees grow all over New England, New York, and Quebec (but the proprietors snicker a little behind their counter when they do). Open 9 a.m. to 5 p.m. daily, May to Oct; closed Sun from Nov to Apr. Call Harman's Cheese and Country Store at (603) 823-8000.

Across the street is the **historical museum.** Housed in three buildings, the exhibits show, through an exceptional collection of old photographs, artifacts, carriages, and furnishings, the daily life of early settlers and Sugar Hill's heyday as a summer resort. Here are the kitchen from a stagecoach tavern with its original furnishings, a blacksmith shop, the ornate wagon of a local hotel, and a genealogical library. A small admission fee is charged. Open Thurs, Fri, and Sat late June through Labor Day, 1 to 4 p.m. Call (603) 823-5336 or visit www.harmanscheese.com.

Within walking distance of both of these is **Hilltop Inn.** This is one of those places that friends hesitate to tell you about because they are afraid it will become so popular there won't be room for them. The 1895 Victorian home is decorated with period furniture but offers every modern comfort. Big beds, plenty of pillows for late-night readers, flannel sheets, and antique linens are just a few of the luxuries. But the real charm of the Hilltop Inn is its owners, Meri and Mike Hern. Their offbeat sense of humor and irrepressible enthusiasm make old friends out of strangers from the first rumble of Mike's contagious chuckle. Meri's breakfasts are so good, with fresh-baked breads and elegant main dishes, that we keep hoping to be snowbound there so she'll have to cook dinner for us, too. It's possible, since the inn is open year-round. Rooms range upward from $45 in low season. Write Hilltop Inn, 1348 Main St., Sugar Hill 03585; (603) 823-5695 or (800) 770-5695; www.hill topinn.com.

Since its heyday as a summer resort, Sugar Hill has had a flourishing arts community and hosts the **North Country Chamber Players**' annual summer festival in the meetinghouse in July and August. Members of this organization hold first-chair positions in major orchestras. For a complete schedule of concerts, write Box 99, Franconia 03580, or call (603) 444-0309 or visit www .northcountrychamberplayers.org.

The **Sunset Hill House** was one of the grandest of the White Mountains resort hotels, on the crest of a hill with mountain views in all directions. A boardwalk connected it to the village so that ladies could stroll up to watch the sunset without soiling the hems of their gowns. The main building is gone now, but a second one dating from 1882 has just been restored to an opulence that made the original hotel famous. Guest rooms are beautiful and comfortable, with a view from every window. The dining room overlooks the Presidential Range, which on clear evenings is bathed in a rosy reflection of the sunset known as alpenglow. Dinner guests may have trouble giving the menu the attention it deserves until after dusk claims the mountains, but the flavors of dishes such as duckling sauced in chutney, brandy, and almonds can compete with any view on equal terms. There is no off-season here, with sleigh rides, cross-country trails, golf, hiking, and maple sugaring available from the front door and ski slopes minutes away. Write Sunset Hill House, Sunset Hill Rd., Sugar Hill 03585; (603) 823-5522 or (800) 786-4455; www .sunsethillhouse.com.

In the valley of the Gale River, east of Sugar Hill, **Franconia** was once the center of an iron industry that thrived from 1811 until the 1850s. The ore came

The Day the World Didn't End

The Millerites were followers of William Miller, a clergyman of the early 1800s who prophesied the end of the world on October 22, 1844. Sugar Hill had a particularly active group of Millerites, many of whom were so convinced by his preaching that they raised no crops that year, secure in the knowledge that there would be no winter to provide for. Others sold or gave away their livestock as the day approached and devoted themselves to prayer and fasting.

On the ordained day, they gathered at the cemetery on the little rise at the west side of town, which you can see above you as you head toward Lisbon on Route 117. They wore long, flowing white robes, the proper dress for ascending to their eternal reward. The end of the story is probably no surprise to you: The world didn't end on October 22. But other locals had a lot of fun over them, especially with one gentleman who was giving his unsaved neighbors a last-minute exhortation that morning and fell asleep afterward next to a small pile of hay. The objects of his sermon lit the hay on fire, and when the man awoke to the smell of smoke and crackling of fire, he was certain the end had come and he'd gone to hell.

from mines close to Sunset Hill House; the vein was the richest then known. The giant *stone furnace iron* where ore was smelted still stands by the river, near the LaFayette Regional School on the east side of Route 116, just south of its junction with Route 117. An interpretive center and outdoor panels explain the process that turned ore into wrought-iron bars. Inside the building, which is open irregular hours, is a scale model of the furnace, cut away to show its interior. This is the only iron furnace remaining in the state.

South of the village, off Route 116, the **Robert Frost Place** is a small weathered farmhouse with its mailbox marked R. FROST. Along with Robert Frost memorabilia and autographed first editions, there are a slide show, a nature trail marked with lines of his poetry, and a rare collection of the poet's less-known work: Christmas card verses. Open late May to July 5 Sat and Sun 1 to 5 p.m., Wed through Mon, 1 to 5 p.m, July through Columbus Day. You can walk the trail after hours but mustn't disturb the poet in residence. Donation of $5 adult, $4 senior, $3 ages six to eighteen suggested. The Frost Place is in Franconia; call (603) 823-5510.

The Ammonoosuc

Bethlehem, now a quiet town stretched out along a ridge, was once a major resort capital of the White Mountains. Along its main street stood thirty of the biggest and the grandest hotels, a summer-long procession of splendor and gaiety. They are gone now, but the elegant cottages that surrounded them are still there—some serving today as bed-and-breakfasts—and so is the pure, pollen-free mountain air that attracted the first visitors.

Its quiet streets and airy location make Bethlehem a good base for exploring the national forest, where the ban on commercial activity leaves no lodging for those who don't enjoy camping.

There are, it is said, more architectural styles in Bethlehem than in any other New England town. It's easy to believe. But the most unusual must be *The Bells,* a pagoda-shaped, three-story cottage on Strawberry Hill Street. For a self-guided tour that reveals some of Bethlehem's lively architectural and social heritage, get a copy of the booklet *An Illustrated Tour of Bethlehem,* sold locally for $2.

The Rocks, west of Bethlehem on Route 302, is a late-nineteenth-century farm estate now in the care of the Society for the Protection of New Hampshire Forests. The double stone walls, the buttresses, and the lower story of the Victorian barn were built of stones cleared from the rolling pastures and meadows that surround the house and barns. A free leaflet describes the sights along a 2-mile self-guided trail, past a highly original sawmill-pigpen and a bee hive, and on through forest and wetlands. Another self-guided trail, this one through the Christmas tree plantation, describes the growing of trees and some of the estate's history as it leads to a scenic overview.

Seasonal activities are planned on weekends year-round, with a Halloween festival, hay-wagon tours of the Christmas tree plantation (along with cut-your-own sales), a winter forest festival with logging demonstrations, snowshoe tours, maple sugaring, and a wildflower festival. Nature trails and gardens are free and open dawn to dusk. Maps are available describing cultural history, the process of growing Christmas trees, and the forest habitats. There are fees for special programs, and registration is necessary for some. The Rocks is on Route 302, Bethlehem 03574; call (603) 444-6228 or visit www.therocks.org.

Off Prospect Street and also managed by the same society is the *Bretzfelder Memorial Park,* seventy-seven acres of forest, pond, mountain brook, and picnic areas connected by walking and cross-country trails. A leaflet tells about the various trees, and signs along the trails explain the natural history and ecology. The story of Mr. Bretzfelder and his favorite tree (the tree is still alive even after major surgery) is told on a sign by the entrance. On Wednesday evenings in July and August at 7 p.m., take an evening ramble to explore some aspect of the park—its nocturnal animals, wildflowers, or other subject. No admission is charged; call (603) 444-6228 for dates and a description of the programs; www.therocks.org/bretzfelder.php.

In the center of town is *Angelica's,* a seafood restaurant whose chef/ owner travels to New Bedford, Massachusetts, three times a week to buy from the fishing boats. The menu offers seafood prepared in a variety of ways, and the chef does very well with any of them—including fried clams, shrimps, and scallops that arrive at the table crisp on the outside and perfectly cooked on the inside. In nice weather, ask for a table on the wide porch, overlooking their beautiful gardens and Bethlehem's wide main street. Angelica's Restaurant, 2085 Main St., Bethlehem; call (603) 869-5420.

Maplewood was not just the largest and grandest of the local hotels; it was a village of its own with a Victorian railroad station, farms to provide food for its dining rooms, a sugar bush that once yielded one hundred gallons of syrup each spring, a golf course, and a casino with a ballroom, movie theater, and bowling alley. The hotel is gone, but the village of Maplewood is still on the map. The restored casino with its stone tower still guards the golf course, and four wonderful old "cottages"—great hulking things with porches and gabled windows—are situated in a row just east of the casino.

Beyond them is a little shrine by the side of the road with a lovely story to tell. From the beginning of the century until 1949, underprivileged boys from a Boston industrial school were brought up in the summers to work as caddies at Maplewood. In 1958 a number of the former caddies, many of them prominent and successful, built the shrine. To this day these men gather at Maplewood for reunions.

Not far from Bethlehem, on its way to Whitefield, Route 142 drops down a long, steep hill. At the very bottom, just as the road curves to the left, is the tiny brown workshop of a man who has been honored by the president and whose work is on permanent display at the Smithsonian Institution. *Newt Washburn* is a fourth-generation Abenaki basket maker, one of fewer than half a dozen who have continued in this art. He designs and makes his own tools, the knives and splitters with which he turns an ash log into a finely woven basket. On a full-size basket each splint is the thickness of a growth ring separated from the log, but for smaller baskets Newt splits each splint in half to keep its thickness

Something for Every Taste

The Art Deco *Colonial Theater* on Main Street is being restored and brought back to life as the town's entertainment center. Its schedule features art and foreign films, live music and performances, and even a matinee for parents with babies so they can enjoy the movie without their children disturbing patrons who don't have kids. For a current schedule, call (603) 869-3422 or visit www.bethlehemcolonial.org.

in proportion to its width. Newt will show you the whole process, from log to basket, and his scrapbook, too. This is a rare chance to order museum-quality Abenaki baskets, although there is no stock for sale ready-made. Newt Washburn's workshop is in Bethlehem Hollow; call (603) 869-5894.

As you arrive in Littleton on Route 302, **Bishop's Homemade Ice Cream Shoppe** is in a white house on the right. If you can think of any excuse to stop and try this ice cream, do it. You can sit at picnic tables on the lawn or inside the upbeat green-and-white ice-cream parlor while you enjoy the old favorite flavors—both blueberry and maple are extraordinary—a wide variety of homemade yogurt flavors, or one of their unique recipes. For calorie watchers or those with cholesterol problems, there are sorbets rich with the taste of real fruit. The Bishop's Bash is filled with chunks of brownie, walnuts, and chocolate chips. Open daily noon to 10 p.m. from mid-April until mid-Oct at 183 Cottage St. in Littleton; (603) 444-6039.

Opposite Bishop's, Mt. Eustice Road travels under I-93, just beyond which a short lane leads to the **Wallace Horse Cemetery.** Inside a small corral are three graves and a family stone; on the fence a placard explains the touching story of the team of matched bay Morgans, buried here with all their regalia, the only "children" of the Wallaces from 1889 until the death of the horses in 1919. As touching as the story recounted here are the pennies that visitors have placed on the stones.

Throughout northern New Hampshire you will see photographs of the White Mountains "the way we were" during the golden age. Most of these were reproduced from stereoscopic view cards, which, when seen through the double lenses of a special viewer, jumped into a three-dimensional landscape or scene. They were the forerunner of the Viewmaster and were a prime source of home entertainment. The major manufacturer of these cards was the Kilburn Brothers Stereoscopic View factory in **Littleton.**

Look where any river in New Hampshire drops more than a few feet in a short distance, and you are almost certain to find evidence of an old mill foundation or pieces of a former dam. You'll find them on small streams, often in places long overgrown with forest.

In Littleton you can see one of these brought back to life. At **Littleton Grist Mill,** between Main Street and the river, you can see the giant waterwheel that turned more wheels inside the understory of the mill, connected by belts to a series of other wheels and belts, only a small part of a complex system that once powered a fulling mill, three gristmills, and several others. The cog wheels are made of wood, with teeth more than two inches in diameter. You can buy flours ground at the mill, along with whole grain cereals and mixes for pancakes, scones, and breads, in the mill shop.

A Real Deal

The White Mountain Attractions Association offers an irresistible bargain on admissions to seventeen of the most popular places in the mountains. For about half the price of the normal entrance fees, you can buy a *White Mountains Value Pass,* a single pass that admits two adults to each of the member attractions. Since nearly all the biggies are members of the White Mountains Attractions Association, the pass pretty well covers the north country. But unlike most season passes, these are transferable, so two different households can share one, or you can loan it to friends.

The attractions include natural wonders (The Flume Gorge, Lost River Gorge, and Polar Caves) and New Hampshire's low-key kids' park and recreation sites—Santa's Village, Six Gun City, Story Land, Clark's Trading Post, Whale's Tale Water Park, and Fields of Attitash. In addition are the major mountain-top rides: the Cannon Mountain Aerial Tramway, Loon Mountain, Wildcat Mountain Gondolas, and—worth a big chunk of the cost by itself—the Mt. Washington Cog Railway. Other scenic rides, including the *Conway Scenic Railroad,* Hobo Railroad, and Mount Washington Auto Road, are also included on the pass.

The number of these passes sold is limited, so it's a good idea to order them early—they are mailed on April 1 each year. The value of the admissions is about $600, and the cost of the pass is about $295. They are good until each attraction closes at the end of the season. Order from White Mountains Attractions, PO Box 10, VPB, North Woodstock, NH 03262; call (800) 346-3687 or log onto www.visit whitemountains.com.

The mill is at 18 Mill St.; (603) 444-7478 or (888) 284-7478; www.littleton gristmill.com. It is open daily May through Dec and Wed through Sat in winter and spring. Admission is free.

In 2003, the National Trust for Historic Preservation named Littleton a Great American Main Street Community. One look at the six-block Main Street, bookended by the 1895 town hall at one end and the 1832 white Congregational church at the other, will tell you why. One side is lined with classic brick mercantile buildings, interrupted by the white Doric-columned facade of 1850 Thayers Inn and the 1940 metal-wrapped Littleton Diner. The other side is more eclectic, ranging from the 1909 Beaux Arts Masonic temple and 1935 Federal Court Building to the last of the nineteenth-century homes that once looked down on Main Street from shaded lawns. The last remaining one is now the Community House, and its elegant interior is preserved and open to the public.

Learn about the architecture and history by picking up a copy of the 16-page walking tour booklet, which identifies and tells the story of more than 20 historic landmarks. Main Street was the original route of an 1820 coach road, and Thayers Inn was built to house the increasing traffic along it. The rest of the town grew as mills took advantage of the power generated by the 144-foot drop in the Ammonoosuc River, some 60 feet below Main Street.

The Village Book Store is the place to find, along with best sellers and an excellent children's section, a tremendous array of books about the White Mountains. A stairway from the bookstore leads down to the New Hampshire League of Craftsmen's stunning new gallery, overlooking the gristmill and the Ammonoosuc. Back up on Main Street, *Chutters* claims the world's longest candy counter, 112 feet of sweet stuff that includes all the long-ago penny candy favorites. At Rae's Smoke Shop, as much museum as shop, you can buy handy cigar boxes without having to buy the cigars that came in them.

Step inside Parkers Marketplace to see some of the original interior of the Parker Mansion, home of the business partner of Sylvester Marsh, builder of the Mt. Washington Cog Railway. From the library lawn, a statue of the fictional character Pollyanna encompasses the scene with outstretched arms. She was the creation of local author Eleanor Porter, and her exuberant spirit is a good match for Littleton's own. This lively Main Street has taken a lot of local initiative to maintain in the face of the north country's long-term economic woes.

Tim and Biruta Carr, owners of *Tim-Bir Alley* restaurant, are back in Littleton, after several years in Bethlehem, now in a classy setting on Main Street. Tim-Bir Alley provides an exceptional, if expensive, dining experience. The menu changes daily, featuring what might include sole with wild mushrooms and shrimp in a Chardonnay sauce, salmon in a sunflower-seed crust, or maple-glazed pork tenderloin. Fresh-from-the-oven biscuits and small breads arrive with the salad that accompanies each entrée. Desserts are equally memorable, such as plum-and-almond tart and maple cheesecake. No credit or debit cards are accepted. Tim-Bir Alley, 7 Main St., Littleton; (603) 444-6142.

Fossils are not common in New Hampshire, and one of the few places where they are found is atop a rock formation overlooking Littleton. The *Kilburn Crags* are the result of great masses of layered, fossil-bearing rock being heaved into an almost vertical position. The fossils aren't just lying about; it takes some effort to find them, but serious geology buffs may find brachipods and ferns here. To reach the crags, continue on Route 118 past the Dells (a pleasant picnic area). Half a mile after it separates from Route 135 in a left turn, look for a sign on the left side of the road with a small pull-out for

sweettalk

If you "collect" world record holders, be sure to stop in *Chutters.* The *Guinness Book of World Records* says they have the longest candy counter in the world, and who are we to argue? The address is 43 Main St., Littleton; (603) 444-5787; www.chutter.com.

parking. There is no trail, but you can walk along the edge of the field to an old woods road. Follow it to the top, just over half a mile of steady but not difficult climbing. If fossils don't interest you, the view down over Littleton is worth the climb. Watch for moose, which are plentiful here.

Avoid the interstate here by taking Route 18 to the Connecticut River, which forms both the Vermont border and a huge lake behind **Moore Station Dam.** One of the major power-generating dams in the northeast, it has a visitor center with displays explaining the dam, as well as a picnic area and boat launch on the reservoir. The center is open June to mid-Oct, Thurs through Mon. For launch information contact the Connecticut River Joint Commission at (603) 826-4806; www.crjc.org/boating.

Route 135 plays hide-and-seek with the Connecticut River through valley farmland to Woodsville. You can either return to the Littleton area on Route 302 or take Route 112 from Bath to Franconia and **Kinsman Notches.**

In **Bath** be sure to stop at the **Brick Store,** which has been open in the center of town since 1804 or maybe even earlier. Without being "ye olde general store," this emporium manages to retain the feel and much of the merchandise of an old country store while remaining a useful shopping place for local residents. Top shelves are lined with old tins, a thread cabinet, and other vintage store memorabilia, and the homemade fudge is displayed in a glass case. There's a wheel of cheddar on the counter and four shelves of buffalo-plaid wool shirts, a hot item here in the winter. Notice the slanted counter fronts that make room for hoopskirts. If you stop here for a sandwich (if you don't find one you like in the fridge, they'll make one up for you), enjoy it sitting on the front porch with a view of Main Street and the old Mobil sign with the red Pegasus. Open weekdays 6 a.m. to 9 p.m., Sat 7 a.m. to 9 p.m., and Sun 8 a.m. to 9 p.m. The store is on Route 302; (800) 964-2074.

Behind the store is the **Bath Village Bridge,** a covered bridge so long that motorists are asked to turn on their headlights when entering it. Built in 1832 at a cost of $3,500, it still has its original arches. Be sure to notice its construction (all covered bridges are not built in the same way), a fine example of a Burr arch structure. At 400 feet, it is the longest in New Hampshire and one of the oldest still in use in America.

Bath has two other covered bridges, one of which is just off Route 112 in the village of Swiftwater. Farther along Route 112 and the Wild Ammonoosuc (don't let this confuse you—there are three different Ammonoosuc Rivers in the area), where the road parallels the river for a stretch, there is a spot where hopeful prospectors have had moderate luck panning for gold. You may see their vehicles parked along the road. Route 112 leads to Kinsman Notch.

ALSO WORTH SEEING IN THE WESTERN WHITE MOUNTAINS

The Flume,
Franconia Notch; (603) 745-8391; www
.visitnh.gov/flume/index.html.
Open daily 9 a.m. to 5 p.m. mid-May
through late Oct. A deep natural chasm
with sheer granite walls.

The Aerial Tramway,
www.cannonmt.com.
Carries passengers to the top of 4,200-
foot Cannon Mountain, daily mid-May
through Oct.

Clark's Trading Post,
Route 3, Lincoln; (603) 745-8913;
www.clarkstradingpost.com.
Open spring and fall weekends, daily in
July and Aug.
Spotless and good wholesome fun
for kids, with enough to keep adults
amused, such as steam train rides
and a Victorian main street. The bears
clearly enjoy performing as much as the
audience enjoys the show.

Northeast of Bath on Route 302 is ***Upper Village,*** a cluster of eight homes remarkable enough to make almost anyone ease up on the gas pedal. The most imposing are three grand brick mansions built in the early 1800s. Also set in the carefully manicured grounds, which cover both sides of the road, are other homes and huge, yellow clapboard barns with steep-pitched roofs, all in pristine condition. You expect to see a sign with the name of a museum, but these are private homes. Jeremiah Hutchinson moved to Bath in the winter of 1781 with his wife and twelve children. As you might imagine, it took two sleighs to bring them. There's no place to stop safely, but look as you pass at this family village of extraordinarily well-preserved Federal-style homes, unlike any other in the state.

Just south of Lisbon, on the east side of the road, is another group of historic homes, although of a much different sort. Early mills frequently provided housing for their workers, whose wages were often too low for them to afford adequate housing on their own. The company houses were built in rows, all alike. Most of the houses are long gone elsewhere, but eleven of them stand here in their original row.

Lisbon offers another view of the state, one that you have glimpsed from the hardscrabble farms on the backroads. This is a town with lots of guts and little money, but every year it looks just a little bit more prosperous. They have a ***Lilac Time Festival*** toward the end of May. A real hometown event, it has pancake breakfasts, chicken barbecue, races, a golf tournament, a quilt show, a flea market, crafts, bands, singers, and a Saturday night dance. It's a lovely and uncrowded time to visit, before summer attractions have opened. For this year's dates and schedule, write the Lisbon Chamber of Commerce, Lisbon 03585, or call (603) 838-2862 or visit www.lisbonnh.org.

Beyond Lisbon is Woodsville and Route 10, which heads south overlooking the beautiful Connecticut River valley and the Vermont and New Hampshire farmlands that line it. Haverhill is the first town, and although *Haverhill Corner Historic District* is not as well known as neighboring Orford's Bullfinch-inspired Ridge Houses, it has some fine early homes that befitted its position as the northern terminus of the first Province Road from the seacoast. You'll see magnificent examples of Federal architecture along Court Street, including fan doorways and double chimneys. The road dwindles to a lane and then a trail, but you can trace bits of it elsewhere in the state. Equally fine brick buildings stand above the town common and bandstand, where you are welcome to use the public picnic tables.

Just north on Route 10, in North Haverhill, you'll pass *The Big Scoop* (603-787-6588), a bright pink cabin with picnic tables at the corner of Hazen Drive. The name says it all, and we can't imagine how they can make five scoops balance on a cone.

More Places to Stay in the Western White Mountains

BETHLEHEM

The Grande Victorian Cottage
Berkley St.
(603) 869-5755
www.thegrandevictorian
.com
Grand it is, with ten guest rooms decorated in antiques. Some have private baths; rates moderate.

The Mulburn Inn
Main St.
(603) 869-3389 or
(800) 457-9440
www.mulburninn.com
The former Woolworth estate, filled with architectural details, including fine woods, curved window glass, and an art deco bathroom; rates moderate.

FRANCONIA

Lovett's Inn by Lafayette Brook
Route 18
(603) 823-7761 or
(800) 356-3802
www.lovettsinn.com
A national register property restored as a B&B, with an eclectic dining room.

NORTH WOODSTOCK

Jack O'Lantern Resort
Route 3 (south of exit 30 from I-93)
(800) 227-4454
www.jackolanternresort
.com
A family resort with golf, tennis, and swimming. The moderate rates at the inn, motel, or cottages can be with or without meals at the resort's two dining rooms.

More Places to Eat in the Western White Mountains

BETHLEHEM

Rosa Flamingo's
Main St.
(603) 869-3111
Contemporary restaurant with a varied menu and an outdoor cafe in good weather.

FRANCONIA

Franconia Inn
Easton Rd.
(603) 823-5542
www.franconiainn.com
Well-prepared dishes;
moderate. Breakfast is
served, too.

LITTLETON

Italian Oasis
106 Main St.
(603) 444-6995
Italian food, with an outdoor patio in the summer.
Has its own microbrewery
and live music on Fridays.
Traditional Italian dishes are
inexpensive.

Littleton Diner
145 Main St.
(603) 444-3994
www.littletondiner.com
The really old kind of diner,
before stainless steel
streamlined their look,
right in the center of town.
Their breads are baked
with whole grains, ground
within earshot of the diner,

at Littleton Grist Mill.
Inexpensive.

The Miller's Fare
16 Mill St.
(603) 444-2146
A cafe with a deck that
looks out over the Ammo-
noosuc River just down-
stream from the dam. Big
sandwiches, freshly made
soups, and salads. Closed
Mon; open 8:30 a.m. to
2:30 p.m.; limited hours in
winter.

NORTH WOODSTOCK

Woodstock Station
80 Main St.
(603) 745-3951
Busy for three meals a day
during the summer; look for
off-season dining bargains.
Live entertainment nightly
and an adjacent brewpub.
Entrees are inexpensive.

SUGAR HILL

Polly's Pancake Parlor
Route 117
(603) 823-5575
www.pollyspancakeparlor
.com
Freshly made and served
with real maple syrup (their
own); pancakes are served
from 7 a.m. to 2 p.m. on
weekdays, 7 a.m. to 3 p.m.
on weekends in the sum-
mer. They grind the organic
whole grains right there, too.

Sugar Hill Inn
Route 117
(603) 823-5621
www.SugarHillInn.com
Four-course prix-fixe dinners, by reservation only,
might include such dishes
as agnolotti filled with porcini mushrooms in a sage
butter or a savory navarin
of lamb and spring veg-
etables. Tastings at 4:30
p.m. (you'll need to reserve
for these, too) feature
comparative wines, beers,
cheeses, or caviar.

TO LEARN MORE ABOUT THE WESTERN WHITE MOUNTAINS

Franconia Notch Chamber of Commerce,
Franconia 03580; (800) 237-9007;
www.franconianotch.org.

Waterville Valley Region Chamber of Commerce,
Campton 03223; (603) 726-3804 or
(800) 237-2307 in New England;
www.watervillevalleyregion.com.

White Mountain Attractions Association,
200 Kancamagus Highway,
Route 112 at exit 32 off I-93,
North Woodstock 03262;
(800) 346-3687;
www.visitwhitemountains.com.

THE NORTH COUNTRY

The north country isn't for everyone. The nearest mall is hours away; if the local grocery-store-cum-tackle-and-bait-shop doesn't have it, you won't find it here. Nightlife consists of swapping fishing or birding stories in front of the fire or soothing muscles tired from canoeing, hiking, or skiing. If there is a Jacuzzi in this part of New Hampshire, it's well hidden.

But if the sight of a moose with a full rack of antlers drinking from a pool at the side of the road makes your heart beat faster, and if the cry of a loon is your favorite song, this is your Serengeti. You'll meet people here with character, not the "ayuh" and hayseed-style characters but the real stuff. There is a ready wit born of the sense of humor necessary to those who choose the backwoods as home. It's tent-and-canoe country, with a few fine lodgings for those who prefer their adventures to end in time for a full-course dinner.

Route 3 stays close to the **_Connecticut River,_** which at Stewartstown ceases to be the border between New Hampshire and Vermont. Travelers who have seen the Connecticut River flowing through southern New England will hardly recognize this meandering little brook as the same river. Just north of Stewartstown is a sign marking the crossing of the

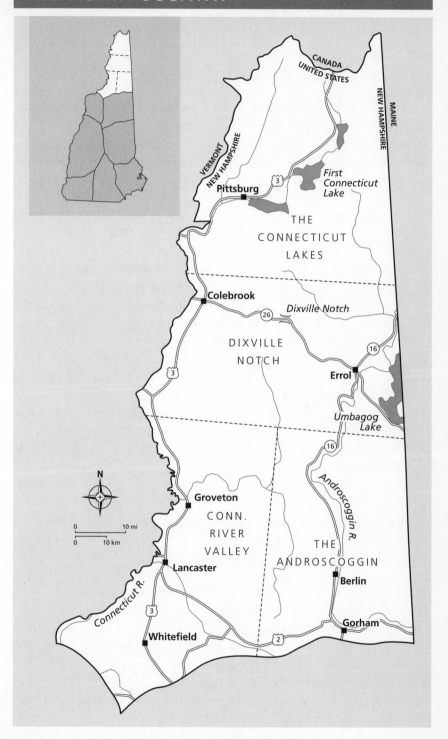

CANADA
UNITED STATES

VERMONT
NEW HAMPSHIRE

MAINE
NEW HAMPSHIRE

Pittsburg

3

First
Connecticut
Lake

THE
CONNECTICUT
LAKES

Colebrook

26

Dixville Notch

DIXVILLE
NOTCH

16

Errol

Umbagog
Lake

16

3

N

0   10 mi
0   10 km

Groveton

CONN.
RIVER
VALLEY

Androscoggin R.

THE
ANDROSCOGGIN

Lancaster

Berlin

Connecticut R.

3

Whitefield

Gorham

2

forty-fifth parallel. From that point north you are closer to the North Pole than to the equator.

Connecticut River Valley

The **Mountain View Grand Resort** has been a part of the White Mountains for over a century, but its recent rebuilding and renovation has restored its elegance and charm. It sits like a palace in a sea of green forest high above the valley floor, providing views that go for miles. Like most resorts, the Mountain View offers a wide range of activities, including a golf course with the most distracting views in New England. Accommodation rates start at $289, but look for special packages that can save you money. Mountain View Grand is on Mountain View Rd., Whitefield; (603) 837-2100 or (866) 484-3843; www .mountainviewgrand.com.

A bit farther down Mountain View Road, **The Spalding Inn** strikes just the right balance between elegance and informality. First opened in 1926 on the site of a former hotel, the inn accommodates guests in bright, airy rooms in the main lodge, in a converted carriage house that was part of the former hotel, and in trim cottages close to the pool and tennis courts. Unusual in White Mountain hotels, the Spalding has a fine bowling green (they'll show you how to play) and a real British-style court for lawn croquet. But the view across the lawns and gardens from the wide front veranda may tempt you to spend your time just watching the flowers grow. Special arrangements allow guests to use the adjacent Mountain View golf course.

The dining room menu changes nightly and might include the inn's hallmark dish, Duck Bombay. Be sure to mention any special diet, since the chef is especially creative in designing alternatives, both at breakfast and dinner. Birders will find binoculars and field guides handy by the terrace window and will enjoy the bird photographs taken by the innkeeper's daughter. Another daughter's paintings decorate the walls of the parlors, and the innkeeper herself is responsible for the tasteful decor featuring her own collection of antiques. Rates are moderate, and include a full breakfast. The Spalding is at 199 Mountain View Rd., Whitefield; (603) 837-9334 www.thespaldinginn.com.

A short distance away on Route 116 is **Jefferson,** an unadorned town set along a ridge facing the mountains. Only the outbuildings remain of the Waumbek Hotel, which once dominated its crossroads, but there are still accommodations in town at the **Jefferson Inn** (www.jeffersoninn.com). A new ell has been added to the original 1896 Victorian house with its tower and wraparound porch, along with woodwork and other architectural details that either match or fit the style of the original house.

The Lost Virgin

In 1759, after repeated Indian raids from Canada had left New Hampshire farms and villages in flames, Robert Rogers of Dunbarton led a group of his famous Rangers on a raid on the village of St. Francis, home of a group of Indians converted to Catholicism by the French, who encouraged Indian raids by paying a bounty on white scalps during the French and Indian Wars. The Indians were busy celebrating their most recent raid when the Rangers attacked, killing and scattering the Indians. Leaving, they carried with them a pair of candlesticks and a large silver image of the Virgin Mary from the church, rich from ransomed captive settlers.

On their return, the Rangers were forced to break up to avoid their pursuers, and the group with the Virgin, trying to cross over Jefferson Notch, floundered in the thick forests and rough terrain of the Israel River. Searches for the treasure were fruitless and were abandoned until the gold candlesticks carried by another band turned up on the shores of Lake Memphremagog in 1816. The silver Virgin is still missing, although tales abound of her appearing aglow in the night to lost hunters in the area. Keep a sharp lookout for the statue in the Jefferson Notch area, but don't get lost in the still-thick woods.

Quilts warm most of the beds, and antiques are mixed with more recent furnishings, creating a nice balance of comfort and style. Families will enjoy the inn's suites and ample recreation space, as well as the two sociable horses in the barn. Couples will find cozy rooms stylishly decorated by the energetic owners, who have added a historical theme and their personal art collection. The delicious European breakfast dishes have to compete with the birds outside the window for your attention. More than twenty-five species visit here, including indigo buntings. Reasonably priced from $115 to $145 in peak season. The inn is open all year at 6 Renaissance Lane (Route 2), Jefferson 03583; call (603) 586-7998 or (800) 729-7908, or visit www.jeffersoninn.com

Meet some veterans of the Iditarod and their friends at **Muddy Paw Sled Dog Kennel** in Jefferson, where in the winter you can visit sled dogs "at home" and learn harnessing, hook-up, and sledding commands before taking to the trails—with an experienced musher, of course. This is one of the rare places that actually teaches visitors how to drive a dogsled, instead of just taking them for rides. Of course there's nothing wrong with just going for a ride, and they're happy to do that, too. As for the dogs, they're happy as long as they are running with a sled behind them, a fact that's clear to see from their excited yipping when the teams are being selected and their crest-fallen faces if they're not on one. Muddy Paw Sled Dog Kennel, 32 Valley Rd., Jefferson; call (603) 986-0697 or visit www.dogslednh.com.

EVENTS IN THE NORTH COUNTRY

North Country Moose Festival,
late Aug, Colebrook

Lancaster Fair,
early Sept, Lancaster
(603) 788-4531

Logging Competition and Fall Festival,
June and Sept, at Northern Forest Heritage Park, Berlin;
(603) 752-7202
Lumberjack competitions, log building demonstrations, and other activities.

Just before reaching Lancaster, Route 3 passes over a shoulder of **Mount Prospect,** a low peak easily spotted because of the stone tower at its summit. The tower and the stone-and-stucco "lodge" beside it were built by a man to whom the north country and everyone who travels there owes a tremendous debt. John Wingate Weeks was a U.S. senator and cabinet member to two presidents but is remembered most as the father of the White Mountain National Forest. It was the "Weeks Law" that authorized the government to buy and preserve forest areas in the East.

The tower and buildings are now in a state park encompassing 420 acres on the mountain. The lodge contains an outstanding collection of local birds, historical displays on the White Mountains, and a gallery of photographs that reflect Weeks's prominent role in world affairs and the friends who visited the estate. Free lectures on historical and ecological topics are held at the lodge on Thursday evenings throughout the summer. The lodge and tower are open from 10 a.m. to 5 p.m. Sat and Sun from mid-June until Labor Day. Admission is $7 ages twelve and older, $3 ages six to eleven, New Hampshire residents free. For a current schedule of evening programs call (603) 788-4004 or (603) 788-3155, or visit www.nhstateparks.org.

Just north of the park is **Lancaster,** seat of Coos County, where descendants of its original settlers, who came in 1764, still live. Lancaster has completed its section of the **New Hampshire Heritage Trail,** which will one day provide walkers with a route from the Canadian to the Massachusetts borders. The 15 miles through Lancaster are not only complete, but they have a free brochure mapping the route and describing the historic houses along the way through the center of the town. One of the buildings is the Stone House on Main Street, once the only granite house in the state and built from a single boulder (there went another glacial erratic) in 1836.

Also on the route, and on yours as well, is the **Wilder-Holton House** at the junction of Routes 2 and 3, the first two-storied house in the north country, built in 1780, on the National Register, and now the historical society museum. Inside, along with fascinating information on the bizarre story of the Brunswick Springs Hotel, just over the river in Vermont, the museum has a children's room with dolls and a sled, a closet filled with vintage clothing, and household utensils, including a hand-operated vacuum cleaner. Every alternate Sunday from the end of June until the end of September a flea market is held on the lawn, where you can sometimes find amazing bargains. The house is open on flea market days and other times by appointment; call (603) 788-2073 or (603) 778-3004.

Leave Lancaster on Route 135 south to find the Mt. Orne Covered Bridge across the Connecticut River. The double-span truss bridge was built in 1911 to replace another that was destroyed in a log-jam in 1908. This section of the river was filled with logs every spring, carrying them from the northern forests to lumber mills and shipping centers on the spring melt-off.

Route 135 follows the river closely, past farms that take advantage of the rich soil deposited by floodwaters. At Dalton, a long iron rail bridge crosses the river, and almost under it is a put-in popular with canoe and kayak paddlers. This is in the middle of a 125-mile stretch of flat water, one of the longest and most scenic stretches of easy river paddling in New England. About 7 miles south of Dalton village, a lane to the right leads down to the river, where alongside a scenic riverside picnic area with tables, there's another boat launch.

Following the Connecticut River from Lancaster in the other direction, Route 3 heads north, past northern New Hampshire's largest antiques shop. *Potato Barn Antiques Center* holds a little bit (or a lot) of everything, especially vintage clothing and hats and old tools. Some rooms are like museums, with display shelves filled with examples of lanterns or lamp chimneys or woodworking planes. It's open Apr through Dec Thurs to Mon 9 a.m. to 5 p.m., Jan through Mar Fri to Sun 10 a.m. to 4 p.m. Potato Barn Antiques Center, Route 3, Northumberland; call (603) 636-2611 or visit www.potatobarnantiques.com.

Farther north, just before Route 3 reaches *Groveton,* Route 110 branches to the right (east) and travels along the upper Ammonoosuc River. To the north lies the *Nash Stream Watershed,* an area whose future has been the subject of an intense battle among land developers, the state, and several conservation groups. Forty thousand acres of it have finally been secured as public lands, a mixed habitat for hawks, falcons, and smaller birds in a forested valley. Access is via Emerson Road, about 2 miles east of Groveton. Follow it another 2 miles to a fork and then go left. After about 4.5 miles of dirt road, a right fork leads uphill to Little Pond Bog, a fine spot for fly-fishing high above the valley. In the winter this area is crisscrossed by cross-country ski trails.

If you continue straight ahead less than half a mile instead of taking the right, you come to *Pond Brook Falls,* a series of waterfalls known to very

Flat Water on the Connecticut

North of Lancaster the Connecticut River runs for a mellow 9 miles or so, providing a pleasant three- or four-hour paddle that is only slightly assisted by the current. The only white water in sight is upstream from the put-in, which is just across the river in Guildhall, Vermont. Cross the bridge about 7 miles north of Lancaster, not far past the fairgrounds on Route 3 at Northumberland. The put-in is downstream below the bridge. Take out at the state boat-launch ramp just below the bridge at Lancaster, on the New Hampshire bank. Except for the put-in point, you'll be in New Hampshire all the way, since the river is New Hampshire's. Of course, spring runoff creates a whole different set of conditions, so don't expect gentle, flat water on any river then.

few people outside of Groveton and Stark. Just after crossing a culvert you will see a pull-out area to the right. Park there and follow the trail a short distance to the lower falls (watch for moose tracks—this is a favorite path for them, too). You'll hear the falls before you see them, and then you'll see only part of them. Continuing uphill, the path ends at a second falls; from here the best route is over the sloping granite ledge alongside the rushing water. Except during spring runoff, there is plenty of room on this 50-foot-wide span of rock for both you and the brook.

Keep going upstream for an ever-changing series of falls, some gushing through narrow chutes and others spread in a filmy veil across a wide ledge. As you reach the top of each, you look up to see another of a different size and shape. This is New Hampshire's sampler of waterfall styles. Do be careful after a rain or in the early spring when the rocks are wet, since they can be quite slippery to climb. On wet days, go through the woods next to the falls where the footing is more secure.

Back on Route 110, continue on to visit **Stark,** a mountain town clustered around its covered bridge under Devil's Slide, a 700-foot precipice. During World War II, Stark housed a camp for German prisoners of war. The remarkable story of how these men, taken prisoner in North Africa, became friends of local farmers during their long winters together is told in *Stark Decency* by Allen Koop. East of the village, on Route 110, a state sign marks the site of the camp. In the field behind the trees, the fireplace in the dining hall, holding messages from children of former prisoners, is all that remains to tell the tale.

The well-kept house with a terrace overlooking the river, just over the covered bridge in Stark, is the ***Stark Village Inn Bed and Breakfast,*** offering three antiques-furnished guest rooms and a great deal of homey comfort to travelers. Hiking, canoeing, fishing, climbing, cross-country skiing, and bicycling begin at the doorstep of this restored farmhouse, and photographers could spend the day sitting on the front porch capturing the river and the bridge in all their different moods and lights. A full country breakfast is cooked on the big black woodstove in the kitchen; in summer guests can eat on the terrace overlooking the river. Low rates make this a bargain as well as a treat. Write to them at 16 Northside Rd., Stark 03582, or call (603) 636-2644.

Rock hounds take note: At Diamond Ledge on Long Mountain and also on the south slope of Percy Peak, about 200 feet below the summit, amethyst is found in the surface rock; topaz is also found at Diamond Ledge. You will need to get thorough directions locally or use a topographic map.

Between the towns of Stratford and North Stratford on Route 3 is **The Foolish Frog.** This unexpected roadside museum is the personal three-decade collection of Carol Hawley and Francis McMilleon. The museum contains hundreds of frogs made in every imaginable material, ranging from plastic toys and novelties, to beautifully carved Indonesian frog deities, a frog-shaped flute from Colombia, baskets, batiks, puzzles, pottery, bottle stoppers, potholders, and mechanical banks. It's fascinating to see how this creature has been interpreted by artists all over the world. A small section displays frogs for sale, including several unusual toys. A discreet box stands near the door for donations, which help the collection to grow. Open May through Oct at 302 Route 3, Stratford Hollow; (603) 636-9843.

The Connecticut Lakes

The town of **Pittsburg** is geographically the largest in New Hampshire, more than 20 miles wide and covering more than 360 square miles. The entire tip of New Hampshire, from the Maine to Vermont borders to the international border with Canada, lies within its boundaries. The whole town was an independent nation for three years beginning in 1832. Claimed by both New Hampshire and Canada, and with no decisive action taken by either to settle the issue, the Indian Stream Territory was left in chronic limbo. Tiring of this, and not wishing to be governed by either contender, the citizens voted their independence at a town meeting. This finally brought them to everyone's attention. After three years and a few altercations among the local militia, a Canadian sheriff's posse, and a small company of New Hampshire militia, the Republic of Indian Stream became the town of Pittsburg.

Within Pittsburg's borders lie all four of the Connecticut Lakes and Lake Francis, and mile after mile of forests, mountain streams, bogs, and assorted wilderness lands. Pittsburg's main (almost its only) road borders each lake in turn until it finally climbs the "height-of-land" to the Canadian border station.

("Height-of-land" is a term commonly used in the north country to describe the high point of any of the area's many ridges.) At nearly any point you may see deer or moose by the roadside.

What is unique here is the series of pristine water bodies. Uninhabited by man, these provide habitat for wild shorebirds found in few other places. Loon populations are increasing here. You can put in a canoe on nearly any pond, and you are welcome to roam over the woods roads built by the timber companies as long as they are not barred. The whole area abounds with trout.

Coon Brook Valley, a long, wide, marshy area cut by a woods road, is a sure place to see moose at almost any time of day. To find it, look for a road marked MAGALLOWAY TOWER entering Route 3 from the right. Go a few yards north and take the road entering from the opposite side of Route 3. Just drive in and park in an open spot—you may even see moose before you park.

For an adventure into the outer reaches of the wilderness, but one that requires only a short hike, search out ***Garfield Falls.*** Take the above-mentioned gravel road marked MAGALLOWAY TOWER, following the tower signs until you reach the height-of-land. At this point a dirt road to the tower goes off to the right, but you should keep going. About 2 miles after you pass Paradise Camp on your left, you will go down a hill and see a road bearing off to the right (the road straight ahead of you may be blocked just below this). Follow the road to the right 1.1 miles to where it makes a sharp left turn and crosses a bridge. Take the dirt road right at the turn.

It's narrow, but unless there have been heavy rains, it is easily passable without four-wheel drive. In another 1.1 miles the road opens out into a yard (an open area where logs are stored). Park there and follow the trail into the woods on the left side of the road. It may take a minute to find it if there have been logging operations there recently, but it is close by a tumble of large rocks.

Garfield Falls is only a five-minute walk from here, through a forest carpeted in the spring with trillium, clintonia, bunchberry, wood sorrel, and occasional moose droppings that look like piles of nutmegs beside (or in) the trail. The falls will be to your left, dropping off the facing side of a chasm into a pool almost directly under your feet. It comes through a zigzag chute and then bounces off the boulder with such force that it has worn a depression in the face of the cliff as well as a cave at its base where its velocity creates a whirlpool. Below the falls the river is split by a giant boulder, from which you can get an excellent view of the falls—and the deeply undercut bank that you were just standing on!

This is not a trip to begin with bald tires, with a near-empty gas tank, or in a downpour of rain, but it is quite an easy one. The distances aren't great, just slow to cover. Before you curse the timber companies for their cutting throughout this area, remember two points. First, you are traveling on their roads, which are the only access to these areas in case of forest fires. Second, their cutting, done with the techniques that they now employ, creates a far more inviting habitat for birds and animals than dense forest provides.

A little farther up Route 3, just above Second Connecticut Lake, another timber road to the right leads to **Scott Bog** and **East Inlet.** The road curves down into a valley and across a stream to a rough T, where you should go left to find Scott Bog or right to find East Inlet. The latter is a former log drive impoundment from which logs were floated out on the spring thaw. In 1987 Champion Paper Company donated 426 acres of pristine pond and moose pasture here, including a tract of virgin spruce and fir, to The Nature Conservancy. The Scott Bog-East Inlet area is considered by birders to offer the best sightings in the north country, with spruce grouse, Canada jay, sixteen warbler varieties, and the rare black-backed woodpecker. Sightings of eighty to ninety species in just a few days are quite common here.

Wandering around on these woods roads is a lot easier and less nerve-wracking with the inexpensive map "Roads and Trails, Connecticut Lake Region," printed on waterproof paper and available at most stores in the area.

The Connecticut River, barely a trickle now, crosses the road above Second Connecticut Lake, and the tiny **Deer Mountain Campground** (603-538-6965) sits on its northern banks. Its twenty campsites are rustic: no hot showers, flush toilets, or camp store here, but there is plenty of quiet, and the riverbanks are alive with birds. The **Moose Falls Flowage,** just north of the campground, is a good place to put in a canoe. The campground is open from May until the end of Oct and is administered from nearby Lake Francis State Park; (603) 538-6965 or www.nhstateparks.org.

Third Connecticut Lake has a boat ramp right off Route 3, but Fourth Connecticut Lake takes a bit more effort. Only about an acre in size, it is reached by a trail from the U.S. Customs station at the Canadian border. The trail, which is actually the cleared swath along the border, is "steep and rugged," as the map warns. Because it is rocky, it is not a hike for street shoes. Park and sign in at the customs station, where they will give you a trail map. It is only about 0.5 mile to the seventy-five-acre site that Champion Paper Company donated to The Nature Conservancy in 1990. Be sure to walk around the upper part of the lake to find the spot where the first few drops of the mighty Connecticut River trickle from the rocks.

The best way to enjoy this area is to settle in for a few days, and the best place to do that is in a comfortable log cabin or lodge overlooking a lake. **The Glen,** at 118 Glen Rd., a former private estate, looks as though it had grown there with the tall spruce trees that line the shores of First Connecticut Lake. The big lodge, which has been welcoming guests for more than thirty years, is a convivial place, with a huge stone fireplace and comfortable Adirondack log and maple furniture; you can also opt for the seclusion of your own cabin. The atmosphere here is comfortable, not cute. There are no frilly curtains or designer sheets, but you won't be roughing it either.

All meals are included in the rate ($100 to $190), and they'll pack you a box lunch; they will even fill your thermos with hot coffee when you leave for your day's adventure. Dinners in the dining room are generous, including such entrees as Wednesday's special, haddock filet with shrimp and scallops, served with vegetables, pilaf, and wine. The whipped cream on your chocolate cream pie is real, and the vegetables in the salad bar are crisp and fresh. Meals prepared to suit special diets are treated with the same careful attention. Nonguests are welcome to dine there with reservations. But you can expect one distraction while you're eating: The bird feeders outside the dining room windows are aswarm with hummingbirds.

The tone and warmth of The Glen is set by its owner, Betty Falton. She helps guests choose places to hike, fish, bird, or just wander around, suggesting routes and telling about her own favorite nooks and crannies. Betty keeps rental boats moored on various lakes so you won't have to haul them around, or you can bring your own. She loves her "neighborhood," but she stresses that this is not the place for everyone's taste. "If you can't walk to the brook without seeing something interesting, you don't belong here," she is quick to tell prospective guests.

When the full moon rises over Mount Magalloway, reflecting in the lake and outlining the spiky silhouettes of the fir trees around the lake, it looks like the stage set for *Rose Marie*. If the lure of the wilderness charms you, there's no finer place to enjoy it. The Glen is open from mid-May to Oct, when you can call for reservations at (603) 538-6500. From Dec to Apr call Betty at (508) 475-0559 or (800) 445-GLEN, or visit www.theglen.org.

South of Pittsburg you have a choice of roads. Route 145 covers the same route, but in a straighter line. At least on the map it's straighter—if you ironed out the hills, the length would probably be the same. The view from the hilltops, past hillside farms and forests to the skyline of mountains to the south, makes it a nice change from Route 3's river-bottom route.

Fishing friends of ours rave about the hearty homemade food at **Tall Timber Lodge,** a rustic backwoods sporting resort of cabins and a B&B-like lodge, with licensed guides on staff, a fly-fishing school on summer weekends, and fly-tying classes in the winter. Thanks to a bottom-release dam, the waters are cool even in August, which allows three months of prime trout fishing. It's a rendezvous for snowmobilers in the winter. Tall Timber is at 609 Beach Rd. in Pittsburg; (603) 538-6651 or (800) 83-LODGE; www.talltimber.com.

Don't think that just because this area is remote, it doesn't have fine dining. **Rainbow Grill,** the restaurant at Tall Timber Lodge, brings regulars who think nothing of driving an hour or more for the mesquite-grilled duck or venison sausage with blackberry-cognac sauce. Fish and sauces are interchangeable to suit individual taste, though to ours, the boneless trout sautéed in lemon butter needs no further embellishment. The Drambuie-based Highland Sauce plays well with the filet of Atlantic salmon that has been basted in olive oil as it's grilled. Wed through Sun evenings the Rainbow Grill serves a full dinner menu; other nights a shorter tavern/dinner menu. Rainbow Grill, Beach Rd., Pittsburg; reserve at (603) 538- 9556.

South of Pittsburg, Stewartstown has several landmarks, including the marker identifying the **45th Parallel,** the point exactly midway between the North Pole and the Equator. In the little village of West Stewartstown is a unique furniture and home décor store. **Northern Rustic Furniture** works with craftsmen to provide beautifully designed furnishings for northern living, items as small as wrought-iron hooks or as large as beds crafted of peeled logs. Beautifully grained tree burls are hollowed to form waste baskets, while shelves and frames are edged in white birch. The large showroom displays furniture for all rooms, from bentwood chairs and a dramatic red-cedar dining table to peeled log futon frames, bunk beds, and a king-sized pine canopy bed. Décor accessories include hand-wrought iron chandeliers and an eye-grabbing stag-horn wine rack. The genial owners are a goldmine of information about the area, too (they were the ones who introduced us to the Rainbow Grill). Northern Rustic Furniture, 866 Washington St. (Route 3), West Stewartstown; call (603) 246-7025 or visit www.northernrusticfurniture.com.

Across the street, **The Spa** has grown from a 1927 family diner to a full restaurant serving three meals a day from an extensive menu. Whether it's a heaping plate of ham and eggs with home fries for breakfast or seafood platter at dinner, it will be good and very reasonably prices. The pies are all made right there. The Spa, 869 Washington St. (Route 3), West Stewartstown; (603) 246-3039.

Beaver Brook Falls drops almost onto Route 145, about 2.5 miles before you reach **Colebrook.** You will see small parking areas on both sides of the road before you see the falls. Be prepared for a surprise, especially if it has rained recently—somehow one doesn't expect the 35-foot straight drop

notyourtypical dayinmay

On May 2, 1798, a man crossed the Connecticut River just south of Colebrook on foot, across the ice. Locals observed stoically that the breakup was a tad late that spring. At least the mosquitoes, usually thick by May, didn't bother him.

of a waterfall to appear out of the woods, particularly on the side of the road. Below, a series of cascades spill from pool to pool. At the foot of the falls is a small park with picnic tables and a swimming hole. If you aren't going into the tip of the state, you can get to the falls via Route 145 out of Colebrook (the sign is marked Clarksville), making the 5-mile side trip before going on to Dixville Notch.

Dixville Notch

Unlike most of New Hampshire's other notches, which run north and south, Dixville lies east and west. Route 26 follows the Mohawk River all the way from Colebrook to the notch itself. About 3 miles outside of Colebrook, look for East Colebrook Road going up the hill to your left. The road continues upward, giving fine views over the notch.

For many visitors, the goal and the reward of the long trip to this far-off tip of the state is staying at the world-class grand hotel set just below the head of the notch. *The Balsams* is unique in so many ways that we'll mention only a few. Once one of many large resort hotels where city families came to spend the summer before the days of air-conditioning, The Balsams is still thriving, having weathered the tough financial climates as well as it has weathered its natural climate. It has turned the harsh winters to advantage by opening a family ski area and miles of cross-country ski trails, keeping Lake Gloriette cleared for skating, giving snowshoe lessons, and offering the free use of snowshoes.

Its success is even more surprising because of the hotel's remote location, but therein lies another unique feature. Unlike the other big hotels that were built in the busy White Mountain circuit, The Balsams stands alone, with none of the tourist attractions of the more heavily traveled routes. It is a gracious and highly civilized oasis in a vast wilderness, and its owners have turned that fact to their advantage. They have provided so many activities, sporting opportunities, social events, and gastronomic pleasures that it would take a week to enjoy them all. In the summer, you can enjoy golf, hiking, walks with a staff naturalist, fishing in the lakes and streams, boating, canoeing, tennis, moose watching, swimming, dancing, movies, cooking lessons, a daily sports program, and the opportunity just to sit on the wide veranda and look at the mountains.

Long gone are the days when the White Mountain resort hotels depended on having a captive audience at dinner; today all these grand dames use their dining rooms—and menus created by their award-winning chefs—to lure guests. But The Balsams has put food first for decades, putting it on the New England culinary map. The resort's signature display of the entire menu each evening is a welcome feature, so you see exactly how each menu item is served. Near the front of the dining room, guests can circle a table with plated samples of each item on the menu—the soups, the salads, the appetizers, and the main dishes.

Dinner might begin with the choice of chilled Peaches and Cream Soup, crab cake with guacamole, ginger-poached Gulf shrimp, or gnocchi in roasted tomato cream garnished with thin spears of asparagus. Entrees also change nightly, perhaps including roasted chicken with strawberry-rhubarb chutney or sashimi-grade ahi tuna with mixed Asian greens. Chocolate mousse, apple tarte with cinnamon ice cream, or a simple bowl of perfect raspberries might be offered for dessert.

Unlike many luxury resorts where families can eat together in the dining room only before the normal dinner hour, The Balsams welcomes all its guests, whatever their age, to all its facilities. Children are welcome to join fly-fishing lessons, for example, and a whole menu of spa experiences are geared to a child's attention span. To help youngsters through the dining experience, a class in dining room manners is part of the regular daily Camp Wind Whistle program for ages five and up, and included in the hotel rate. The camp pro-vides activities for kids and free time for parents all day if they want it, and babysitting is available. But we find that many families choose as we do, to play together.

Non–hotel guests are welcome to visit the historic room where the resi-dents of Dixville gather every four years at midnight to cast the nation's first ballots for the presidential election. Write The Balsams, Dixville Notch 03576; call (603) 255-3400 or (800) 255-0800 in New Hampshire or (800) 255-0600 elsewhere, or visit www.thebalsams.com.

Between meals at The Balsams, explore the notch. You can vary your level of exercise, beginning with a walk around the Lake Gloriette walking trail, a 1.4-mile loop, with the hotel's *Natural History Handbook* as your guide. This informative little book explains the geology of the notch and helps you identify its abundant wildflowers and birds. More energy is required for the climb up to **Table Rock,** especially if you take the rock-strewn trail that goes almost straight up from the notch. A more gentle ascent can be made by a trail begin-ning near the Balsam/Wilderness Ski Area entrance road. Table Rock overlooks The Balsams, the lake, and the notch, but it's no place for the acrophobic.

At the point where the trail drops steeply to Table Rock, another trail leads away from the ledges. If you follow it for a few yards you will come to a deep split in the rock face. This ice chasm has snow and ice in it even during the hottest summer days. Although there is no sign leading to it, you won't have trouble finding it; you just have to know it is there. Be careful: It can be dan-gerous if you get too close to the sharp edge.

After hiking, be sure to stop for a refreshing drink of pure mountain spring water at the newly built **Spring House,** an exact reproduction of the original, which was a popular destination for a Sunday drive. Many locals remember the spring as the scene of their first kiss or even the place of their marriage proposal. There must be something about the water.

The **Balsams Wilderness Ski Area** is part of the resort but is also open to nonguests. Its trails tend toward intermediate skiers and beginners, which makes it a good place for family vacations. A few more challenging runs are available for more advanced skiers. The resort has sixteen trails, 80 percent of which are covered by snowmaking. The slopes have a vertical drop of approximately 1,000 feet. Another of the great appeals of the resort is the Nordic facility: 15,000 acres of northern paradise with 95 kilometers of trails winding through them, making this one of the finest cross-country sites in the northeast. Eighty-five kilometers of those trails are regularly tracked and groomed, most to 14 feet in width. Watch for moose, deer, and other wildlife and expect to see at least their tracks during your outing. For information check the Web site www.thebalsams.com.

The Flume is on the other side of the notch, and on your way there you can appreciate how wild this notch is compared to Franconia, Pinkham, and even Crawford Notches. It's a real notch, where you go over a hump in the road, through a cleft in the cliffs, and down a steep, winding road squeezed between two tree-covered walls. The difference is geological: The surface rock here has been tilted on end so that its strata stand upright, causing the craggy eroded points of rock that give it such a wild aspect.

Authors' Note

We arrived at The Balsams right after a heavy thunderstorm, when the wind howled through Dixville Notch and rain pelted us in a brief but violent torrent. The sun had come out as we pulled up, and in front of the hotel we found an assemblage of bellmen, waiters, housekeeping staff, one of the owners, and several guests, all looking anxiously at the cliffs behind the hotel. One of the bellmen left the group to help us unload but kept looking upward, attentive and hospitable as ever, but clearly preoccupied. More people came out of the hotel—the head of guest services, a couple more waiters, and two men in tennis whites, all looking intently up at the cliff.

"Is something the matter?" we finally asked.

"Oh, yes," the bellman answered anxiously, squinting up at the cliff again. "The peregrine falcons have a nest up there, and we're afraid that the storm may have dislodged it or hurt the fledglings." Only at The Balsams would the world virtually stop for a nest of rare birds.

Sharpen Your Winter Skills

The Balsams has teamed with L. L. Bean to create a series of winter activity workshops to teach snowshoeing, cross-country skiing, and orienteering. Four-day *Outdoor Discovery School* workshops are designed to teach beginners and to help more experienced winter enthusiasts improve their skills. The easy pace includes three days of training, one dedicated to each sport, and all equipment is provided (a good chance to try out the latest models and designs in Nordic skis and snowshoes). Cost for the Outdoor Discovery School is $150, in addition to The Balsams regular room and meals rate.

About a mile past the head of the notch look for a picnic area on the left. The geology changes back to granite here, as Flume Brook carves a gorge more than 200 feet long with sides so straight it almost seems to have been built from cut blocks of stone. It is 40 feet deep in places, as the brook drops from pool to pool and finally over the ledge. Walk along the rim, and in the spring look for trillium and white and pink lady's slippers beside the trail. They are protected species, so enjoy them in place.

Just a few yards down Route 26, this time on the right, is the road to a second picnic area. **Huntington Cascades** is reached by a short path to the brook and then a short walk upstream. The falls continue above the one that you can see from the base, but there is no trail up the steep slope beside the falls, so most visitors simply enjoy the lower section as it rushes in its curving path over the rocks. If you do go exploring here, be careful and stay away from the edge, which has been undercut by the brook. In case you wondered, the little cemetery by the entrance to the parking area contains the remains of some of the area's earliest settlers.

The 5 miles of road between Huntington Cascades and the town of *Errol* is a prime stretch for moose viewing, so drive slowly and keep watch. You can't miss the Errol International Airport, whose building is so tiny that its long name has to be abbreviated to fit across its façade.

Staying at *A Peace of Heaven Bed and Breakfast* is like having a small place in the wilderness all your own. Travelers who once stayed in Rooms With A View (now closed) will recognize Sonja and Charlie Sheldon, who now run this small, three-room B&B in Millsfield, between Colebrook and Errol on Route 26. Rooms are beautiful, as you would expect from Sonja, and all have private bath and come with full breakfast. One room has a separate entrance and is fully wheelchair accessible. Rates are a reasonable $90 for a double. They will also arrange special outing packages for guests, including biking, canoeing/kayaking, photography, snowshoeing, cross-country skiing, and other of the delights of the Great North Woods. Located on Route 26, Millsfield; (603) 482-3443; www.apeaceofheavenbandb.com.

At *L. L. Cote's* you'll find anything you need for camping or outdoor sports, from a backpackers' stove and hand-tied fishing flies to archery targets and long underwear. In the back is the famed white moose. Open daily 8 a.m. to 5 p.m., and until 6 p.m. on weekends. It's easy to spot on Main St., Errol; (800) 287-7700 or (603) 482-7777; www.llcote.com.

Each of the two roads leaving from the far end of Errol's main street will take you to the Maine border. Route 16, to the left, offers a pleasant drive along the upper Androscoggin and the Magalloway Rivers.

Both Route 26 and *Lake Umbagog,* whose southern tip it passes, continue on into Maine, and just before the border is New Hampshire's newest state park. In 1999 the state purchased the Lake Umbagog Campground, creating *Lake Umbagog State Park* and protecting all but 10 percent of New Hampshire's share of the lake's shore from development. The park preserves the nesting grounds of bald eagles, loons, and ospreys and retains the character of the campground's thirty-eight campsites, designed primarily for "canvas campers," and the thirty additional sites that can be reached only by boat. Cabins and sites with electric hookup are also available. The farthest of the "remote sites" is 11 miles from the main campground, about as far off the beaten path as you can get without carrying your camping gear on your back. Take your canoe or kayak and lose yourself for a day on this beautiful, pristine lake.

A Note about Our Less Appealing Wildlife

While May's lilacs are safe as the state's flower, there is talk every spring about changing the state bird from the purple finch (which we rarely see) to the mosquito or blackfly, which we see all too often. Unless you have allergies to their bites, these springtime insects are merely an annoyance. They don't carry malaria or yellow fever as their tropical relatives do, and slapping them is a source of moderate exercise.

But in the north country, especially in May and June, it is wise to be prepared with long sleeves, long pants, and shirts with collars when these voracious creatures are at their worst—evenings and mornings and in the deep woods.

Everyone has a favorite brand of repellent; we favor Natrapel for most places, the only repellent we know of with EPA approval that comes with a propellant-free spray and a recyclable bottle. Natrapel is a New Hampshire product, created by people who know mosquitoes and blackflies intimately. For sources call (800) 258-4696, write Tender Corporation, P.O. Box 290, Littleton 03561, or visit www.tendercorp.com.

Outdoor Adventures

Lucie LaPlante Villeneuve is a wilderness guide and outdoor educator who knows the backwoods of New Hampshire's north country and its nature, from the delicate springtime wildflowers to the moose that populate the forests. And she revels in introducing these woods, lakes, ponds, rivers, and mountains to those who would like to know them better. She can arrange, outfit, and guide day or overnight (and longer) canoe and kayak trips, snowshoe hikes with a picnic, winter survival training, and backcountry skiing excursions. She teaches orienteering, nature photography, archery, and camping skills and can lead moose-spotting tours on foot, skis, bicycle, or in a canoe or kayak. Her Web site is an excellent source of information—and pictures—on northern wildlife. To arrange or join a tour, contact **Outdoor Escapes** at (603) 528-0136 or visit www.outdoorescapesnh.com.

These sites are isolated, at least half a mile apart, and are not for beginning campers but for the woodswise and the waterwise. They offer real camping that is very hard to find. You can rent canoes, kayaks, and boats at the campground. Open from Memorial Day to mid-September; you can reserve sites. Lake Umbagog State Park is on Route 26 in Errol; (603) 482-7795. For reservations for this and other state parks, call (603) 271-3628 or visit nhstateparks.org.

In Errol, *Saco Bound* rents canoes and kayaks, and operates a full transportation service so you can put in at one place and be picked up at a different location. In the summer they offer reasonably priced guided day trips complete with a barbecue lunch. They operate a white-water canoe and kayak school at Errol, as well as a campground for their customers with sites spaced for multiday trips. Saco Bound is headquartered at 2561 East Main St. (Route 302) in Center Conway; (603) 447-2177 or (603) 482-3817 during the season, or visit www.sacobound.com.

The Androscoggin

South of Errol on Route 16 begins a scenic stretch where the road and the **Androscoggin River** travel side by side through **Thirteen Mile Woods.** The river is wide and for the most part gentle, and there are put-ins at several different points. If you have ever held a paddle, you will long to be on the water in this flat reach where the trees overhang the river. There is even a campground, the **Mollidgewock State Campground,** right on the river and designed primarily for canoeists. It is open from mid-May to mid-Oct. Be sure to call them at (603) 482-3373 for information or (603) 271-3628 for reservations, since its half-mile frontage on calm water and rapids is a favorite teaching area for groups learning white-water techniques. More information is available at www.nhstateparks.org.

Motorists will find good places for a riverside picnic or to just sit and watch the river traffic go by. Below the Thirteen Mile Woods is another area frequented by moose, where it is not unusual to see them beside (or in) the road.

North of Berlin look for the stone cairns in the river, among the last reminders of the days of the logging drives that were common in this country during the nineteenth and early twentieth centuries. These midriver cairns served as the point from which the great chain booms were secured. These captured and held a vast flotilla of logs during the annual spring release of the timber that had been harvested during the winter. As trees were cut during the winter, the logs were hauled into impoundment ponds. During the runoff, the dams holding these ponds were released. The water and logs broke into a wild frenzy of energy and wood that found its way downstream into the sawmills and paper plants of New England.

Berlin (pronounced with the accent on the first syllable) is a paper mill town; you can't miss the smokestacks of the James River Corporation. It has been a paper town ever since the first logging camp was established in 1825, although the first paper mill didn't open until 1852. At one time it was estimated that the paper produced in Berlin annually would cover a road 15 feet wide that would run nineteen times around the world. The mill brought immigrants from Canada and as far away as Russia. These ethnic groups have mixed and moved, but a few traces remain from the days when church services in the community were conducted in five different languages.

Berlin's lumbering and papermaking history is explored at ***Northern Forest Heritage Park,*** a growing museum that displays historic artifacts and photographs. Displays explain how the timber was cut, moved during spring log drives, and either shipped for use elsewhere or converted into paper. A regular schedule of festivals celebrates the wide range of ethnic groups drawn to the

And You Thought You Spoke the Language

You have already learned how to pronounce the name of the state's capital like a native, but the road map is filled with names that will expose you as a foreigner the minute you try to say them. In the north country, Berlin and Milan are pronounced BURR In and My In, respectively. They had European pronunciations until World War I, when they changed for political reasons.

mills and lumber camps and the unique lifestyle they made together. Although its biggest era was the late 1800s, lumbering is still important to the north country, and its modern operations are included, too. Other programs are planned in the summer, so it's wise to call ahead. The museum is open year-round, Mon through Fri from 10 a.m. to 7 p.m., and it is located at 961 Main St.; (603) 752-7202. Their Web site, www.northernforestheritage.com, is very informative.

While in Berlin, inquire at the information booth about moose tours, which began at Heritage Park. These take visitors by van to some of the most likely locations for spotting moose, showing a video about the local logging heritage on the way. Tours are usually held every evening from mid-May through Columbus Day weekend. Call (603) 752-7202 or (603) 752-6060 for reservations, or take your chances by appearing at the park. Times vary according to daylight hours.

Saint Anne's church, a classic French-Canadian brick structure, rises like a fortress in the center of town, enormously tall, with an oversized statue on top. But far more unexpected is *Holy Resurrection Church.* Take Mount Forist Street, which intersects with Main Street near the post office, and follow it up the hill. When we say up, we mean almost straight up what may well be New Hampshire's steepest street. Just before the street ends, go left on Russian Street, still going uphill, and look to your right. Six polished, gold-leafed, onion-shaped domes crown a gem of a Russian Orthodox church on the corner of Petrograd Street. Each dome is surmounted by a double patriarchal gold cross; the rest of the church is white. It sits above the city overlooking the smokestacks and rows of company housing below, a poignant and rare reminder of the homesickness of the many peoples who were propelled into this strange and new land.

For a fine view over the mountains to the west, take the *Cates Hill Scenic Route,* turning right off High Street onto Hillside Avenue. The road continues to climb until it reaches a ridge of cleared meadows with a backdrop of mountains. You can reach Hillside Avenue from Route 16 north of town by taking the road marked Coos County Home and continuing to the top of the hill.

On Jimtown Road, just off Route 2 west of Gorham, is a very pleasant campground at *Moose Brook State Park.* Its forty-six sites are well spaced in open forest, with a few at the edge of a field. An ingenious warming pool brings the icy-cold waters of Moose Brook up to a more suitable temperature before it flows into the swimming pool downstream. There is a picnic area near the swimming pool. Be sure to notice the architecture of the administration building, which is a classic of Civilian Conservation Corps (CCC) construction. The park is open from late May through Labor Day; (603) 466-3860; www.nhstateparks.org.

Across from the town hall on the common in **Gorham,** the **Victorian railway station** has been turned into a museum by the local historical society. The collection emphasizes the years when the railway was the lifeblood of the region but contains other memorabilia as well, including a stereoscope visitors can actually use to view the collection of historic cards. Outside stands a fine collection of rail cars, including a beautiful steam engine and its coal car from the Grand Trunk Railway. 19 Railroad St.. Hours vary; call (603) 466-5338 or (603) 466-5570.

If you think that heading into New Hampshire's most remote northern corner means leaving fine dining behind, think again. There are a number of choices, one of which is just on the other side of Mt. Washington. In a former bank building on Main Street, **Libby's Bistro** is so good that people think nothing of driving the 45 minutes from North Conway to have dinner there. We've driven even farther for a taste of Liz Jackson's Forever Braised Beef or Truffled Tallegio Fonduta with roasted vegetables and polenta fries. The eclectic dining room, with its rich colors and well-spaced tables, sets the perfect background for a menu that's just as eclectic. On Friday nights in the winter, Liz features a particular cuisine, maybe Mexican, maybe Italian, or maybe a "Friday in Paris" menu that includes Hunter's Cassoulet and a shrimp and scallop stew with Normandy influence, served with a garnish of crispy fried mussels. The cassoulet brims with rabbit, duck, Cornish hens, and smoky bacon. Although menu prices are moderate, the four-course Chef's Table menu is a real bargain at $32, and includes a choice of three entrees, perhaps Pork Lyonaise with porcini mushrooms or a sole roulade and crab cake with lemon cream. Desserts get equal attention from this talented chef; the Chef's Table menu might offer coffee caramel pot de crème with hazelnut shortbread on a cold winter night, or on a summer evening finish with Liz's own citrus-Prosecco sorbet with pomegranate seeds, clementines, and cookies. For those fresh off the hiking trails who prefer a more casual menu and atmosphere, the downstairs pub is a cozy place for a drink or dinner. The quality matches the upstairs standard—the food is from the same kitchen. Libby's Bistro is open Wed through Sat from 5:30 to 9 p.m., at 111 Main St., Gorham; call (603) 466-5330 or visit www.libbysbistro.com.

Shelburne is best known for The Shelburne Birches, a stretch of Route 2 lined with beautiful white birch trees. These are striking at any time of year—their paper-white trunks contrasted against summer's green, autumn yellows, or casting shadows on the snow. Just past the birches, the big white **Mt. Washington B and B** is enviably positioned to catch views of the summit of Mount Washington from the rocking chairs on its west porch. Two of the two-room suites have whirlpool tubs, all have private baths. The informal, comfortable atmosphere and the genial owners make this an ideal place to relax, and the delicious breakfasts fortify more ambitious guests for nearby hiking trails and kayaking in Reflection Pond. Mt. Washington B and B is at 41 Route 2, Shelburne 03581; call (603) 466-2669 or (877) 466-2399, or visit www .mtwashingtonbb.com.

The *Old Man of the Valley* in Shelburne is virtually unknown, despite a modest sign on the south side of Route 2 between Gorham and the Maine border. Park in the pull-out just east of the sign. Walk back to the sign, where a short trail enters the woods. A short distance ahead is a large stone with the profile of a man on one side. Surely, you say, this has just been sculpted to look this way, but a walk around the stone shows a jumble of perfectly natural planes that form the face when viewed from the front.

More Places to Stay in the North Country

JEFFERSON

Applebrook Bed and Breakfast
Route 115A
(603) 586-7713 or
(800) 545-6504
www.applebrook.com
Eight rooms and two suites. Moderate.

Josselyn's Getaways
306 North Rd.
(800) 586-4507
Real log cabins sleep four to ten and have full kitchens; $95 to $125 for a two-person cabin.

PITTSBURG

Magalloway Mountain Lodge
45 Stewart Young Rd. (First Connecticut Lake)
(603) 538-6353 or
(800) 538-6659
www.magallowaymountain lodge.com
Housekeeping units with baseboard heat, open all year and convenient to snowmobile trail system.

Mountain View Cabins and Campground
Route 3
(603) 538-6305
www.mountainviewcabins andcampground.com
Log cabins open year-round, located on the main snowmobile trail system. All have central heat, some with fireplaces or wood-stoves, too.

SHELBURNE

Philbrook Farm Inn
881 North Rd.
(603) 466-3831
www.philbrookfarminn.com
A comfortable, old-fashioned place where families come year after year; $120 to $150, with breakfast and dinner.

Town and Country Motor Inn
Route 2
(603) 466-3315 or
(800) 325-4386
www.townandcountryinn .com
Well-kept motel with a swimming pool; moderate.

TO LEARN MORE ABOUT THE NORTH COUNTRY

North Country Chamber of Commerce,
Colebrook 03576;
(603) 237-8939 or (800) 698-8939;
www.northcountrychamber.org.

Northern White Mountains Chamber of Commerce,
164 Main St., Berlin 03570;
(603) 752-6060 or (800) 992-7480;
www.northernwhitemountains.com.

More Places to Eat in the North Country

BERLIN

Northland Restaurant & Dairy Bar
1826 Riverside Dr. (Route 16)
(603) 752-6210
North of town on the road to Milan, the Northland is a local institution with a pleasant dining room, reliably good food and low-to-moderate prices. In the summer the dairy bar serves up generous scoops of excellent ice cream.

ERROL

Northern Exposure Restaurant
Main St.
(603) 482-3468
Don't look for innovative nouvelle anything here, but expect well-prepared generous portions of favorites, plus a surprise or two—such as venison burgers. The pies are made in-house. Open Sun through Thurs 5 p.m. to 8 p.m., Fri and Sat 5 a.m. to 9 p.m.

GORHAM

Saladino Italian Market
152 Main St.
(603) 466-2520
You know you are in the right place by the wonderful aromas of a real Italian market. The sandwiches are wonderful, or stock up on provisions for your camping trip and make all the surrounding campers jealous.

Yokohama Restaurant
288 Main St.
(603) 466-2501
Pan-Asian menu, with particular emphasis on Japanese food; entrees $6 to $12. Closed Mondays.

PITTSBURG

The Glen (see chapter text) serves dinner to non-guests by reservation.

WHITEFIELD

Grandma's Kitchen
186 Lancaster Rd.
(603) 837-2525
Breakfasts and pies are what Grandma's is famous for, but the burgers are outstanding, the sandwiches generous, and the prices unbelievably low, which probably accounts for why it's usually full. Everything is prepared from scratch here, from handcut fries to the sliced turkey in the sandwiches.

Index

About the Authors

Barbara Radcliffe Rogers and Stillman Rogers have, jointly and singly, written and illustrated more than thirty books, most of them on travel, wildlife, and gardening. Titles include *Galapagos, Safari, Drive Around Portugal, Big Cats, Giant Pandas, Exploring Europe by Boat, Drive Around Italy's Lakes and Mountains, Travellers Milan and Italian Lakes, Adventure Guide to Canada's Atlantic Provinces, Adventure Guide to New Brunswick and Price Edward Island, Adventure Guide to the Chesapeake Bay, Eating New England, Secret Providence and Newport,* and *The Rhode Island Guide.* They have written and illustrated several books in the *Children of the World* series and written several others in the *Enchantment of the World* and *Cities of the World* series, describing the lives and cultures of children from Argentina to Zambia. Barbara has written articles for *Yankee* magazine, *Country Journal,* the *Boston Herald,* the *Los Angeles Times,* and others, including a monthly column for *New Hampshire Magazine.* Stillman's photographs have illustrated hers and other articles.

In *New Hampshire Off the Beaten Path,* they write about their home state. Although they have explored its trails and backroads since childhood, they still find it as fascinating as the most exotic locales in their wide repertoire of travels.